Can Israel Survive in a Hostile World?

Can Israel Survive in a Hostile World?

by
David Allen Lewis

New Leaf Press

First printing: June 1994
Second printing: October 1996

Library of Congress Catalog Number: 93-87251
ISBN: 0-89221-260-8

Cover photo of wounded soldier courtesy of the *Jerusalem Post*, by Ariel Jerozolimski.

*This book is gratefully
dedicated to my gracious
wife, Ramona.*

*Also to
David Ben Joseph,
Elizabeth, Cassandra,
Rebecca, Thomas, and
Joseph Neil.*

Acknowledgments

Profound thanks to Mary Hitchcock for her unstinting loyalty, fervent spirit, clear vision, and not least for extremely long hours of labor in making this book come into existence.

To my publisher, Tim Dudley of New Leaf Press, gratitude that cannot be fully expressed. Truly a leader among men, a man for this hour, Tim has transformed New Leaf into an instrument of witness that reaches effectively around the whole world. Tim has been so supportive of our work, that we shall never be able to express our thanks adequately.

To Barry Hitchcock, a volunteer with pure motives and a strong heart. Without Barry, who carries so much of the load of work for this outreach, we would be in distress. He is a comfort to us, a true friend.

Thank you Rita, Nancy, Chuck, and Robert for all your help. This list is not complete. There is not enough space to contain the names of all the volunteers and givers of encouragement who should be listed here. God bless them all.

Contents

Prologue

On the tawny shores of the blue Mediterranean there is a minuscule nation whose survival always hangs by the slenderest of threads. Never has there been a moment that her existence has not been threatened.

Surrounded by hostile neighbors who have unrelentingly sworn her destruction, she never knows when the next katusha rocket will explode or when a full scale war will break.

Beset by malicious media, greedy politicians, manipulators, and opportunists, she holds on to life with the most tenuous grasp.

This wife of Jehovah, will she survive? Will the days of rest and restoration come at last? Or, is the modern state of Israel only a momentary aberration upon the pages of history?

Having passed through the furnace of affliction, the Jews are now hounded by revisionists who tell survivors, including Schindler's Jews, that they invented the Holocaust to get sympathy.

Threatened by civil war, Israel must contemplate the possibility of imminent destruction.

In the Diaspora, Jews find themselves under attack. Anti-Semitic incidents are on the rise. Many American Jews seek not to be noticed, fearful of accusations of dual loyalty.

Thrust upon us by her detractors is the demand that we must question the identity of Israel. Who are these Jews? Are they the impostors of all time? What connection do they have to Abraham? How can black Ethiopian Jews be Abraham's children? Some deny Israel's identity, assigning descent from the "ten lost tribes" to Europeans. The theological deviants say that the Jews of today are cursed — not of Abraham, but descendants of the old Khazar tribes of Russia.

This Christian writer has no Jewish ancestry and no divided loyalties. My loyalty is one. It is to God, and under the aegis of providence my hopes and actions of good will then extend to my nation, to Israel, and to all the peoples of this benighted planet. We wish ill to no one.

In these pages you will read of the biblical meaning of Zion. Discover here those Christians who have caught a vision for Jerusalem, who battle racism, prejudice, and hatred for the Jews.

What if the peace accords become treaties and really work? Could there be a Middle East Common Market? What impact would this have on the Gentile nations?

Above all let the Word of God convince you of what Deity has at stake in Israel. The holiness of God and the return of the Jews to the land will captivate you. Shades of blindness will be removed from eyes of the uninformed and the misinformed.

This book is not for the fainthearted, the bigot, nor the ignorant. It is designed to help serious, thoughtful people get an insight into the major issues of our times.

We deal with the most serious of problems and the darkest of fears. But our message is a message of hope, both for the present and the far future.

The final answer is that Israel will survive. But we all have serious choices before us. The Church, the Jewish people, politicians, and nations are undergoing a litmus test. Under God's watchful eye, performances are evaluated and futures predicated. We know the ultimate outcome, but there is a long, long road to travel from Wichita, or Sidney, or Toronto to the New Jerusalem.

The choices we make will determine the quality of life for the whole world from now until God's visible intervention in human affairs takes place and the Messianic kingdom is ushered in.

Foreword

Nothing blesses a teacher more than to see one of his former students doing a greater work than he could possibly do. I am indeed blessed as I recognize that one of them, Dr. David Allen Lewis, has become one of the world's foremost prophecy teachers and evangelists. His many visits to Israel keep him in touch with significant events that he is able to interpret in the light of what the Bible says. This book is the cry of his heart to a hurting world and a largely indifferent Church.

Like John the Baptist, Dr. Lewis is a voice crying in the wilderness of confused and contradictory events as he points to the Lamb of God who takes away the sins of the world. Like John the Baptist, he also fearlessly cries out against the sins of the world around us and lets us know the dangers that are ahead.

With the renewed spread of various forms of amillennialism and post-millennialism on one hand, and the spread of pagan New Age philosophies on the other, many are being led astray. Post-millennialism in both its older and newer forms puts the return of our Lord in that far distant future and dims the blessed hope of the Church. Neither post-millennialism nor amillennialism have any place for the future restoration and blessings of national Israel in their theological systems. Even premillennialists are in danger because of the spread of literature that encourages doctrines that rob one of the sense of the imminence of Christ's coming. They spiritualize the Bible in such a way that they rob it of its plain meaning. Thank God that there are still outstanding Bible scholars who uphold the truth.

Some things Dr. Lewis says will shock you — and they should. Bible believers need to wake up and become concerned about the growing, spreading anti-Semitism that so subtly twists both the facts and the Scriptures. We also need to learn the lessons of history, especially the history of pre-World War II Germany. The German Christians were terribly deceived by Hitler. A sleeping Church today could just as easily be deceived.

Even more important, we need to pray and act in support of Israel. Dr. Lewis gives an account of his own spiritual journey and what it means to be a Christian Zionist. His answers to those who oppose or disregard Israel are biblical and convincing. May the Lord stir your heart as you read and re-read this book. Then pass it on to others who may need a new vision and a fresh understanding of God's plan for His chosen people.

— Stanley Monroe Horton, Th.D.
Distinguished Professor Emeritus
of Bible and Theology
Assemblies of God Theological Seminary

Introduction

Early in my life I was deeply influenced by three books in addition to the Bible. The Bible has always been first. Those three books were *The Pursuit of God* by A. W. Tozer, *The Ultimate Intention* by DeVerne Fromke, and *God's Fool.*

I have lost my copy of *God's Fool* and think I remember that the author's name was George Patterson. The sentence from *God's Fool* that is burned into my mind is a statement by the author, "I am a man with a passion for God."

Jeremiah had a fire burning in his bones and he had to speak out.

The apostle Paul anguished, "Woe is me if I preach not the Good News."

The author's introduction is supposed to be an explanation of why he wrote the book. Here is my reason:

I had to.

David Allen Lewis
Spring, 1994
Springfield, Missouri

1

A HOSTILE WORLD

Understanding the Concept of Evil

> *For the earth is the Lord's, and the fulness thereof* (1 Cor. 10:26).
> *... The whole world lieth in wickedness* (1 John 5:19).
> *And I will punish the world for their evil, and the wicked for their iniquity . . .* (Isa. 13:11).

God created the earth a paradise. Through collaboration with the enemy mankind has birthed a fallen world system. It is corrupt and shows little evidence of improvement. There is more evidence for devolution than evolution.

The Holocaust is a glaring, recent example of the depravity into which mankind is capable of descending. Tiny minorities have, from time immemorial, stood against the darkness, holding back the black night of evil. Only by the grace of God has humanity been spared from final self destruction.

> Of man's first disobedience, and the fruit
> Of that forbidden tree whose mortal taste
> Brought death into the world, with all our woe,
> With loss of Eden.[1]

Thus opined John Milton in *Paradise Lost*. Can we also hope with Milton, to "See golden days, fruitful of golden deeds with joy and love triumphing?"

EVIL STALKS THE EARTH

Evil is not abstract, it is personal. There is a devil and he is at work. "The Lord said unto Satan, Whence comest thou? Then Satan answered the Lord, and said, From going to and fro in the earth, and from walking up and down in it" (Job 1:7). In a day when our children carry guns, rob, plunder, vandalize, and kill each other and their elders, humanity drinks Victor Hugo's "fourth goblet of wine," the goblet of brutality.[2]

Our best humanitarian efforts are dashed against rocky shores along the sea of despond. UN forces enter Somalia to rescue the starving and end up killing them. Israel is now asked to entrust her security into the hands of these same UN peace enforcers. Oh! Brave New World of Orwellian newspeak — war is peace. Hate is love. Land for peace. Once Israel battled the Midianites, but now must enter conflict with the far more subtle media-ites.

In the midst of the peace talks of 1993 we learned that the previous year was our worst war year since 1945. Fifty-two nations were at war at the close of 1992. Today, the situation is worse. "For when they shall say, Peace and safety; then sudden destruction cometh upon them, as travail upon a woman with child; and they shall not escape" (1 Thess. 5:3). In all the annals of history there are less than 300 years noted as times of universal world peace. Earth is a nasty neighborhood to live in. It is like New York's Central Park at night. "But evil men and seducers shall wax worse and worse, deceiving, and being deceived" (2 Tim. 3:13).

The quest for peace is legitimate, highly desired, but on God's terms not man's. ". . . Peace, peace to him that is far off, and to him that is near, saith the Lord . . . . But the wicked are like the troubled sea, when it cannot rest, whose waters cast up mire and dirt. There is no peace, saith my God, to the wicked" (Isa. 57:19-21).

CHOICES BEFORE US

Historically two peoples, Israel and the Church, have been called, chosen, and used of God to hold back the powers of darkness that ever threaten to engulf the world. Alas, the assignment has not been fulfilled. Most Christians and Jews have failed miserably in their God-given tasks. The darkness deepens. Ignorance of the real issues of our times is abysmal. Some Christians do not even know the meaning of the word Holocaust. Is it too late for reformation? Can a quest for truth and justice be reborn? Can this generation succeed where others have failed? It seems barely possible, but it is possible. "See, I have set before thee this day life and good, and death and evil" (Deut. 30:15). We have major choices before us. Our reaction to these choices will determine the quality of the future we live in from now until the dawning of the Messianic Age.

SPIRIT OF MOLOCH

For Israel the Holocaust is never history. It is always looming, potential. This world is a wicked place. "Hatred of the Jew has been humanity's greatest hatred. While hatred of other groups has existed, no hatred has been as universal, as deep, or as permanent as anti-semitism."[3]

The Psalmist pondered the threat of genocide: "They have said, Come, and let us cut them off from being a nation; that the name of Israel may be no more in remembrance" (Ps. 83:4).

Moloch[4] lives, he prowls the planet, seeking to devour. The Elberton, Georgia, New Age monument calls for the death of 5 billion people so the remaining New Age master race of 500 million can manage the planet in balance with nature. The first of 10 New Age commandments orders, "Maintain humanity under 500 million in perpetual balance with nature." A powerful secretive organization, makers of the Georgia Guidestones, scheme for the elimination of five billion human souls. We know that all Jews and Bible Christians are on that hit list. Almighty Jehovah, we pray that they will fail in their evil aspirations! Let Messiah, our deliverer, save us from the plot of your ancient enemy.

> Molech, scepter'd king,
> Stood up, and the strongest and the fiercest spirit,
> That fought in heav'n; now fiercer by despair.[5]
> — John Milton

WARS AND RUMORS OF WARS

Angola, Cambodia, Cyprus, El Salvador, Georgia, Haiti, India/Pakistan, Iraq/Kuwait, Israel/Syria, Lebanon, Liberia, Mozambique, Rwanda, Western Sahara, Somalia, and the former Yugoslavia are scenes of violence and unrest. Ironically, these are places where UN peacemaking forces are either present now or shortly will be. Are these the stalwart soldiers the Western nations want to mandate the new "peace" in the Middle East?

Other areas experiencing war and insurgency are Algeria, Armenia, Azerbaijan, Afghanistan, Burundi, Gabon, Ireland, Korea, Macedonia, Mexico, Sierra Leone, South Africa, Sudan, Tadzhikistan, and Zaire. These hot spots of violence are killing fields and this is only a partial list.[6]

The streets of the USA and Canada are no longer safe. Germany boils over with mayhem and riots. IRA bombers hit London time and again. The former Soviet Union is exploding. Neo-Nazism rises again, screaming the age-old slogans of hate and death. Louis Farrakhan spouts his vitriolic brand of race hatred for hours over C-Span II, broadcast from the Javits Center in New York.

ISRAEL, TARGET OF WORLD WRATH

In this fallen world one nation, above all others, has been singled out and targeted for destruction. From its beginning the nation of Israel has been threatened with extinction (see Ps. 83:4). The Arab world, never threatened with extinction, longs for the destruction of Israel. A war of attrition and gradualism is now being waged in the name of peace. A handshake is a cheap gesture when promises are broken. On the other hand if the promises are fulfilled it could augur a time of tranquility for both parties. "Now faith is the substance of things hoped for, the evidence of things not seen" (Heb. 11:1).

On September 19, 1993, just six days after he signed the peace accord on the White House lawn, Yassir Arafat spoke the following words to 19 foreign ministers gathered for their regular semi-annual meeting in Cairo, Egypt. "Our first goal is the liberation of all occupied territories and return of all refugees, self-determination for the Palestinians and the establishment of a Palestinian state whose capital is Jerusalem. The agreement we arrived at is not a complete solution, but only part of a transitional phase . . . which accomplishes a small part of our rights. It is only the basis for an interim solution and the forerunner to a final settlement, which must be based on complete withdrawal from all occupied Palestinian lands, especially holy Jerusalem."

Arafat considers "occupied Palestinian lands" to be all of Israel including Tel Aviv, Beersheba, Eliat, and Gesher Haziv. The goal is still to completely destroy Israel and finally occupy all of the land. Can there be peace? We hope so. There is no advantage for the killing to continue.

On September 13, shortly after the signing, Arafat spoke to his

Palestinian people on Jordanian television: "When we say the Palestinian state is coming, it will undoubtedly come. This is historical inevitability. And history makes no mistakes . . . [the Palestinian flag] will fly over the walls of Jerusalem, the churches of Jerusalem, and the mosques of Jerusalem."

The PLO covenant demands the destruction of Israel. Though promises to change the document were made, at the time of this writing no changes have been forthcoming. If you want the true sentiments of the Arab leaders, disregard what they say on the White House lawn, and in press conferences, for the benefit of the Western media. Pay attention to what they say to their own colleagues in the Arab world. "The words of his mouth were smoother than butter, but war was in his heart: his words were softer than oil, yet were they drawn swords" (Ps. 55:21).

Jean Kirkpatrick, former United States Ambassador to the United Nations said on September 13, the day of the signing: "The PLO was created for the specific purpose of destroying the Jewish state and replacing it with a Palestinian state. In its brief history, the PLO has achieved an extraordinary record of murder and mayhem against Israeli diplomats, athletes, soldiers, and ordinary civilians, and has mobilized a remarkably successful attack against Israel in the U.S. and among the world's diplomats . . . . Yassir Arafat is a man made for war. His kingdom is an army that has made war on all from whom it could hope to profit — on Jordan, Lebanon, Kuwait, Hamas, and on other factions of the PLO . . . . Rabin knows that Arafat is a specialist in violence, conspiracy, and deception and that his forces in Fatah are well-trained in the arts of war, and little else. A miracle would be required for such men to become peaceable citizens of a peaceful community."

Can any good come out of the peace process? Maybe, just maybe. We shall see. We hope, but find it hard to trust those who have such a poor track record. We pray that all the parties involved will see the value of honest negotiations for an honest peace.

> The Jews have been objects of hatred in pagan, religious, and secular societies. Fascists have accused them of being Communists, and Communists have branded them capitalists. Jews who live in non-Jewish societies have been accused of having dual loyalties, and Jews who live in the Jewish state have been condemned as racists. Poor Jews are bullied, and rich Jews are

resented. Jews have been branded as both rootless cosmopolitans and ethnic chauvinists. Jews who assimilate are often called a fifth column, while those who stay together often spark hatred for remaining different. Literally hundreds of millions of people have believed that the Jews drink the blood of non-Jews, that they cause plagues and poison wells, that they plan to conquer the world, and that they murdered God himself.

Jews have been perceived as so dangerous that even after their expulsion or destruction hatred and fear of them remain. Attesting to the durability of anti-Semitism is the depiction of Jews as ritual murderers of young Christian children in Chaucer's *Prioress's Tale* in the *Canterbury Tales* 100 years after all Jews had been expelled from England, and the characterization of Jews as usurers who wish to collect their interest in flesh in Shakespeare's *The Merchant of Venice* 300 years after the Jewish expulsion. A contemporary example is Poland, in 1968, when for months the greatest issue on Polish radio, television, and in Polish newspapers was the "Unmasking of Zionists in Poland." Of the 33 million citizens of Poland in 1968, the Jews numbered about 20,000 or less than one-fifteenth of 1 percent.[7]

Today Israel is barely surviving in a very hostile world. Sometimes I think that other than the Bible believers in the Church not too many would care much if she ceased to exist. Multitudes would take great delight in her demise. If the Church does not act as the moral conscience of society, then the morally bankrupt leaders of this world will act as the evolving animals they believe themselves to be.

COMFORTING ISRAEL, IMPLEMENTING GOD'S PLAN

Should Israel come to the brink of extinction it would seem to demand the coming of Messiah. How else could the biblical promises be fulfilled? We have unfortunately treated Israel as our eschatological[8] toy. We sit in prophecy conferences and ponder our speculations, ignoring the clear call to action mandated upon the Church. What is your church doing to comfort Israel?

"Comfort ye, comfort ye my people, saith your God. Speak ye comfortably to Jerusalem . . ." (Is. 40:1-2). We must ask, who is this who is to comfort Israel? Surely it is not Israel comforting Israel. Isaiah envisions here a people not yet called, not yet in existence. The command is to you.

I write to shake you, to challenge you, to entreat you, hopefully to enlist you in this great cause in the end times. Of course the fulfillment of the Great Commission is the prime mandate for the Church of all ages. But, implementing God's plan for Israel and recognizing the legitimacy of Christian Zionism must now also be thrust upon the consciousness of the church of Jesus Christ.

My purpose is to enlist you in the army of emboldened prayer-works warriors who march out on Israel's behalf. To the front lines, soldier. Lift the banner high. No time now for retreat. Nothing less than a frontal assault on the citadels of doubt will suffice for this great battle. "The night is far spent, the day is at hand: let us therefore cast off the works of darkness, and let us put on the armour of light" (Rom. 13:12).

Yes, you believe in Israel's prophetic destiny, but what are you doing to protect her from the yapping hounds of Hades? What bulwark do you erect between her and Beelzebub? What have you done to actively combat anti-Semitism and the liars who say there was no Holocaust?[9]

You treasure your annotated study Bible, and ponder your neat prophecy chart, and well you do so. But do not become smug and overconfident, while reducing prophecy studies to mere intellectual exercise. Prophecy is a call to action and implementation. Remember that while you are saved by faith, you will be evaluated for your works at the Bema judgment seat of Christ (see 2 Cor. 3). The New Testament writer James says, "Faith without works is dead." Are you a spectator or a participant in the end-time drama now unfolding before us? Important question, sojourner, if you ever expect to hear the words, "Well done, thou good and faithful servant."

We treat Israel as our soteriological[10] toy as well. We piously recall that salvation comes to the gentiles through Israel (see John 4:22) and we piously speak of calling "our dear Hebrew brethren" to the cross of Jesus. But alas, our love is conditional. We will love the Jews only if they will convert to Jesus. Otherwise, curses be upon them, and any horrible holocaust they suffer is their just due, since they allegedly are guilty of deicide, the murder of God.

Dr. G. Douglas Young, founder of the Institute of Holy Land Studies on Mount Zion once told me of an outrageous encounter involving well-meaning Evangelicals and a local Jerusalem family of Jews. He had taken a lovely, refined Christian couple to a Jewish home. They were all professional, well-educated people. They all enjoyed a delightful evening of fellowship, tasting of local foods, and engaging in lively conversation. As they were leaving, Douglas was horrified to hear the bright Christian lady say to the Jewish hostess, "Thank you for such a lovely evening. I never knew Jews could be so nice. Why, I could almost forgive you for killing Jesus."

UNCONDITIONAL LOVE

Whatever happened to unconditional love? Does our Father in heaven hear the weak echo of a few radicals in Pilate's judgment hall shouting for the crucifixion of Jesus, or does our Father hear the prayer of His Son on the cross, "Father forgive them?" All of them, Gentiles and Jews. Whoever gave arrogant Christians the right to say the Jews are under a curse? We will dispel that mythology to your satisfaction in this book — if you believe the Bible. Incidentally, regarding the death of Jesus, there is plenty of blame to go around. No need to give it all to Israel. "For of a truth against thy holy child Jesus, whom thou hast anointed, both Herod (Edomite, Roman puppet), and Pontius Pilate (Roman procurate), with the Gentiles, and (last on the list) the people of Israel, were gathered together" (Acts 4:27). *Res ipsa loquitur* (the facts speak for themselves).

Many Christians have relinquished their right and authority to witness to Jews. They know little about the Holocaust, about the Inquisition, the Crusades, the expulsions, the forced conversions, the dark side of Church history. Little is known of the fact that the visible Church has been largely responsible for the anti-Semitism of the past 1,700 years. We have a generation of pastors and evangelists who do not teach the people these things. They were discouraged to research Israelology in our seminaries and Bible colleges. Now they are too busy and seldom have time to read solid meaty books, only searching the Bible for proof texts to buttress their "how to" sermons.

The well-intentioned but ill-informed Christian launches into a poorly considered "witness" to a Jew and meets with objections he cannot counter. Then he walks away to tell of his experience with that smug, bullheaded Jew who refused to believe in Jesus. The poor Jew never saw the real Jesus in that witness. What he saw was a blond-headed, blue-eyed Aryan, whom even Hitler could love.

What if we have misjudged God's timetable, and the present state of Israel is dismantled? God forbid! At any rate, the Jewish people will not be destroyed. There will yet come a day when the final regathering will take place and all the prophecies will be fulfilled, though it take another thousand years. "The Lord also shall roar out of Zion, and utter his voice from Jerusalem; and the heavens and the earth shall shake: but the Lord will be the hope of his people, and the strength of the children of Israel" (Joel 3:16). God's Word cannot be broken. But woe to the church that would allow this to happen in our day. The Dominionists would have a brief day, then the neo-dark ages of New Age terrorism against the Church would roll in upon us. "Dark the night of sin has settled, loud the angry billows roar."[11] I believe in the imminent return of our Lord, but must live my life as if I would finish a normal span of years, for I cannot know the appointed day of His return (see Mark 13:32-33).

INHERITED LIES

The Gentile governments are never going to be protectors of Israel. This is the role of the Church, and great will be the punishment of the Church if she fails to stand in the gap and demand that Israel be preserved. The centuries of dark ages will pale in comparison to the evil that will befall the post-Holocaust Church if we fail in our God-given task in this crisis hour. "O Lord, my strength, and my fortress, and my refuge in the day of affliction, the Gentiles shall come unto thee from the ends of the earth, and shall say, *Surely our fathers have inherited lies,* vanity, and things wherein there is no profit" (Jer. 16:19). (Emphasis added.)

THE CHURCH AND ZION

Christians should be Zionists. It is time to stop pushing the issue aside. Too much is at stake. Shout it from the housetops. Biblical Zionism is simply the idea that God owns the whole world and can give any portion of it to whomever He wills. His Word declares that He has given the land of Israel to the Jewish people. If you believe the plain truth of God's Word you are a Zionist. If you are not a Christian Zionist you simply do not believe the entire Word of God, or you have so grossly misinterpreted it as to make its message unrecognizable.

One need not be affiliated with a political Zionist organization to be a Biblical Zionist, but one cannot believe the Bible without being a Zionist. Beyond personal redemption this is the key issue of our times. If it is low on the Church's agenda of priorities, then it is time to revise the agenda and line up with God's plan as revealed in Scripture. Rise up noble Bereans and put the sensation-seeking Athenians to shame (see Acts 17:10-21).

Our interest in the survival of Zion is a vested interest. What is at stake is the very existence of both the evangelical Church and Israel.

The same forces that seek the destruction of Israel would also welcome the catastrophic ruin of the Church. The Moslems chant, "First we will eliminate Saturday then Sunday." Translate: First we conquer the Jews then the Christians. One billion Moslems are joined by one billion New Agers, plus a motley assortment of cultists, atheists, and Christian skeptics, in wishing that we would no longer exist. And how sad that Israel is threatened by forces in her own ranks, just as the nominal church is rotten from within.

WILL WE SURVIVE?

Can Israel survive in this hostile world? Can the Evangelicals survive in this hostile world? This is actually one question.

Our churches are falling apart morally. Pastors, faced with counseling situations they heretofore could scarcely have imagined, are suffering burnout. Many church leaders fail morally. Only a few Christians join the ranks of protest against the slaughter of innocent unborn babies. It is not a good time. Part of the cause of our quandary is the abandonment of Israel and the cause of Christian Zionism. Rejection of Israel involves reinterpreting the Bible. Accept that and the basis of morality is gone.

Few people who reinterpret the Bible will be on the front lines of any unpopular cause. We are cursed with a curse as surely as God has spoken. The Word of God to Abraham speaks of those who bless or curse the promised seed through Isaac and Jacob: "And I will bless them that bless thee, and curse him that curseth thee: and in thee shall all families of the earth be blessed" (Gen. 12:3).

We reject the idea that we now live in a post-Christian era. This would abolish the promise of ultimate survival of the Church which Jesus declared in Matthew 16:18. However we are in danger of moving into a post-Bible age in the Church. What a tragedy if we lose our foundation in the Word and begin to preach the ideas of men just because they are popular or comfortable.

Many are trying to get the Bible back into the public schools. We should also work to get the Bible back into the pulpits of our churches and classrooms of our seminaries. We thank God for the many pastors and teachers who are true to the whole Word of God. They are true allies, champions of a noble cause. We entreat the rest to return to the foundations of the Word of God.

We can count on the world to curse Israel. It never fails. Betrayal is the action of choice for a bankrupt world system. The French Catholic theologian Jacques Maritain wrote: "Israel . . . is to be found at the heart of the world's structure, stimulating it, exasperating it, moving it. Like an alien body, like an activating ferment injected into the mass, it gives the world no peace, it bars slumber, it teaches the world to be discontented and restless as long as the world has not God, it stimulates the movement of history . . . . It is the vocation of Israel which the world hates."[12]

In his novel *Armageddon*[13] Leon Uris, a Jewish author, has one of his characters saying that Hitler was anti-Semitic because he was anti-Christ. Uris' character pondered Hitler's hatred of Christ and since Hitler could not get at God or His Son he attacked God by trying to destroy the Jews, the chosen.

Marshall Fishwick, an Episcopal historian wrote, "Shortly after World War II, I found myself in Paris. The Nazi chapter had closed; bookstalls along the Seine were open. Spotting a battered copy of Goethe's *Faust*, I began to thumb through the pages. A voice behind me said quietly: 'Ah Monsieur, I see you are interested in the Devil.'

"Turning, I confronted one of those gaunt, drawn, infinitely sad faces which filled Europe in the 1940s. The man's clothes were tattered, his shirt stained. His long thin fingers were bent, like legs of dead crabs. Pain and agony had long been his constant companions. Both eyes burned with an intense flame. Somehow they scorched me. Hesitantly I tried to answer his question.

"Yes, I am.

" 'I have seen him!' the old man said. Then he faded into the crowd."

Fishwick later quotes theologian Charles Journet who warns, "It is dangerous to embark on the question of evil. We risk defeat, and we risk presumption as well." Fishwick asks, "How can we dare to set foot in forbidden territory?

"There are those today who do not believe in the Devil. They are the first fallen: for Satan always begins by trying to convince us that he doesn't exist. The wisest human minds, and the God-made Man, have acknowledged the existence of the forces of evil, and wrestled with them. So must we."[14]

"Be sober, be vigilant; because your adversary the devil, as a roaring lion, walketh about, seeking whom he may devour" (1 Pet. 5:8).

Can Israel survive in a hostile world? Can the Jewish people survive in a hostile world? The answer is yes, but there is more . . . .

Notes

[1]John Milton, *Paradise Lost*, 1667.

[2]Victor Hugo, *Les Miserables*, Translated by Charles E. Wilbour, 1862. "Upon the first goblet he read this inscription, *monkey wine;* upon the second, *lion wine;* upon the third, *sheep wine*; upon the fourth, *swine wine.*"

    These four inscriptions expressed the four descending degrees of drunkenness; the first, that which enlivens; the second, that which irritates; the third that which stupefies; finally the last, that which brutalizes. The swine are again trampling the earth.

[3]Dennis Prager and Joseph Telushkin, *Why the Jews?* (New York, NY: Simon and Schuster, 1983), p. 17.

[4]Moloch: A demon god that demands human sacrifices. "And thou shalt not let any of thy seed pass through the fire to Molech, neither shalt thou profane the name of thy God: I am the Lord" (Lev. 18:21). Also see: 2 Kings 23:10; Jeremiah 32:35; Leviticus 20:2-5; 1 Kings 11:7. Note: There are, in the Bible, two spellings of Molech/Moloch. We use the latter except when quoting other authors, or when quoting one of the Bible passages which uses Molech.

[5]Milton, *Paradise Lost.*

[6]Thomas Eagleton, *News Leader* (Springfield, MO: Gannett, January 1, 1994). Eagleton is a former U.S. senator from Missouri who now writes a weekly newspaper column.

[7]Prager and Telushkin, *Why the Jews?* p. 17, 20.

[8]Eschatology: A branch of theology concerned with final events. Study of end-time prophecy.

[9]Deborah Lipstadt, *Denying the Holocaust — the Growing Assault on Truth and Memory* (New York, NY: Macmillan-Free Press, 1993). This book deals with the revisionist historians who deny that the Holocaust ever took place.

[10]Soteriology: Study of the doctrine of salvation.

[11]P.P. Bliss, "Let the Lower Lights Be Burning."

[12]Jacques Maritain, *A Christian Looks at the Jewish Question.* (New York, NY: Longman's, 1939).

[13]Leon Uris, *Armageddon* (Garden City, NY: Doubleday, 1964).

[14]Marshall W. Fishwick, *Faust Revisited* (New York, NY: Seabury Press, 1963), p. 1, 7.

2

THE HOLOCAUST

Christian Responsibility and Response

> *To any sane observer, there has always been an unfathomable mystery about the systematic evil the Nazi regime perpetrated — like a moral black hole, it seems to defy the laws of nature while being a part of that nature.* — David Ansen[1]
>
> *In the twilight, in the evening, in the black and dark night* (Prov. 7:9).

The Holocaust is an event so horrible that millions have blinded their eyes to its reality. A mysterious mind-numbing force has erased the memory of the Shoah for some. There are people around you who cannot even define the term Holocaust, nor its Hebrew equivalent, the Shoah.

"Holocaust" is the term used to describe the Nazi attempt to exterminate the Jewish people in Europe during the period of the Second World War. The most conservative estimate is that four million people were executed. Most Holocaust scholars put the figure at six million or more. While there have been many persecutions of the Jews in the past this was the first time that genocide became a national political policy. Hitler and his henchmen called it "the Final Solution" for dealing with the "Jewish problem."

The racist theories of the Nazis persuaded millions of Germans and other Europeans that the Jews did not belong to the same human race as white Aryans. According to the Nazi theory there was no common origin of all human beings. Darwin's theory of evolution was used to their advantage. The Jews were seen as having a separate evolution and belonged to a sub-human species. This also applied to black people, in fact to all non-Aryans. If the Jews were allowed to intermarry with white Aryans, it would mongrelize and debase the human race. If Germany did not win the war, the Jews would triumph and their plot for world domination would succeed. Hitler proclaimed himself as the savior of the true human race. Since the Jews were such a terrible threat any means to get rid of them was justifiable, and indeed could be proclaimed as a manifestation of the will of God.

In 1939, as the world stood on the brink of the Second World War, Hitler said, "Today I will once more be a prophet. If the international financiers inside and outside Europe should again succeed in plunging the nations into a world war, the result will not be the bolshevisation of the earth and thus the victory of Jewry, but the annihilation (verichtung) of the Jewish race throughout Europe." Since the Jews were seen as the worst enemies of "true humanity" one purpose of the war would be to get rid of the Jews.

The Jews refused to believe that any such thing could happen, in spite of the ranting of Hitler and other Nazi leaders. They considered Germany to be the epitome of Western Christian civilization. "It can't happen here, not in the center of Western culture." The rest of the world did not take Hitler seriously until it was too late. Holocaust survivors tell us that even while riding the box cars to the death camps, the victims refused to face reality. They were going to be workers.

Children of the Warsaw ghetto, all slaughtered by the Nazis.

While going into the gas chambers they believed the lie that it was shower rooms they were entering. Only when they breathed the first whiff of gas . . . .

FOR A LACK OF KNOWLEDGE

One evening a friend who was in Springfield, Missouri's Battle-field Mall, observed a young woman (she appeared to be in her thirties) coming out of the movie *Schindler's List*.[2] Schindler was a "good" Nazi who spent millions of dollars and great effort to save Jews from death. She was weeping and saying, "I didn't know that this ever happened, I did not know about the Holocaust." According to recent polls, 25 percent of Americans and Canadians profess that they never heard of the Holocaust.

"My people are destroyed for lack of knowledge . . . . they regard not the work of the Lord, neither consider the operation of his hands. Therefore my people are gone into captivity, because they have no knowledge . . ." (Hos. 4:6; Isa. 5:12-13).

The word "Holocaust" comes from a third century Greek word *Holokaustos,* referring to "the burnt sacrificial offering of the Jews dedicated exclusively to God." The Holocaust was Hitler's fiery offering of human sacrifice to Satan, just as in the days of the heathen Amorite god, Moloch.[3]

Having glimpsed the horror of history, some choose to deny that the Holocaust ever happened. Some books by allegedly learned scholars call the whole thing a hoax, perpetrated by the Jewish people themselves.[4]

Saint Paul rightly says that Satan is capable of blinding the minds

Gas furnaces for disposal of Jewish corpses.

of those who refuse to believe the truth. "In whom the god of this world hath blinded the minds of them which believe not . . ." (2 Cor. 4:4). In this passage the "god of this world" is Satan.

How any person can deny one of the most documentable events, the Holocaust, is beyond me. And yet historical revisionists use twisted logic, and bald-faced lies to make just such a denial, adding that if there was any large scale killing of Jews, it was the fault of the Jews themselves.

General Dwight David Eisenhower gave a statement to the press on April 15, 1945 after having visited some of the Nazi death camps. He said, "The things I saw beggar description . . . the visual evidence and the verbal testimony of starvation, cruelty, and bestiality were . . . overpowering . . . . I made the visit deliberately in order to be in a position to give *first-hand* evidence of these things if ever, in the future, there develops a tendency to charge these allegations merely to propaganda."

The waters are further muddied by the fact that there are self-hating Jews who play into the hands of the enemies of Israel, as is so graphically revealed in books like Sander L. Gilman's *Jewish Self Hatred.* A tiny, radical minority of Jews pander to those who deny the Holocaust, falling over themselves to proclaim that there were no gas ovens nor gas chambers, and no mass killing of Jews. No *reliable* historian takes these people seriously.

ISRAELOLOGY, THE LOST DOCTRINE OF THE CHURCH

In his compelling dialogue on Christian-Jewish relations in the Epistle to the Romans, chapters 9, 10, and 11, Saint Paul makes some vital observations. The passage clearly establishes that God still has a plan for natural (national) Israel. Some commentaries on Romans treat the entire Epistle with weighty word-by-word analysis, except for these three vital chapters. Other commentaries only lightly pass through these important three chapters. Arnold Fruchtenbaum's book *Israelology: The Missing Link in Systematic Theology* has addressed this major flaw and weakness of Christian systematic theology.

Examine the syllabus of the Romans courses taught in some of our Bible colleges and seminaries, and you will find that in many the ninth, tenth, and eleventh chapters of Romans are ignored completely. This was first called to my attention by a respected colleague, Dr. Amos Millard, a professor of Bible in an Evangelical college.

Church creeds detail a long list of doctrines dealing with many legitimate theological ideas, yet are strangely silent on the destiny of national Israel. As far as I am able to perceive, there is only one church denomination that gives official recognition to the concept that there is a future for the nation of Israel. Surely there are other denominations that have such a statement in their creed? If you know of one, please inform us as we are anxious to expand our research in this area. Most Evangelicals tend to base their beliefs on sound interpretation of the Scripture, so an acceptance of national Israel in God's plan is common in these groups. It is common, but by no means universal.

Charles B. Williams writes in his commentary on Romans, "What does Paul mean when he says, 'All Israel shall be saved?' It is a hyperbole [exaggeration] . . . . It means that vast hosts of Israel at some time will accept Jesus as their Messiah . . . . Surely, he is not saying that Israel will all be restored to the Holy Land in a physical and political sense."[5]

It is a wonder to me how some authors want the Bible to be literal in matters of historical data, instruction for church ordinances, and redemption, but see only allegories and hyperbole when it comes to Israel. Indeed Romans 11:26 has nothing to do with the physical restoration of Israel to the land. So why did Williams inject a denial here? The return of the Jews to Eretz Israel is firmly established in scores, if not hundreds, of other biblical passages. Why a denial that does not even fit into the text being examined? Does it show a bias on the part of the author against the restoration of Israel to her land?

Our faith does not rest on denominational creeds. Our faith is grounded on the record of the 66 books of the Bible. Further, when we speak of a plan for national Israel we are not referring to the salvation of individuals. That is a personal matter worked out between the person and God. In another chapter, we will show that God is still in covenant with the nation of Israel, through the Abrahamic covenant, which was and is unilateral and unconditional (see Gen. 12 and 15).

JEW, ISRAELI, HEBREW, TRIBE

In the light of the Abrahamic covenant Paul cautions the converted Gentiles of Rome not to boast against the natural branches (Jewish people) that have grown out of the root of Abraham. The terms Jew, Israelite, Hebrew, etc., had become interchangeable by the time the New Testament was written. We also use the word "Jew" in its present common usage, applying to all who are of natural Israel. Note how Paul describes himself with these various terms: "I also am an Israelite, of the seed of Abraham, of the tribe of Benjamin" (Rom. 11:1). "Circumcised the eighth day, of the stock of Israel, of the tribe of Benjamin, an Hebrew of the Hebrews; as touching the law, a Pharisee" (Phil. 3:5). "But Paul said, I am a man which am a Jew of Tarsus" (Acts 21:39). (Also see Acts 22:3.)

Romans also says that the tree still belongs to Israel. It is their tree. We Christians are former Gentiles, wild branches grafted into the natural tree of Israel. The *Wycliffe Bible Commentary* correctly establishes that Abraham is the root of us all.[6]

Note that Paul reminds the converted Gentiles in Rome that you do not support the root, but the root supports you (see Rom. 11:18). "And if some of the branches be broken off, and thou, being a wild olive tree, wert graffed in among them, and with them, partakest of the root and fatness of the olive tree; Boast not against the branches. But if thou boast, thou bearest not the root, but the root thee . . . . For if thou wert cut out of the olive tree which is wild by nature, and wert graffed contrary to nature into a good olive tree: how much more shall these, which be the natural branches, be graffed into *their own olive tree?"* (Rom. 11:17-24). (Emphasis mine.)

While Israel can easily explain her existence without the Church, the Church cannot explain her existence without Israel. Jesus was Jewish as were His disciples and followers.

JESUS AND THE EARLY DISCIPLES WERE JEWISH

The only Bible Jesus and His followers had was the Tenach, (Old Testament). The entire body of Christian Scripture was penned by Jewish authors, with the possible exception of Luke and Acts. At the very first the Church was entirely Jewish in its membership. In fact, the Early Church, in its primitive days, was never thought of by the Jewish people, in or out of the Church, as anything more or less than a Jewish sect. It was not until after the Bar Kochba revolt in the year A.D. 135 that the Jewish and Gentile elements in the Church finally separated and went their own ways. The way the Gentile branch of the Church followed tragically led directly to the Holocaust. Thus a contemporary United Methodist theologian, Roy Eckardt, told me that he believes that the Holocaust was not an isolated incident, but merely indicative of the general trend the Church has always taken. Can this be true?

THE CHURCH DIVIDES

The sad saga of Early Church history records that animosity arose in the Gentile Church against the Jewish believers and Jews in general. As time went on the Church became more and more anti-Semitic.

This situation reached a zenith when Constantine granted the edicts of toleration. While Christianity was not actually made the state religion by Constantine, and while Constantine never was a convert to Christianity, he submitted to baptism by sprinkling upon his deathbed, thus adding "Christ" to his list of pagan Roman deities — not an uncommon practice in the pagan world of multiple gods. Nevertheless, under the edicts of toleration Christianity was popularized, and tens of thousands of unconverted pagans were baptized into the Church because it was the popular social or politically expedient thing to do.

THE DARK ROAD

Malcolm Hay, Fr. John T. Pawlikowski, Fr. Edward Flannery, and other Roman Catholic authors, along with many modern Protestant writers such as Roy and Alice Eckardt, Reinhold Niebuhr, Franklin Littel, Herman Voss, and David Rausch, have extensively documented the historic anti-Semitic bias of the Church.

A well-documented book, *Thy Brother's Blood*, by Malcolm Hay, a French Catholic historian, is one of the finest documents on the subject of Christian anti-Semitism ever written. It has been published under various titles.[7]

Consider the harsh words of Saint Ambrose, who said that the Jewish synagogue was "a house of impiety, a receptacle of folly, which God himself has condemned."[8] It is no wonder that his followers then went out and set fire to the local synagogue.

In the fourth century, Saint Gregory of Nyssa eloquently declared the Jews to be, "Slayers of the Lord, murderers of the prophets, adversaries of God, haters of God, men who show contempt for the law, foes of grace, enemies of their father's faith, advocates of the devil, brood of vipers, slanderers, scoffers, men whose minds are in darkness, leaven of the Pharisees, assembly of demons, sinners, wicked men, stoners, and haters of righteousness."[9]

Saint John Chrysostom must have had some good qualities, for Cardinal Newman wrote of him, "A bright and cheerful gentle soul, a sensitive heart, a temperament open to emotion and impulse; and all this elevated, refined, transformed by the touch of heaven, — such was St. John Chrysostom."[10]

A Protestant theologian wrote, "Chrysostom was one of the most eloquent of the preachers who, ever since apostolic times, have brought to men the Divine tidings of truth and love."[11]

It must have been difficult for the Jewish people of his time to see his good points for in his homilies against the Jews, St. John Chrysostom said, "The synagogue is worse than a brothel . . . the temple of demons . . . and the cavern of devils . . . . I hate the synagogue . . . . I hate the Jews for the same reason."

Martin Luther, beloved among Protestants and Evangelicals made strong anti-Semitic statements late in his life. "All the blood kindred of Christ burn in hell, and they are rightly served, even according to their own words they spoke to Pilate . . . . Verily a hopeless, wicked, venomous, and devilish thing is the existence of these Jews, who for 1,400 years have been, and still are, our pest, torment, and misfortune. They are just devils and nothing more." Malcolm Hay comments, "His doctrine provided many suitable texts for Hitler's program of extermination."[12]

Today various hate groups reprint Luther's pamphlet, *The Jews and Their Lies* to support their vengeful attacks on the Jews.[13]

In 1558 the Protestant preacher Jodokus Ehrhardt wrote, "We ought not to suffer Jews to live amongst us, nor to eat and drink with them."[14]

Six million died. Christian anti-Semitism paved the road that led to the Holocaust.

Following the precedent of Saint Ambrose he also recommended that "their synagogues should be set on fire."[15]

STRANGE BEDFELLOWS — NAZIS AND THEOLOGIANS

Our beloved Church became a Haman to the Jews, bringing on the dark ages, the horrors of the Inquisition and the bloody Crusades, ultimately producing the climate in which Hitler could succeed with his diabolical plot.

Donald McEvoy writes, "While we know that Hitler and his Nazi cohorts were anti-religions secularists, and there is no way in which their actions can be equated with the tenets of the Christian faith, it remains a fact of history that the Nazi terror arose in the midst of a nominally Christian nation with a minimum of active opposition from the church." These words from the pen of Donald W. McEvoy points out a problem that has implications for the church today. "Many church leaders actively endorsed and applauded the rise of the Third Reich. A high percentage of the Nazi leaders remained in full communion with the churches even while engaging in their murderous acts.

"Christianity's role in the Holocaust must not remain hid-

Jews waiting execution, treated as less than animals by the Nazis.

den or unstated. It must be faced, no matter how painful an undertaking that may be.

"Two realities must be considered in our assessment of the church's role. First the Nazis inherited a religious and social climate of anti-Semitism which had been fostered by the church for centuries. The Final Solution was deeply rooted in what has been rightly described as the church's 'teaching of contempt for the Jews.' It was relatively easy for the totalitarian state to exploit the traditional anti-Jewish teachings of the church, which said, in effect, 'You have no right to live among us as Jews,' and turned it into the murderous declaration, 'You have no right to live.' "[16]

Can we be offended at the Jewish scholar who indicts Christianity as the prime cause of anti-Semitism for the past 1,800 years? It might be convenient if we could ignore the dark side of our heritage, but if we ever hope to improve conditions in the world it would be more practical to face up to history, ourselves, and our society.

What a perverse joke it is when present day replacement theologians accuse their premillennial brethren of being socially irresponsible in the face of the drastic, crisis needs of our world, while they themselves are promoting evil hatred for the nation of Israel through their tired, old, worn-out anti-Semitic theology. How have they managed to resurrect these ancient errors and breathe such new vigor

ARBEIT MACHT FREI: Sign at one of the slave labor and death camps: Work makes you free.

into them until they are now sweeping like an "ill wind that bodes no good" throughout the ranks of evangelicalism?

Dr. Roland Pritiken, a retired Air Force general, recently sent me an interesting list of comparisons between pre-Nazi Germany and conditions in America today. There is indeed cause for concern.

The Church in pre-Nazi Germany was preaching the twin doctrines of Christian anti-Semitism. They are the *doctrine of replacement and the doctrine of contempt*. The theology of replacement contends that the Church has replaced Israel and that God no longer has any purpose for Israel. Contempt declares that the Jews crucified Jesus therefore they are under a curse and whatever happens, including the Holocaust, is their just dessert. We should not concern ourselves.

While both of these errors had been refuted, nevertheless Hitler's henchmen were able to quote both Roman and Protestant theologians in justifying their heinous acts against the Jewish people. Thus in a Christian nation, out of a perverted Christianity came the Holocaust, costing the lives of six million Jews and also 50 million other casualties, lives lost as a direct result of the Second World War.

EVANGELICAL RECORD BLIGHTED

My Evangelical brethren cannot boast that our colleagues performed any better in the Nazi era. As noted earlier, the late Dr. Oswald Smith, pastor of the great People's Church in Toronto, Canada, came back from Germany with a glowing report in the mid-1930's. He spoke of over 14,000 Evangelical pastors who felt that Hitler was the answer to Germany's problems and that probably the neo-Nazi movement would bring spiritual revival to Germany. Later Dr. Smith realized the awfulness of what was happening in Germany and recanted, but it was too late. Dr. Smith was a man of true greatness and humility. He had simply made a tragic misjudgment of the situation in Germany. Such errors are costly.

We still have time to speak out and prevent another Holocaust in our times, but the handwriting is on the wall. If we are silent history will repeat itself.

Is the Church in America different today from the Church in pre-Holocaust Germany? I hope that it is, but I have some deep concerns. Perhaps the 14,000 Evangelical pastors that Dr. Smith spoke of were not actively anti-Semitic. Perhaps they were simply unconcerned. As Pastor Martin Neomuller wrote from a Nazi prison cell: "When they came for the Jews I did not protest because I am not a Jew. When they came for the Catholics I did not protest because I am not a Catholic. When they came for me, there was no one left to protest."

We have heard some strange things from modern churchmen in recent years. After Israel was savagely attacked by Syria and Egypt on the Day of Atonement, October 1973, Father Daniel Berrigan, a well-known anti-Israel priest, accused Israel of behaving like a "criminal" and "racist state." Then Henry Pit van Deusan, former president of the Union Theological Seminary, likened the Jewish nation to Nazi Germany. To this, Methodist theologian Roy Eckardt commented, "Whenever Israel is assailed, certain suppressed, macabre elements in the Christian soul are stirred to sympathy with the assailants."

WHAT HAVE WE LEARNED?

We wonder if the Christian world has drawn any lessons at all from the Holocaust. We should have. When the greatest events of mankind's history are finally recorded they will include the Creation of earth, the fall of man, God's provision of redemption through Jesus, the destruction of Jerusalem in A.D. 70, the Reformation, two World Wars, the Holocaust, the re-establishment of the nation of Israel, and the second coming of Christ.

Being an Evangelical I should not presume to speak for the older churches. My colleagues in the National Christian Leadership Conference for Israel, Dr. William Harter, Presbyterian; Dr. Franklin Littel, United Methodist; Reverend Edward Flannery, Roman Catholic; Reverend Isaac Rottenberg of the Reformed Church; and a host of others have documented the anti-Semitic and anti-Israel bias that has

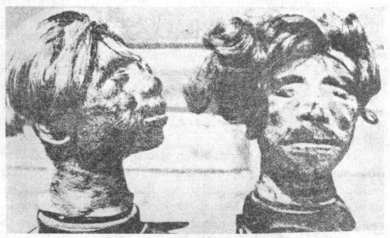

Proud work of Nazi taxidermist — mounted Jewish heads.

been consistently manifested by the National and the World Council of Churches.

I have heard a Roman Catholic nun, the great and compassionate scholar Sister Rose Thering, professor emeritus of Seton Hall University, lament the Vatican's long refusal to recognize the state of Israel. Therefore, concluding that there are strong voices in the old-line churches, calling for repentance in that quarter, I will speak primarily to my own Evangelical brothers and sisters. Even as I write these lines the news informs me that the Vatican is relenting and will recognize that Israel has a right to exist.

In the past we Evangelicals have prided ourselves in using the Bible as our mandate for action. Some of us have boasted confidently of the strong support for Israel and resistance against anti-Semitism that exists in our ranks. We still have great strength in these areas, but a certain erosion of these values is in progress. New waves of anti-Semitism are sweeping through our own churches. Strange new anti-Semitic doctrines are being promoted, and whenever there is anti-Semitism, a Holocaust could happen again.

Kingdom Now, Dominion, Theonomy, Restoration, and Reconstruction are labels attached to vigorous Evangelical movements which not only differ with our eschatology, but which also have an agenda for political takeover, establishing a world theocracy before the return of Christ, to abolish democracy, do away with pluralism, and put the Jews in their place. There are, of course, exceptions. Not all of the people in these groups have the same agenda for world action. Some Evangelical Protestants who plan to rule the world before the Second Coming realize that first they must conquer the Church. Even now, while much of the Church sleeps, the secular media is calling attention to this aggressive movement.

We learn from time to time of secretive and in some cases hidden networks existing among the Charismatics and Pentecostals. We learn of new ones beginning regularly. There are also open conferences and conventions designed to effect major theological changes in our churches. "Their" leadership is encouraged to stay put in our ranks and work for control within. Newly appointed Charismatic apostles exert a self-aggrandizing authority to which some of my own brethren are willing to bow. The thirst for political power in the ecclesiastical world is wondrous to behold.

Why are the Pentecostals and Evangelicals targeted for hostile takeover? Who will be the pope of the Pentecostals? With control of

176,000,000 denominational Pentecostals and 156,000,000 Charismatics at stake, that is a foremost question! Which apostle will your pastor be asked to bow to? How will they overcome existing church governments and capture the clergy in classical Pentecostal churches? Will the cry "Unity at any cost" be the nemesis of those stubborn people who insist on believing that Israel and the Jewish people are still significant to the plan and purposes of God? Are you even aware of what is going on?

Will the silencing of my voice and that of my colleagues open the door for a future holocaust? Does anyone even care?

Even though a time of wrath will come upon the whole world, *woe to those by whom it comes*. Blessed therefore are those who do the will of God regardless of personal cost. Blessed are those who resist evil in all forms at all times.

The existence of the anti-Semitic Christian doctrines I speak of are further evidenced by an outpouring of attractive books and literature promoting theological anti-Semitism and thus potential hatred for the Jewish people.

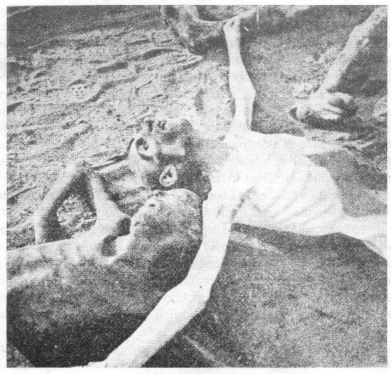

It could happen again.

Kingdom now theology is primarily amillennial. Dominionism is post-millennial. It is only fair to note that there are amillennialists and post-millennialists who are strongly pro-Israel, but their numbers are small. One notable example is Rev. Ivan Rogers, a leader in the Open Bible Standard Church, a Pentecostal denomination. Rogers, an amillennialist, does not openly espouse any of the groups listed above. Ivan is a true man of God. He is supportive of Israel.[17]

Not all of the leadership in these groups mentioned are actively anti-Semitic, but most of them teach that God no longer has any plan for the nation of Israel (replacement theology). Some speak harshly and even confirm that they would not be bothered to see the state of Israel crumble. They feel that the existence of Israel is an accident of history, not a fulfillment of prophecy. Some are blatantly anti-Semitic.

Almost daily the news decries the spread of Neo-Nazi activity. Recently a group of five radicals from Texas were apprehended in Washington, DC. The FBI reported that their possessions included an M-16 grenade launcher, machine guns, rifles, shotguns, handguns, and silencers along with a Nazi flag. Law enforcement officials here in our area tell me that these Aryan groups are now common all over America. Our formerly quiet, rurally-oriented area is a hotbed of Neo-Nazi activity. Our Evangelical colleagues (in part) are properly shocked at these media revelations. These Nazi groups unfortunately fly the flag of Evangelical or Fundamentalist Christianity. We disown them.

But it is not enough to speak of Aryan radicals in our culture. Never mind the fact that right here in southern Missouri we are surrounded by skinheads, the Order; the Covenant, the Sword, and Arm of the Lord; and Pentecostal Nazis; and that the Ku Klux Klan has moved its international headquarters to Harrison, Arkansas, within 70 miles of my front door.

It concerns me that in my own hometown Dominionist books with theologically anti-Semitic overtones are on the bookshelves of local religious bookstores. The concept of replacement has been preached on a local religious radio station. It is preached in local churches. I would venture to say that it is in your hometown as well.

We speak of the Holocaust as an historic phenomenon. But if we allow these ideas to advance in our churches, if we are silent, as so many were silent in Germany, it could happen here. It could happen again.

THE HOLOCAUST IS NOT MERE HISTORY. IT IS POTENTIAL

The TV cameras were running. We were in the Yad Vashem Holocaust Memorial in Jerusalem. We were involved in the production of a Christian documentary on the Holocaust. Out of the shadows stepped an elderly Jewish man who called out, "Mister, I was there. It really happened." Rolling up his sleeve, he thrust out his arm, revealing a tattooed number on his wrist. "Look, look, I was there. Don't let them tell you it never happened." His embarrassed wife pulled at his coattails until he backed away from the lighted area.

We watched his retreating figure fading back into the darkness. We heard his final, plaintive cry, "Mister, listen to me. Mister — *it could happen again.*"

PRAYER

Almighty God, we confess our sins and the sins of the Church. As the ancient prophets of Israel confessed the sins of their nation — sins of which they had no personal guilt — so we confess the sins of our Church and our nation. We have not pleased You when we have participated in slander against the Jewish people. Forgive us for remaining silent when we should have spoken out against evil hatred of Your people, Israel. Forgive us for being intimidated in the face of anti-Semitism.

Having confessed our sin we pray that You will give us the resolve and courage to act upon our faith. Anoint us by thy Holy Spirit to receive Your truth. Let our belief be our mandate to action. May we never again be silent when anti-Semitism raises its ugly head in our midst. Strengthen us in this determination.

In the name of the Lord Jesus Christ. Amen.

Notes

[1]David Ansen, review of the movie *Schindler's List* (New York, NY; *Newsweek:* December 20, 1993), p. 113.

[2]*Schindler's List*, a movie about the Holocaust, directed by Steven Spielberg.

[3]Michael Marrus, *The Holocaust in History* (New York, NY: New American Library, 1987), cited by Rosio in *Hitler and the New Age.* See Rosio p. 50 footnote #5) p. 23.

[4]Arthur R. Butz, *The Hoax of the Twentieth Century* (Richmond, Surrey, England: Historical Review Press, 1976).

[5]Charles B. Williams, *A Commentary on the Pauline Epistles* (Chicago, IL: Moody Press, 1953), p. 298.

[6]Everett Harrison, Ed., *The Wycliffe Bible Commentary* (Chicago, IL: Moody Press, 1962/1974, 10th ed.), p. 1217.

[7]Malcolm Hay, *Thy Brother's Blood* (New York, NY: Hart Publishing Company, 1975). This book was first published in 1950 under the title *The Foot of Pride* (Beacon Press); in 1960 under the title *Europe and the Jews*; The book is now published under another title, which we cannot recall. Your librarian may be able to help you.

[8]Hay, *Thy Brother's Blood*, p. 25.

[9]Hay, *Thy Brother's Blood*, p. 26.

[10]Hay, *Thy Brother's Blood*, p. 27.

[11]Hay, *Thy Brother's Blood*, p. 27.

[12]Hay, *Thy Brother's Blood*, p. 167.

[13]Martin Luther, *The Jews and Their Lies* (Eureka Springs, AR: Christian Nationalist Crusade, ncd), reprint of Luther's work. This organization may no longer be represented in Eureka Springs. They may be operating under another name in California.

[14]Hay, *Thy Brother's Blood*, p. 168.

[15]Hay, *Thy Brother's Blood*, p. 168.

[16]Donald W. McEvoy, *Jerusalem Courier* (Springfield, MO: Christians United for Israel, 1989), Vol. 8, #1.

[17]Ivan A. Rogers, *End-Time Interviews*, a set of two audio cassettes (Marshfield, Wisconsin: Israel to Israel, ncd).

3

ANTI-SEMITISM AND THE CHURCH

The Dark Side of History

> *The demonic quality of the phenomenon that turns saints into sadists, savants into muddleheads, and common folk into assassins.* . . . — Edward Flannery
>
> *And the Lord said unto Satan, The Lord rebuke thee, O Satan; even the Lord that hath chosen Jerusalem rebuke thee: is not this a brand plucked out of the fire* (Zech. 3:2).

Some time ago a seminar for church leadership was offered, which I was privileged to attend. The theme of the seminar was *The Family,* and on the whole it was helpful and constructive.

The program included the showing of a film dealing with some of the problems facing the family in today's fractured society. The film featured a well-known lecturer and a number of people who gave testimonies of their personal experiences. A woman giving one of the testimonials told of her unhappy life as an unbeliever. She emphasized how that contrasted with her new life as a follower of Jesus Christ. Her sincerity and enthusiasm were refreshing. However, in the course of her remarks she said, "I found out that Jesus wasn't just a *tripped-out*

Jew," and later, "I knew then that *He wasn't just a Jew.* "

SUBTLETY OF ANTI-SEMITISM

Anti-Semitism is a very subtle thing and unless one is very watchful our terminology can be loaded with racist and anti-Semitic implications. Have you ever said, "I *Jewed* him down on the price?" Or, "He's a real *Shylock.* " Once while negotiating a business transaction a person said to this Christian, of English and French ancestry, "Don't be such a *Jew.* "

It is not my purpose to indict the woman giving testimony in the film for her subtle anti-Semitism. But she could have said, "I found out that Jesus was not just a man. He was the very Son of God." That would have been better than what she said, "Not just a tripped-out Jew."

I do indict the film editor and producer for their insensitivity. This should never have gotten into the final production version of the film.

THE JEW HATING BISHOP

In 1980 I spent some time with the bishop of an Evangelical denomination of another country. He spoke very badly of the Jews. He also had a very light view of the inspiration of the Scriptures. He had recently been in the Holy Land on a guided tour, and commented that his Israeli guide "had a bit of Shakespeare's Shylock in him." His insults intensified as he noted that although the guide had studied the Gospels, and could speak of the events in Jesus' life, "It had no effect on him. It was done only for advantage." It was an insult to the Jewish guide, who was simply trying to do his job to the best of his ability.

I told him that the Israeli government had invited me to teach a two-day seminar for Israeli guides, in which I was asked to explain the Gospel of Jesus so the guides could better identify with their Christian clients. I thought that was a thoughtful and fine thing. The seminar was a real success and benefit, not only for the guides, but for the Christian tourists they serve. Over 100 guides took the course. Their attitude was very positive, the dialogue was lively.

The bishop lectured publicly in a church located in Texas. Sitting in the meeting, listening to his message, I was not at all surprised to find that the prejudice he displayed in private was just as remarkable in a public setting.

DISCUSSING BEGIN AND SADAT

The bishop described his impressions of Prime Minister

Menachem Begin of Israel and Anwar Sadat, president of Egypt. He spoke only ill of Mr. Begin, who came off very badly in his presentation. He had only the highest praise for Mr. Sadat.

I certainly appreciate the peace efforts of Mr. Sadat as well as those of Prime Minister Begin, but I think the bishop could have been a little more evenhanded in his evaluation. The bishop spoke of God's purpose in Egypt. He made absolutely no mention of the purpose of God for Israel.

He said, "While Sadat may not know the Son or the Spirit, he certainly knows the Father." Of course Sadat was a Moslem and worshipped Allah as his God. There is no relation between Allah and our Father. Jehovah and Allah are two different God concepts. The bishop called for prayer for Egypt. He made no request for prayer for Israel even though the Bible commands us to pray for the peace of Jerusalem (see Ps. 122).

Of Mr. Sadat he said, "He has had an encounter with God. He quoted David, Solomon, Jesus, and Moses." (Let's not forget he also quoted the Koran, the words of Mohammed, prophet of Islam.) We were told in glowing terms of Sadat's proposal for the building of a religious complex at Mount Sinai consisting of a mosque, a church, and a synagogue. He declared that Sadat was a man chosen of God, for the destiny of Egypt.

WITHOUT GRACE

This ungracious church leader described Prime Minister Begin in slanderous terms, describing him as a cold, calculating, and unappealing person. This contrasted with his description of the Egyptian leader who was a man of pathos, power, and strong appeal.

His words did not describe the Begin I personally knew and met with on 15 occasions, in his home and in the prime minister's bureau in Jerusalem.

Let's be realistic. Neither Sadat nor Begin were Christian. One was a Moslem, one a Jew. With the Jewish prime minister we share a heritage in the Old Testament. Mr. Begin held a Bible study weekly in his home for a circle of friends who wished to study the Bible with him. This is not something he publicized — it is something he did privately out of personal conviction.

In my first meeting with Begin, in his home, I had strongly urged him to have such a weekly Bible study and prayer time with his friends and an inner circle of political leaders. Mr. Begin was knowledgeable concerning the prophecies of the Old Testament, and loved to discuss them with us. I was privileged to take several Evangelical leaders to meet with Prime Minister Menachem Begin. He did not hide his warm feelings toward Christians.

One needs to remember that it was Begin who invited Sadat to come to Jerusalem in 1978 to discuss a peace accord. It was not Sadat who initiated the peace process between Israel and Egypt. Furthermore, Egypt needed the treaty that finally was signed a lot more than Israel needed it. Egypt gained the Sinai, the Abu Rudis oil fields, and the Mitla and Gedi strategic passes. Israel got a piece of paper from a nation that could never hope to defeat Israel militarily. Israel gave land for peace. Now it is time to give peace for peace. After normalization of relations everything else can be peaceably negotiated.

The bishop was a very prejudiced person, so typical of Christians who despise the Jews. He was ready to believe every media distortion that was aimed against Israel. He was not interested in dialogue that involved a presentation of facts which would make Israel's case look more favorable. He scorned my biblical views as so much superstitious literalist nonsense, saying that I was duped by "those Machiavellian Jews."

PRAY FOR THE PEACE OF JERUSALEM — AND HER NEIGHBORS

We should pray for all the people of the Middle East and for the peace of Jerusalem and all of her neighbors. We pray that Israel and her neighbors will reach a level of negotiation and agreement that will allow a normalization of relations, free trade, and exchange of agricultural, medical, and other technology. Is that so bad?

Would it be fair to say that the bishop is an anti-Semite? According to the common use of the term, the answer is yes. "The term anti-*Semitism* was coined by a German agitator, Wilhelm Marr, in 1879 to designate anti-Jewish campaigns then appearing throughout Europe. Since that time the term has been universally applied to any form of behavior, activity, or literature which evidences hostility toward the Jews."[1]

The expression "anti-Semitism" appeared in a book by Marr, *The Victory of Judaism Over Germanism.* The book sounded a warning to the German-Aryan people. To Marr, anti-Semitism indicated a positive thing, a war against the hated Jews.[2]

OBSCENE ANTI-SEMITISM

An allegedly "Christian" publication spewed forth this can of garbage: "The Jew, in order to carry out the plans of white genocide, has set about to build a "colored" army. The Jew has filled America with niggers, wet-backs, chinks, spicks, whops, dagos, and mulattos, in all sizes, shapes, shades, and varieties. The Jew then set up the Federal and State social programs so that his colored vermin could breed freely, while taxing the white working people so heavily that they could not afford to have families. These colored people make a good living by breeding and having colored bastards . . . . Violence cannot be avoided! These bestial creatures do not understand any-thing but brute force." We have file drawers filled with anti-Semitic literature of this caliber. This mean-spirited type of writing is not rare at all.

The author of that article slammed those preachers who believe that the Bible promises regarding Israel are to be understood literally. He said that Jesus was not a Jew, but an Aryan. He portrayed Christ as being anti-Jewish. The author forgets that Jesus was an orthodox Jew and had what is comparable to a bar-mitzvah at age 12, which was the occasion of his being in the temple in Jerusalem as recorded in the Gospels. Jesus never attended church or Sunday school. He attended the temple and synagogue. The Early Church was entirely Jewish until the conversion of Cornelius. The Bible is written entirely by Jewish authors with the possible exception of one author, Luke.

Jesus said, "I am not sent but unto the lost sheep of the house of Israel" (Matt. 15:24). We view the very existence of Israel a fulfill-ment of Bible prophecy, both of the Jewish and Christian Scriptures.

CAN THE LEOPARD CHANGE HIS SPOTS?

Many who have ignorantly espoused Jew-hatred have made an about-face. Gerald Winrod, a Fundamentalist anti-Semite, published the *Defender Magazine*. One of his followers, Rev. Elmer Josephson, ". . . experienced a spiritual crisis after succumbing to the world conspiracy theory and the *Protocols of the Learned Elders of Zion*. He joined Winrod in 1937 because Winrod was 'one of America's top communist-fighters.' Soon after, Josephson took a second glance at his life in the light of Scripture and found he was 'traveling a very perilous path.' He left Winrod and has since operated Bible Light, a ministry supportive of the Jewish people and Israel."[3]

While Winrod never changed his mind about the Jews, his successor, now president of The Defenders organization, Rev. Hart Armstrong, rejects any form of anti-Semitism and is a friend and supporter of Israel.

An observation by David Rausch is appropriate here: "Evangelicals have received considerable bad press because of anti-Semites such as Winrod. Many scholars have taken for granted that the more theologically conservative one is, the more anti-Semitic one becomes. My research has shown that nothing is historically further from the truth. The fundamentalist-evangelical movement has traditionally been a firm supporter of the Jewish people and has staunchly opposed anti-Semitism. During the Holocaust, conservative Christians tended to believe that the Jewish people were being exterminated, while more liberal Christians were labeling the reports of atrocity as propaganda."[4] How could a Christian be anti-Semitic? To be anti-Semitic is to cooperate and agree with the devil. Satan's desire is to destroy the nation of Israel and thereby nullify the promises of God.

In another chapter we refer to Christians who use Israel as their "eschatological toy." Some prophecy buffs see the Jews more as objects than people. An even more serious matter are those Christians who distort prophecies and use them against Israel and the Jewish people.

Paul Carlson shows keen insight, "If liberal Christians are guilty of sacrificing Isaac on the altar of higher criticism, some conservative Christians who identify the church as the Chosen People of today have been guilty of outright anti-Semitism.

"One noted Reformed theologian, for example, has gone so far as to hint of a Messianic Age purged of the Messianic people. In his diatribe against the Jews, he writes: 'The continuance of this bitterly anti-Christian racial group has brought no good to themselves, and there has been strife and antagonism in practically every nation where they have gone. . . .' The veiled vision of this well-known evangelical is that of a Judenrein utopia — a millennium without Jews."[5]

Hal Lindsey is the most prominent figure in the field of popular prophecy literature. His *Late Great Planet Earth* is the best-selling book on end-time prophecy ever written, other than the Bible. Lindsey also writes weighty material for scholars and researchers in the Church. In *The Road to Holocaust* he exhorts the Church: "Those who know and understand the prophetic era in which we live must also strive to prevent the Church from creating the kind of philosophical atmosphere that can lead to another period of anti-Semitism. Let the true Christian never again give a theological framework from which unscrupulous men can promote another holocaust for the children of Israel."[6]

"The authentic Christian can only deplore that the Church and his/her co-believers were actively — or passively — involved in this tragic story, especially in its latest and most gruesome manifestation, the Holocaust. . . . The sin of anti-Semitism contains many sins," writes Edward Flannery in *The Anguish of the Jews*, "but in the end it is a denial of Christian faith, a failure of Christian hope, and a malady of Christian love. . . . And the ultimate scandal: that in carrying the burden of God in history the Jewish people did not find in the Christian churches an ally and defender but one of their most zealous detractors and oppressors. It is a story that calls for repentance."[7]

CHRISTIAN TASK FORCE

Frank Eiklor, president of Shalom International, is a man whose soul is on fire for God. Raised in an anti-Semitic atmosphere, he made a radical life change in 1979. He became a committed Christian Zionist. Frank suggests that Christians organize a Christian Task Force to combat anti-Semitism. Whenever a swastika is painted on a synagogue or a Jewish grave, let the members of the CTF go out and clean it up. Eiklor recommends: "If a newspaper letter or article exhibits contempt of Jews, task force members can answer those accusations in a collective letter with the names of all task force members affixed, to assure maximum impact."[8] Eiklor adds, "Sentimental rhetoric is not enough. The urgent need for action against anti-Semitism is a call to Christian conscience. A Christian task force against anti-Semitism in your city, with you involved, is an undisguised, unmistakable message to the purveyors of hate: 'Not in our town.' "[9]

As loyal sons and daughters of the Church of Jesus we recognize that we have a long and sometimes sordid history behind us, most of it not of our doing. We nevertheless take the responsibility of history on our shoulders. We repudiate the errors and cruelty of the past. We ask God for forgiveness and reformation within the Church. Our inheritance from the past is flawed, but it need not be our future. To all the enemies of Israel who would plot a future Holocaust, we say, "No! You will not succeed." Israel will survive!

Notes

[1]Richard E. Gade, *A Historical Survey of Anti-Semitism* (Grand Rapids, MI: Baker Book House, 1981), p. 7.

[2]Charles Patterson, *Anti-Semitism — The Road to the Holocaust and Beyond* (New York, NY: Walker and Company, 1982), p. 28ff.

[3]David A. Rausch, *Legacy of Hatred* (Chicago, IL: Moody Press, 1984), p. 103.

[4]Rausch, *A Legacy of Hatred*, p. 103.

[5]Paul R. Carlson, *O Christian! O Jew!* (Elgin, IL: David C. Cook Publishing Co., 1974), p. 72.

[6]Hal Lindsey, *Road To Holocaust* (New York, NY: Bantam Books, 1989), p. 282-283.

[7]Edward H. Flannery, *The Anguish of the Jews — Twenty-three Centuries of Anti-Semitism* (Mahwah, NJ: Paulist Press, 1985), p. 295.

[8]Frank Eiklor, *A Time for Trumpets — Not Piccolos* (Orange, CA: Promise Publishing Co., 1988), p. 102ff.

[9]Eiklor, *A Time for Trumpets — Not Piccolos*, p. 103.

4

THE HEBRON MASSACRE

A Tragedy for Jews and Arabs

> *The voice of the daughter of Zion, that bewaileth herself, that spreadeth her hands, saying, Woe is me now! for my soul is wearied because of murderers* (Jer. 4:31).
>
> *Woe is me for my hurt! my wound is grievous: but I said, Truly this is a grief, and I must bear it* (Jer. 10:19).

Hebron was the home of Abraham the Patriarch, and later the capital city of David's kingdom for seven and a half years before Israel united and established a new seat of government in Jerusalem, 3,000 years ago. It is one of the oldest cities in the world.

In modern times two major massacres have written macabre pages of history with a pen dipped deep in the blood of Hebron's inhabitants. The first was the slaughter of the Jews by the Arabs in 1929. The second, Baruch Goldstein's murder of 29 Arab worshipers in the Mosque of the cave Machpelah.

February 25, 1994, was a day that will long be remembered as a day of infamy, of tragedy, a beginning of new sorrows for the Palestinians and the Israelis. Historians will note how the dreadful

Hebron massacre ripped from the Israelis their bargaining power in the peace negotiations. History will note that the hopes of the Palestinians were also dashed. It will set Israelis against each other. Unwarranted and unprecedented concessions are already being made by Israel's lamenting leaders. "Israeli Prime Minister Yitzhak Rabin called PLO chairman Yassir Arafat to express his regret, saying 'As an Israeli I am ashamed of this deed.' "[1]

ISRAEL'S FLAWS

Like America, Canada, England, Australia, or any other country, Israel is a nation with flaws. They do a lot of things wrong. They make serious mistakes. Sometimes they are their own worst enemies.

An Israeli military officer handed the PLO a trump card. Dr. Baruch Goldstein, a member of the tiny Kach party, a follower of the late Rabbi Meir Kahane, committed an act so violent, so appalling, that it caused the whole world to gasp. Israel's enemies will use this act of senseless violence as a club with which to beat on Israel. Most unreasonable demands can now be made. As a gesture, Israel is already making new concessions, beginning with the untimely release of 1,000 terrorists being held in Israeli prisons. The pressure mounts.

A shudder of fear rippled throughout the collective soul of humanity, for down deep in the gut of mankind is an intuitive knowledge that the Mid East is the cockpit of the world. It is the dynamite-keg fuse of Armageddon. What happens there affects the entire planet. Here, in the spiritual realm are massed both the protective angels of God and the howling demons of hell. The invisible war manifests itself in the physical world.

> Have your eyes caught the vision?
> Has your heart felt the thrill?
> To the call of the Master
> Do you answer I will?
> For the conflict of the ages
> Told by prophets and by sages
> In its fury is upon us
> Is upon us today.
> — Anonymous

PRAY NOW!

If ever you pray for the peace of Jerusalem and all her neighbors, redouble your efforts and pray now. Only a few in the secular media or political arena can appreciate this, but prayer is the first and best hope, not a last resort. "We've done all we can, I guess all we can do now is pray" are words that must weary the heart of God. Prayer should be first, not last.

No one can justify the tragic massacre in Hebron. That calamitous act threatens to derail peace negotiations between the Palestinian Arabs and Israel.

BARUCH GOLDSTEIN

Dr. Baruch Goldstein, a 38-year-old physician from Kiryat Arba, which is adjacent to Hebron, opened fire with an automatic weapon in the midst of hundreds of Moslem worshipers, killing about 29 people. Goldstein, a captain in the Israel Defense Forces, was in uniform and the weapon he used was army issue. He opened fire on hundreds of praying Moslems in the Mosque of the Cave Machpelah, burial place of the patriarchs Abraham, Isaac, and Jacob-Israel and their wives, except for Rachel who died in childbirth on the road to Bethlehem.

Neither the nation of Israel, nor its government should be held responsible for the act of one emotionally disturbed man, any more than the people of the USA should be held responsible for the mass murders perpetrated by insane killers in our midst. But as we watch the media we see the blame already being transferred to the Israeli people and their government.

REPORT DIRECT FROM JERUSALEM

Here is a phone report just received and taped from our Jerusalem based correspondent, Thomas Brimmer:

On Thursday evening, February 24, Dr. Baruch Goldstein, an American-born Jew, was attending an Erev Purim service in the building in Hebron that serves both as a mosque and a synagogue. Purim is the Jewish holiday when the Book of Esther is read. It tells the story of the conflict between Mordecai and Haman, who wanted to slaughter all the Jews in Persia (Iran). That took place 2,703 years ago in 355 B.C. when Mordecai, the Jew, outwitted Haman and saved his fellow Jews.

Meanwhile, as Goldstein and other Jews from Kiryat Arba were having their service and reading the book of Esther, Moslem worshippers in the same building, were celebrating their holy month of Ramadan.

> During Ramadan the Moslems fast during the day and feast at night.
>
> As the Jews were reading *Esther,* the Moslem preacher, the Imam, was preaching a sermon against Israel. He called for Jihad, holy war, to stamp out the evil Jews. The Moslem men began to chant, "Death to the Jews! Kill all the Jews! Jihad! Jihad! Jihad! Destroy the cursed Zionist State."[2]

What tortured thoughts went through the mind of Goldstein, who no doubt recalled when the Moslems slaughtered 60 Jews in Hebron, in 1929, virtually wiping out the Jewish population there. The few Jewish survivors moved to Jerusalem. His mind would think of how, in 1936, the resettled Jewish community was again driven from Hebron in the Arab uprising, that took the lives of over 500 Jews in Palestine. Could the Moslem chant, "Kill the Jews" also have reminded him of the slaughter of Jews in the Intifada (uprising) that began in 1987, and which continues to this day?

Brimmer sounded distressed as he said,

> Tension mounted. A shouting match developed into a scuffle between the Jews and Moslems. Shouting,

The mosque at Hebron covers the Machpelah Cave where Abraham, Isaac and Jacob are buried. It served both as a mosque for the Moslems and as a synagogue for the local Jews.

pushing, shoving, then the brawl broke into some fist fights. The Israeli security police rushed into the mosque to break up the riot, and to force the Israelis to leave the Machpelah and go home. The soldiers had to use physical force on the Jews to get them out. They became abusive against their fellow Jews. The Jewish men were angry that they were put out but not the Moslems. They felt that unfair discrimination was being exercised against them. Finally they left and went their way. Goldstein was among them.

We need to see Goldstein realistically. There is some background one needs to know to understand him. A follower of the late Rabbi Meir Kahane, he believed that the Arabs had to be entirely driven out of Israel. His hatred for the Arabs was notable. Goldstein had been an army reserve doctor for many years. A black mark against him was that during the 1982 Lebanon conflict he refused to treat Arabs who were wounded. Other Israeli army doctors and nurses were appalled at this behavior.[3]

U. S. News & World Report commented: "Baruch Goldstein, a Brooklyn-born physician who hated Arabs so much that he refused to treat them in his West Bank emergency room, donned an Israeli Army uniform, walked into the Mosque and fired an automatic assault rifle into a crowd of Palestinians gathered for Ramadan prayers. . . . Israeli Prime Minister Yitzhak Rabin called the massacre 'the crazed act of psychopaths. . . .' "[4]

As revised news reports continue coming out we learn that *U.S. News & World Report* was incorrect. Goldstein did in fact treat many Arabs in the West Bank. It is possible that he changed toward the end of his life's sad journey.

Tom Brimmer told us,

> The man had a history of blind hatred toward the Palestinians. Israeli officials now recognize that he should have been removed from the army long ago, but since every man in Israel is a part of the reserves, nothing was done.
>
> I talked to one of the rabbis in the Kach party and he confirmed to me that the death or removal of all Arabs from Israel is still the party goal. Kach represents only

a minuscule portion of Israel's population. The Rabin government says that the party itself must now be banned. Abject apologies have been made publicly.

Dr. Goldstein went home pondering the wicked Haman who wanted to kill all the Jews. He wanted to destroy Arabs. What twisted thoughts he entertained, one can only imagine. He was seething with anger and frustration. Something snapped in his brain and he went over the edge. The next day, he put on his officer's uniform, took his Galil, one of the most powerful field weapons in the world, and four full clips of army issue ammunition. Early in the morning, at dawn, he made his way into Hebron. He arrived at the Machpelah at around 5:30 a.m. Hundreds of Moslem men were at their early prayers.

He was easily able to pass by the Israeli security forces. He was known to them. He was an officer. He was in uniform. They had no idea what he was up to. They assumed that he had a right to be there. He deceived them and made his way into the place of worship.

Once inside the crowded mosque, he positioned himself in the tightly packed room, took out his gun, put in the first of four full clips of ammunition and proceeded to fire 118 deadly bullets into the dense crowd. Every bullet did its damage. He acted alone.

The Moslems near the exits ran out the doors and made their escape, pushing and shoving, screaming in fear and rage. In the process, unfortunately, they blocked the way of the Israeli soldiers who were trying to get in and see what was happening. But the soldiers could not get in, until it was too late.

Dr. Baruch Goldstein succeeded to fire every bullet he had. Then he was killed, beaten to death by the outraged Moslems.

At this moment the revised count is 29 dead and more could die from their wounds. Over 80 were wounded. Twenty more have been killed in rioting that followed.

Earlier this evening at King of Kings Assembly, the church we attend in Jerusalem, instead of having a normal Sunday evening service, we spent the entire time in prayer for God's help. We prayed that the government would act wisely. We prayed that we would act wisely, being strong in the Lord. A word from the Lord came forth indicating that we should take courage and not be fearful. Momentous events are happening around us, but God's presence is here. He can bring forth good from evil. God does not cause such events, but in the midst of man's rebellion, He is not absent. We as believers have a responsibility to act in a manner which is worthy of Messiah in spite of all else around us."[5]

IS ISRAEL TO BLAME?

There is no justification for Dr. Goldstein's wanton act of destruction of human lives. And there is no cause to blame the people of Israel or the government of Israel for this calamity. Anyone can see that what Goldstein did not only hurt the Arabs, but also hurts Israel's honest efforts to achieve peace in the Middle East.

You would not want to be characterized by the deeds of American mass murderers such as John Wayne Gacy, nor Jeffrey Dahmer who killed 17 people and ate parts of their bodies, nor like cult leader Charles Manson, who inspired his followers to multiple murders. If Israel is to be held responsible for the act of one man, then by the same standard all Palestinians are guilty for the multiplied acts of murder and terrorism perpetrated by Palestinian terrorist organizations, and that would be simply ridiculous.

I cannot blame our president for what acts of violence U.S. citizens may commit as individuals. So please do not use a double standard with Israel. There is a tendency to blame Israel for an act of one individual. I would not want to blame my Palestinian friends Mussa and Janet, Nick and Ermina, nor Dr. Anis Shorrosh for the wild acts of a demented Arab terrorist. Rev. Benny Hinn, a Christian evangelist, is an Israeli Arab of Palestinian ancestry. He would not want to be blamed for the vicious terrorist acts of Abu Nidal. Let's keep our perspectives clear.

The average Israeli is dismayed by the demented act of Dr. Goldstein. What he did was a cruel and selfish thing. Did he not know that this would create a backlash against his own people, whom he was called to defend? Instead he is their heartache and source of defamation.

I assure you that Dr. Baruch Goldstein was not representative of most of the people of Israel. Alas, this world has such a poor record for human abuse.

This tortured world is far from God and far from peace. The Arab world is fraught with violence, mostly directed against fellow Arabs. A mild political protest was launched in Hama, Syria, a few years ago, challenging the Alawi government of Hafez al Assad. President Assad sent in his troops and in a few days killed from 20 to 30,000 of his own people because they were Sunni Moslem protesters. Assad is an Alawi Moslem, which sect comprises only 5 percent of Syria's population.

Saddam Hussein of Iraq uses poisonous gas to kill thousands of his own Kurdish citizens. Iran slaughters Bahaists and Christians. India slaughters its religious minorities. The PLO is responsible for terrorist activities costing thousands of lives. Radical Moslems bombed the Twin Trade Towers in New York, and on and on the list goes.

Earth is a ghetto of violence. Survival grows more difficult. Using Israel as a scapegoat will not help matters. The nation of Israel cannot be held accountable for the actions of one irrational man.

"Woe unto them that seek deep to hide their counsel from the Lord, and their works are in the dark, and they say, Who seeth us? and who knoweth us?" (Isa. 29:15).

Notes

[1] *The News Leader* (Springfield, MO: Gannet Newspapers, February 26, 1994), p.1.

[2] Thomas Brimmer, phone conversation (Jerusalem: February 26, 1994).

[3] Brimmer, phone conversation..

[4] Louise Lief with David Makovsky, *U. S. News & World Report* (Washington, DC: U. S. News & World Report Inc., March 7, 1994), p. 14.

[5] Brimmer, phone conversation.

5

HITLER AND SATAN

The Nazis, the Third Reich, and the Occult

And it is this very combination of the only-too-human and unimaginably inhuman that makes the Nazis a persistent and nettling mystery for us.[1] — Irving Kristol

The whole Nazi ethos grew out of a magical view of the world, and the history of Nazi Germany was forged by strange fanatics whose actions can only be explained in occult terms.[2] — Nigel Pennick

And the Lord said unto Satan, Whence comest thou? Then Satan answered the Lord, and said, From going to and fro in the earth, and from walking up and down in it (Job 1:7).

Adolph Hitler understood the devil. In his early years in Vienna he met Jorg Lanz von Liebenfels, an anti-Semite, who edited an occult, racist publication, *Ostara*. While it has been shown that Hitler had some weird supernatural experiences much earlier in life, Leibenfels can be credited with leading Hitler into the arcane world of the demonic. Later other occult adepts assisted Hitler along his dark pathway.

For decades I have been researching Adolph Hitler's connection to satanism and the benighted world of the occult. We have found that a number of European writers have dealt with this subject very frankly, and with extensive documentation such as: *Morning of the Magicians* by Louis Pauwels and Jacques Bergier; *The Spear of Destiny* by Trevor Ravenscroft; *Mark of the Beast* also by Ravenscroft; *The Occult and the Third Reich* by Jean-Michael Angebert; *The Occult Roots of Nazism* by Nicholas Goodrick-Clarke; *Hitler's Secret Sciences* by Nigel Pennick; *Gods and Beasts — The Nazis and the Occult* by Dusty Sklar; and others.

This is only a partial listing. We did not have an easy time obtaining some of these books. None of these European authors are evangelicals as far as I can tell. They write from a secularist research approach, and come up with amazing evidence and conclusions. We weigh their findings in the balance of Bible truth. Ravenscroft was himself a metaphysical teacher, hoping to use white magic to defeat the dark powers of the Nazis (a futile approach).

Only one secular American author, as far as I know, even tentatively approached the subject in a book. That author, Robert L.

Hitler — mad genius, searcher for occult and satanic power.

Waite wrote *The Psycho-Pathic God.*

In this chapter I will quote extensively from other writings. Our documentation must be strong, or you might think this author has fantasized the Hitler mystique. The strength of this chapter is the exposure you will receive to the work of many other authors who have seen the inner reality of Hitler and Nazism.

THE NERD WHO WOULD RULE THE WORLD

How is it that Hitler, a failed artist, maladjusted, practically friendless non-entity became one of the most powerful and destructive figures in history? Prepare for a shocking but true answer.

Hitler lived from April 20, 1889, until April 30, 1945 — almost exactly 56 years. The difference between his first 30 and the following 26 years seems to be inexplicable. For 30 years he was an obscure failure, then almost overnight a local celebrity, and eventually the man around whom the whole of world policy revolved. How does that go together?[3]

INTO THE ESOTERIC WORLD OF OCCULTISM

A power beyond himself took over Hitler's soul. He became something "other," something so loathsome that a normal mind is overwhelmed with dread when exposed to the harsh reality of this saddest chapter of all history. What we have to say simply adds to the horror of the Nazi era.

Two Austrian cultists, Jorg Lanz Liebenfels and Guido von List, presented an irrational, pseudo-anthropological package which attracted a number of wealthy backers, despite its foolishness. Lanz's Order of New Templars and List's Armanen boasted several influential members.

In 1909, young Adolph Hitler, down and out in Vienna, came across Lanz's magazine *Ostara,* and made contact with the occultist. The erotic language and racist rantings of this magazine were remarkably similar to Hitler's later utterances.[4]

Hitler became a satanic adept and it transformed him from a nonentity to a monster. It changed the world. It altered the course of history.

GERMANY WAS PREPARED FOR HITLER

Germany had been experiencing an occultic, satanic revival. Madam Blavatsky's Theosophical Society was spreading the word everywhere. People explored astrology, metaphysics, spiritism, and various meditative techniques, such as Tibetan Third Eye and necromancy. There was a good market for the satanic *Sixth and Seventh Books of Moses*. German higher criticism in the Church had all but destroyed confidence in the Bible. There were forms of religion, but no bulwark against the onslaught of demonic deception. Following is an unnerving and strange portent of what lay in Germany's future. The poet Stefan George voiced a widespread mood when, in 1921, he prophesied an age which:

> Brings forth the One who helps *The Man*
> And at the same time mapped out his tasks for him:
> He bursts the chains, restores on fields of rubble
> His order, scourges those who've gone astray
> Back to eternal justice, where the great
> Is great again, and master once more master,
> Obedience reigns, and on the people's banner
> Pins the true sign and through wild storm and terror
> Of the red dawn he leads his faithful band
> To the day's deed — the New Reich's planting.[5]

The level of compromise on the part of many German churchmen is a wonder to contemplate:

> Professor Hauer, of Tubingen, expresses himself thus in a liturgy of baptism of the adherents of the new German faith, "The nurse thanks God and the Fuhrer for the gift of this child: thanks to thee, Fuhrer and friend! Thou hast placed us again on the good road where we have been wanderers. Thou hast saved our souls." Some German Christians formulated the following thesis in 1934: "Thanks to Hitler the time of the German people has come, for it is by Hitler that Christ our Saviour God has become powerful among us."[6]

> And Hitler offered more than new forms for old legends. He provided a new system of values which justified a new morality. Psychologists would call it "an alternative super ego system." It can also be seen as a secular religion, complete with Messiah, a holy book, a

cross, the trappings of religious pageantry, a priesthood of black-robed and anointed elite, ex-communication and death for heretics, and the millennial promise of the Thousand Year Reich. Thus Hitler succeeded, in part, because he appeared to many Germans as a godlike Messiah.[7]

MOLOCH, GOD OF DEATH

Ancient pagan gods were called up from the abyss. Man created a god in his own likeness and they themselves became the new gods of the Reich.

> God in Nazi Germany became Hitler. His world and will were therefore divine; the German had no personality except as it was expressed by this being.
>
> He *cleansed their souls by killing others,* an ancient ritual, practiced by prehistoric man, and now carried out on a worldwide scale. Purification through death — this was the Nazi philosophy.[8] [Emphasis added.]

During Hitler's diabolical reign of terror, the god Moloch came slouching out of his den to accept the sacrifice of 50,000,000 humans offered up on the funeral pyre of the Second World War. The firestorms of death swept across the barren land.

The European authors we have mentioned convincingly explore Hitler's journey into the dark realm of the occult, the demonic.

Joseph Carr (left) with Pastor Earl Karl. Carr wrote the book The Twisted Cross.

Two daring American Christian authors have also written books on Hitler and the devil. One is Joseph Carr who wrote *The Twisted Cross* and the other is Bob Rosio who wrote *Hitler and the New Age*. French eschatologist and Evangelical Christian, Rene Pache commented on Hitler and the demonic:

> Until recently it was considered elegant to deny the existence of the devil. Now it is no longer possible to deny that a supernatural and infernal power leads humanity to its suicide in spite of all the good intentions of the nations and their leaders. Professor C.G. Jung, the famous psychologist of Basle, wrote on this matter, "There are demons of a kind as surely as there was a camp of Buchenwald."
>
> And Dr. Hopeler adds: "That which happened at Maidaneck, at Auschwitz, Mauthausen, etc., was not the work of men merely 'bestial' or 'depraved.' The only valid explanation is that they have been 'possessed and full of the spirit of the devil.' In the death-camps Satan has shown his true face, and the world which until then mocked belief in the devil, has been obliged to state with terror that the prince of the power of darkness really exists. This statement, moreover, confirms fully the Bible: for thousands of years it has exhorted man to fight 'the enemy,' 'the one who is a liar from the beginning,' and Scripture defines the mission of Jesus on this earth by saying that He has come 'to destroy the works of the devil' " (Berner Sonntagsblatt, Sept. 9, 1945).[9]

JEWISH COMMENTARY

Now add to the Christian perspective of Rene Pache the words of a Jewish author, Herbert Leuthy, which appeared in *Commentary*.

> Demonically . . . with Hitler it is impossible to avoid the word . . . the lowest spirit that can possess men — or swine. And unsatisfactory as it is that demonology which takes over the task of explaining what the rational understanding still cannot, it unquestionably comes closer to the phenomenon of Hitler than the notion of barbarism. "Shicklgruber, possessed by demons" — as unspeakably vulgar as it sounds, that is the correct starting point . . . . Hitler as a historical figure; his band

of "old fighters" — that chosen collection of pederasts, drug addicts, rowdies, crackpots and criminals. . . .[10]

ANTI-SEMITISM IS SATANIC

Dr. Michael Brown wrote:

> In reality, there is only one way to explain anti-Semitism: *The devil hates the Jews, and his demented nature is revealed in his treatment of the Jewish people.* While many other nations and groups have felt the fury of his wrath, none have felt it so often, so consistently, and so powerfully as have the Jews.

THE EICHMANN WITNESS

> The Holocaust is inexplicable from a solely natural point of view. There had to be a greater force at work, inciting and provoking the Nazis. The words of Adolf Eichmann toward the end of World War II defy human description:
> "I shall leap into my grave laughing, because of the feeling that I have the deaths of five million people on my conscience will be for me a source of extraordinary satisfaction."

ENTERTAINMENT FROM THE THEATER OF HELL

Brown continues:

> The Nazis were *entertained* by Jewish suffering and torment. Writes Elie Wiesel:
> "Imagine: the chief rabbi of the town forced by German officers to clean the pavement, to sweep it with his beard. And all around, proud soldiers, warriors puffed up with their victories, slapped their thighs in merriment. Imagine: a distinguished officer, a man of good family, orders Jewish children to run, like rabbits, and then he takes out his revolver and begins shooting at the terrified living targets, scattering them, mowing them down. Imagine: no, let us not imagine anymore. In those days, the executioners had more imagination than their victims. They were satanically creative.
> "They used every science and technique. Among them were philosophers and psychologists, doctors and

artists, experts in management and specialists in poisoning the mind.

"These were all driven, all impelled, all given over to the humiliation, degradation, and extermination of the Jews. Only yesterday they were neighbors and friends!

When the Nazis murdered all the patients of the Lodz ghetto hospitals they threw *newborn babies* out of upper-story hospital windows. Precious Jewish infants were splattered on the pavement! But for one teenage SS soldier this was not enough. He asked permission — and was granted permission — to catch the falling babies on his *bayonet.* Is there no limit to hell's depravity?"[11]

Luethy writes, "Historians do not want to descend to the level of popular magazines, of scandal and sensation; they are used to other references. But how else can they reach Adolph Hitler's level? It is hard for history to move on a higher plane than its subject, and everything private in Hitler's life is doubtful, sordid, or disreputable."[12]

THE THULE

It was Meister Dietrich Eckart that led Hitler into the inner court of the occultic Gesaltshaft Thule and taught him to honor Satan for power and glory.

Hitler, occult adept, could mesmerize and control the masses.

The Thule Society, organized in lodge-fashion, was one of Bavaria's most influential organizations.

German occultists with radical anti-Semitic inclinations decided to form a "magic" lodge which they named the Order of Teutons ... Herman Pohl the Order's chancellor. . . . . In 1915 Pohl was joined by Rudolf Glauer, an adventurer of Silesian origin, who held a Turkish passport and practiced Sufi meditation. He also dabbled in astrology and was an admirer of Lanz von Liebenfels and Guido von List, both pathologically anti-Semitic. Glauer went by the name of Rudolf Freiherr von Sebottendorf. . . . He became the grand master of the Bavarian Order Province and he founded the Thule society with Pohl's approval in 1918. . . . The inner circle of the Thule Society was relatively small and was accessible only to the initiated masters of the esoteric. This is where occult and magic rituals were performed with great seriousness. . . . There were crosslinks to the English Brotherhood of the Golden Dawn, to the theosophists of Madame Blavatsky, and to the notorious magician and adventurer Aleister Crowley.[13]

DIETRICH ECKART — HITLER'S GURU

The mentor of the Thule Society, Dietrich Eckart ... participated in Hitler's abortive putsch of March 9, 1923. . . . . Not surprisingly, Adolph Hitler belonged to the sect, as did Alfred Rosenberg and many others.

The main purpose of the Thule Society in the mind of its founders was to constitute a rallying point for all the occult societies of like persuasion and thereby to remerge with ancient Germanic tradition. As to the legend of Thule, from which the sect borrowed its name, what has survived until our own times, through the German *Lied,* is the cult of the Gold Cup. The use of the sacred cup in libations was peculiar to Celto-Nordic peoples. We know from mythology that Isis (whose name means "rainbow") used a gold cup to draw from the Styx the water used by the gods for their oaths. . . . . The origin of the sacredness of the cup used in religious libations is explained in Plato's *Timaeus.*[14]

HOUSTON STEWART CHAMBERLAIN

Joseph Carr wrote,

> Hitler's debt to Chamberlain is mostly religious, for it was the works of Houston Stewart Chamberlain that convinced Adolf Hitler to wed together the notions of religion, race, and politics.
>
> Chamberlain's greatest work was a book titled *The Foundation of the Nineteenth Century*. It was published in 1899 and shortly became a bestseller. The metaphysical-political thesis of the book found easy acceptance in the German mind. In it, Chamberlain tried to bring together the world views of those two contentious giants, Wagner and Nietzsche.
>
> Like Hitler, Chamberlain was an occultic initiate who was driven by an assortment of demons. According to William Shirer, writing in *The Rise and Fall of the Third Reich*, Chamberlain often wrote in the "grip of a terrible fever, a veritable trance . . ." that was so completely dominating that he often failed to recognize his

Houston Stewart Chamberlain — one of Hitler's occultic mentors.

own work afterwards. Shirer recounts an incident that occurred on Chamberlain's trip to Italy in 1896. According to Shirer, Chamberlain's demon became so insistent that he interrupted his journey at Gardonne and locked himself in a hotel room for eight days. He abandoned a piece of music which he had been writing and wrote feverishly instead on a logical thesis that would one day form the basis for his book *Race and History* (a Nazi "scripture").

The mad Chamberlain died in 1927, but not before publicly giving Adolf Hitler his blessing, and anointing him publicly as Germany's "messiah."[15]

DR. RUDOLF STEINER

Although deep into the labyrinthine caverns of damnation from early on in his life, Hitler nevertheless went further and further, and there were willing "masters" at each step of the way to assist him in his diabolical journey. Not all metaphysicians found his favor, however. In fact Hitler banned certain persons and some societies. He could not tolerate the threat of competition they posed.

The occultist who probably received the greatest dose of vitriole from Hitler during the early 1920's was Dr. Rudolf Steiner (1861-1925), founder of the Anthroposophical Society. Doctor Steiner had been raised by Austrian Catholic parents and possessed a keen mind and a quality education. He achieved a certain amount of scholarly acclaim and an academic reputation to match at an early age of editing the scientific works of the German philosopher Goethe.[16]

HITLER, TORTURED SOUL

We do not err in concluding that powerful magicians, occultists, and demonically-controlled men had an inordinate influence on Hitler, whom we believe to have been knowledgeably a Satan worshiper.

Goodrick-Clark's carefully researched and documented book *The Occult Roots of Nazism* makes this point in connection with Jorg Lanz von Liebenfels, Rudolf von Sebottendorf, Guido von List, and others. The influence of List was considerable, right down to the choice of the swastika as the emblem of the Nazi (NSDAP) party. "It

Adolph Hitler

is therefore possible to trace the origin of the Nazi symbol back through the emblems of the Germanenorden, and ultimately to Guido von List."[17]

Hitler was a tortured soul. He did not master the demons, they mastered him, and tormented him.

In *The Insane World of Adolph Hitler,* Chandler Brossard comments:

One of his secretaries reported the following, "He often wakes up in the middle of the night and wanders restlessly to and fro. Then he must have light everywhere. Lately he has sent at these times for young men who have to keep him company during his hours of manifest anguish. It is not unusual for him to wake up with convulsive shrieks. He shouts for help. He sits on the edge of his bed, as if unable to stir. He shakes with fear, making the whole bed vibrate. He shouts confused, totally unintelligible phrases. He gasps as if imagining himself suffocating.

"One evening I witnessed a most remarkable scene. Hitler stood swaying in his room looking wildly about him. 'He! He! He's been here!' he gasped. His lips were blue. Sweat streamed down his face Suddenly he began to reel off figures, and odd words and broken phrases, entirely devoid of sense. It sounded horrible. He used strangely composed and entirely un-German word formations. . . . Then he suddenly broke out — 'There, there! In the corner! Who's that?' He stamped and shrieked in the familiar way."[18]

DEMONIC BABBLING

Hitler manifested a satanic counterfeit of the gifts of the Holy Spirit, but deriving this from the demonic rather than the Divine realm. Manvell and Fraenkel observe:

> He would mutter unintelligible phrases, or figures, or unknown German word-formations.
>
> Not all Hitler's rages must be thought to be assumed. Rauschning describes one which appeared real enough. "He behaved like a combination of a spoilt child and an hysterical woman. He scolded in high, shrill tones, stamped his feet, and banged his fist on tables and walls. He foamed at the mouth, panting and stammering in uncontrolled fury. . . . He was an alarming sight, his hair disheveled, his eyes fixed, and his face distorted and purple."[19]

HITLER'S SPEECHES

I have listened to tape recordings of Hitler's speeches. The raw power of his delivery is jarring. I have watched videos made from Nazi films, most notable of which is *Force of the Will*. Bob Rosio captures the essence of what Hitler's speaking mannerisms reveal. True to form, Rosio comes through with insightful analysis:

> The true heart of Hitler often came to light best through his speeches. He seemed intoxicated by his own voice and often said more than he intended to say. Hate spewed forth like the venom of a cobra. Walter Langer said that "in his speeches, Hitler was a man transformed and possessed." Indeed he was. "He was like a medium in a trance." An evil supernatural power manifested itself through him and took control of his audience. His mastery of the audience was the "transmission of a stronger will to a weaker one." The man who so mesmerized his audience also seemed to mesmerize himself along with them. He began slowly, "making an appeal to the hidden forces in the audience. He counted on the magic of the spoken word to call forth emotion in his audience, while dosing himself with the morphine of his own verbiage. It intoxicated him. He talked himself into an auto suggestive euphoria." Colonel Warimont said, "If I hadn't known otherwise, I would have thought he was drunk or drugged." Hitler, drunk with power and hate, served as a mouthpiece for demonic spirits. "Beyond any doubt Hitler was possessed by forces outside

himself of which the individual named Hitler was only the temporary vehicle."[20]

BLACK MAGIC

Herman Rauschning felt that the secret of Hitler's success lies deep in men's souls. He sensed that many Germans "lived in a magic universe, brushing aside logic and reason."[21]

Bob Rosio's thorough research led him to write:

No one would have credited Hitler with genius of any sort before his astonishing success in politics, before he became "energized" by demonic forces. The real Hitler became the Fuhrer through dark abilities that were not naturally his own. Hitler himself made no attempt to attribute his success to academic ability, pointing instead to this "sense of destiny." He had always maintained that he had been providentially chosen to play the decisive role in history, attributing his ability to make correct and timely decisions to the voices which guided him. He waited for them to speak; when they did, he acted, relying heavily on acquired mediumistic abilities.

Hitler considered two specific periods in his life as his most important formative times: his days in Vienna (1907-1913) and his time spent in Landsberg prison. Both were periods of intensive occult training. He wrote, "Since my days in Vienna, I have extended that foundation very little and I have changed nothing in it."[22]

THE TRUTH IS OUT

The Allies were able to capture 485 tons of written material at the end of World War II, documenting in tremendous detail every area of life in Nazi Germany. Although this material had been ordered destroyed, it was providentially preserved and captured. The entire Nazi machine had ground to a halt with the death of Hitler, as if a spell over the nation had been broken.

The secret that Hitler had so zealously and jealously guarded has come to light. As an occult vessel, an "adept" in the black arts, Hitler avidly did Satan's bidding, the real force behind him. Hitler's descent into demonic possession can be traced by specific facts and by Trevelyan's "imaginative guess." My conclusions come more from research than from revelation. Hitler's life and career, unexplainable, incomprehensible, and unbelievable to the rational mind, become explainable, comprehensible, and believable as a phenomenon of total evil in the light of God's Word.

This is the path that Hitler chose, the path of demonic Gnosticism.[22]

Pennick insightfully wrote, "Eckart is said to have given a last death-bed address to his followers. In it he exhorted 'Follow Hitler. He will dance, but it is I who have called the tune. I have initiated him into the Secret Doctrine, opened his centres of vision and given him the means to communicate with the Powers.' "[23] Pennick links the Nazis with the New Age movement, Theosophy, ley lines, Stonehenge, psychic power grids, etc.

"Therefore hell hath enlarged herself, and opened her mouth without measure: and their glory, and their multitude, and their pomp, and he that rejoiceth, shall descend into it" (Isa. 5:14).

"And I will punish the world for their evil, and the wicked for their iniquity; and I will cause the arrogancy of the proud to cease, and will lay low the haughtiness of the terrible" (Isa. 13:11).

POWER THAT DESTROYS

The realm of occult power may seem attractive, but there is a day of reckoning. There is a price to pay. Why does one need a psychic bag of tricks or a fuhrer when you can go direct to the Sovereign Majesty and King of the Universe, Jehovah God?

The modern German occult revival owes its inception to the popularity of Theosophy in the Anglo-Saxon world during 1880s. Here Theosophy refers to the international sectarian movement deriving from the activities and writings of the Russian adventuress and occultist, Helena Petrovna Blavatsky (1831-91).[24]

Oh, what slavering beast now slouches from Babel to Megiddo? Will he pass by Jerusalem? What marvelous evil is being devised in the caverns of darkness (even a smoke-filled room)? What ultimate conspiracy is even now hatching from the Roman cockatrice egg?

Sometime tomorrow, or the day after, what powerful politician will make a deal with the king of darkness and become the final Antichrist? Antichrist — foretold by Daniel in the seventh chapter of the book that bears his name: "And of the ten horns that were in his head, and of the other which came up, and before whom three fell; even of that horn that had eyes, and a mouth that spake very great things, whose look was more stout than his fellows" (Dan. 7:20). "More stout than his fellows!" Worse than all predecessors! The final beast. Worse than Haman, Hadrian, or Hitler. Looming on the horizon today.

Hail Caesar! Heil Hitler? Hail — who? Who will be next? Many recognize Antiochus Epiphanes, Caesar, Nero, and Hitler as forerunners of the future Antichrist, who will be backed by world leaders as the New World Order becomes a harsh, if doomed and short-lived, reality. The forerunners were merely tools of Satan, preparing the way for the final Son of Perdition, the Beast of Revelation.

MAGIC NEW WORLD ORDER

Nigel Pennick was keen-sighted when he wrote in 1981:

> Far from being just another political doctrine, Nazism was nothing less than a deliberate magical attempt to alter the world [to create a paradigm shift in humanity's perception of reality]. Racial supremacy, the much-vaunted "destiny" of the Nazis, was not their final program. The creation of a new race of supermen, a biological mutation to a higher level of being, was their aim. The new man, the result of selective breeding, equipped with psychic powers, would push forward the frontiers of a new civilization based on a magical technology several orders of sophistication above the clumsy techniques of the present. The new superman, so they believed, would finally transcend the human condition — he would gain unlimited power over the universe and win immortality. He would become a god.[25]

Philosophers and historians have marveled over mankind's inability to learn from the lessons that history teaches. Are we doomed to repeat the mistakes of the past? Author Bob Rosio believes that the study of Hitler, an extreme type of the Antichrist, will help Christians to better understand and prepare to confront the advancing New World Order and the extreme New Age movement, of which Rosio says Hitler was knowledgeably a part.

Rosio's attempts to link Adolph Hitler to the New Age movement may shock some people, but the linkage is not imaginary. It is real. Note the subtitle of his book, *Hitler and the New Age — The Coming Holocaust — the Extermination of Christendom.* This may seem startling, but we have proclaimed for decades that the same pagan forces that would destroy the Jews also aim to destroy the Bible churches.

Rosio describes his book as "a study in the mechanics of evil." An advanced theologian, Bob Rosio describes in plain English the philosophical and spiritual similarities between Nazism and the New Age movement. His explanations probe beyond the slick, public relations slogans of the well-organized New Age movement, exposing the followers' blind, futile attempts to find spirituality and God among the virtues of humankind. He uncovers an intricate network of organizations and individuals whose intentions are far less harmonious than their press releases portray. Rosio says, "Hitler's life [was] . . . an occult phenomenon."

Then consider this: A reunified German parliament has met in the Reichstag for the first time since 1933! The war against Saddam Hussein demonstrated how effective a world peacekeeping agency could be in dealing with some of these problems. Now NATO forces blend with our troops and are under the authority of a coalition of foreign powers.

Our nation's sovereignty is being rapidly eroded, with the help of our political leaders who allegedly have sworn to protect the constitution of our country.

Could this quote, which appeared in a German magazine in 1930, apply today? "Germany holds the key of the New Europe. What happens there within the next months will decide the course of European politics for years to come. Geographically in the center of the continent. Germany is the political and economic hub of Europe."

Rosio's book is a warning to Christians and Jews who have a vested interest in mutual survival against the new Hitler's arising.

I was conferring recently with Joe Carr, a long-time friend who wrote the book *The Twisted Cross*. In this monumental work he carefully documents Hitler's indoctrination into satanism. He speaks with authority on Hitler's use of demon force. He did not hesitate to show the connection between Nazism and the New Age movement. Death threats have not deterred this fearless man of God. He continues to expose the works of darkness.

DER HEILIGE LANCE — THE SPEAR OF LONGINUS

There is one part of the Hitler chronicle that is so uncanny that one wonders if it should be told. At any rate, here it is for your speculation. In the Hapsburg Treasure House (museum) in Vienna, Austria, there are many treasures. The strangest of them is the spear of the Roman soldier Longinus Maximus, who according to legend thrust that very spear into the side of Jesus Christ as He hung on the cross. The legend goes that whoever possesses the spear can release its magical powers for good or for evil.

As the young Hitler gazed upon the spear one rainy day he was filled with a strange power and prophetic foresight. He believed then that it was his destiny to be the Antichrist. He must one day possess the spear to assure his ascent to world power and rulership! During the Second World War Hitler came into possession of "der heilige lance." After the Allies defeated the Nazis they had the spear and finally it was returned to the museum in Vienna, where it can be seen to this day.

The authenticity of the spear and its attendant legend is certainly doubtful. Perhaps it is mere superstitious legerdemain, as indeed, I suppose it to be. Nevertheless, Satan uses superstition as a sort of reverse or negative faith. The devil plays upon mankind's superstitions, the better to manipulate men to his own villainous ends. Hitler believed the myth, and tried to use the spear for evil purpose. This is one more bit of evidence, one more piece in the puzzle, of what motivated Hitler and how he became the almost Antichrist and beast of Revelation. One who wishes to pursue this further may wish to read the following books: *The Spear of Destiny*,[26] by Ravenscroft and *The Mark of The Beast*,[27] by Ravenscroft and Murphy. Of marginal interest would be a novel, *The Legend of the Holy Lance*,[28] by Bill Still. *Caveat lector!* (Let the reader beware.) Ravenscroft is a metaphysician, and while his documentation is at least partly valid, his conclusions may be quite dangerous.

SPIRITUAL BATTLES

This is a time of spiritual warfare. The demons that empowered Hitler are active now. The time of games is over.

Frank Peretti saw only a dim vision of the reality we face in this fallen world.[29]

"For though we walk in the flesh, we do not war after the flesh: For the weapons of our warfare are not carnal, but mighty through God to the pulling down of strong holds; Casting down imaginations, and every high thing that exalteth itself against the knowledge of God, and bringing into captivity every thought to the obedience of Christ" (2 Cor. 10:3-6,9).

Notes

[1]Irving Kristol, *Commentary Reader: The Nature of Nazism* (Atheneum, NY: American Jewish Committee, 1966), p. 29.

[2]Nigel Pennick, *Hitler's Secret Sciences* (Suffolk, England: Neville Spearman Ltd., 1981), p. 1.

[3]Sebastian Haffner, *The Meaning of Hitler* (New York, NY: Macmillan Publishing Co., 1979), p. 3.

[4]Dusty Sklar, *Gods and Beasts — The Nazis and the Occult* (New York, NY: Thomas Y. Crowell Company, 1977), p. 5.

[5]Haffner, *The Meaning of Hitler*, p. 16.

[6]Rene Pache, *The Return of Jesus Christ* (Moody Press, Chicago, IL, 1955), p. 198.

[7]Robert G.L. Waite, *The Psychopathic God Adolf Hitler* (New York, NY: Basic Books, Inc., 1977), p. 417.

[8]Chandler Brossard, *The Insane World of Adolph Hitler* (New York, NY: Fawcett Gold Medal Books, nd), p. 7.

[9]Pache, *The Return of Jesus Christ*, p. 167.

[10]Herbert Leuthy, *Commentary Reader: Der Fuhrer* (Atheneum, NY: American Jewish Committee, 1966), p. 66-67.

[11]Michael L. Brown, *Our Hands Are Stained With Blood* (Shippensburg, PA: Destiny Image Publishers, 1992), p. 159-160.

[12]Leuthy, *Commentary Reader: Der Fuhrer*, p. 67.

[13]Wulf Schwarzwaller, *The Unknown Hitler* (Bethesda, MD: National Press Books, 1989), p. 62-63.

[14]Jean-Michel Angebert, *The Occult and the Third Reich* (Paris: McGraw-Hill Book Company, by MacMillian, 1971/1974), p. 8-9.

[15]Joseph J. Carr, *The Twisted Cross* (Lafayette, LA: Huntington House Publishers, 1985), p. 96-97.

[16]Carr, *The Twisted Cross*, p. 96-97.

[17]Nicholas Goodrick-Clarke, *The Occult Roots of Nazism — The Ariosophists of Austria and Germany, 1890-1935* (Wellingborough, Northamptonshire, England: The Aquarian Press, 1985), p.151.

[18]Brossard, *The Insane World of Adolph Hitler*, p. 41-42.

[19]Roger Manvell and Heinrich Fraenkel, *Inside Adolf Hitler* (New York, NY: Pinnacle Books, Inc., 1973), p. 128.

[20]Bob Rosio, *Hitler and the New Age* (Lafayette, LA: Huntington House Publishers, 1993), p. 66.

[21]Angebert,*The Occult and the Third Reich* , p. 120.

[22]Rosio, *Hitler and the New Age*, p. 116-117.

[23]Pennick, *Hitler's Secret Sciences*, p.18.

[24]Goodrick-Clarke, *The Occult Roots of Nazism — The Ariosophists of Austria and Germany*, p. 18.

[25]Pennick, *Hitler's Secret Sciences*, p.2.

[26]Trevor Ravenscroft, *The Spear of Destiny* (York Beach, ME: Samuel Weiser, Inc., 1973).

[27]Trevor Ravenscroft and Tim Wallace-Murphy, *The Mark of the Beast* (New York, NY: Citadel Press Books, 1990).

[28]Bill Still, *Legend of the Holy Lance* (Lafayette, LA: Huntington House, 1992). While this book is a novel, the preface is of some interest and the appendix gives an "historical" outline about the lance from earliest times. It is probably more accurate the closer one gets to the present in the story. The lance is real. Ravenscroft said it is back in the Hapsburg museum. Bill Still claims, "Now, the lance rests at a secret location, guarded day and night by a contingent of the Order of the Teutonic Knights of the Holy Lance. . . . The belief that the lance is anything but evil is a fiction perpetuated by a very real group of secretive men headquartered in Germany who are already planning for the rise to power of the Antichrist. See p. 226-227.

Frankly, I am curious. If any one of our readers is ever in Vienna, please check at the Hapsburg Museum and see if the "der heilige lance"— the Holy Lance is there. If you find it, please let me know. Please get a list or catalog of any literature available and send it to us. Thank you.

[29]Frank Peretti, *This Present Darkness* (Wheaton, IL: Crossway Books, 1986).

6

WAS HITLER A CHRISTIAN?

A Church Member All His Life!

> Adolph Hitler, a baptized Catholic, who was never excommunicated by Rome, implemented a policy of total destruction because, and only because, he was able to. — Harry James Cargas
>
> Woe unto them that call evil good, and good evil; that put darkness for light, and light for darkness; that put bitter for sweet, and sweet for bitter! (Isa. 5:20).

Adolph Hitler, perpetrator of the worst nightmare ever visited upon mankind was not a Christian, in my definition of the word Christian. However, not everyone defines the word in the same way. Many would say that, being a church member, Hitler was a Christian.

Recent polls indicate that if you ask the average American if he or she is a Christian, about 70 percent will say, "Yes." You may also hear, "I belong to the Presbyterian Church, of course I am a Christian." Or, "Yes, my dad was a Methodist preacher." Or, "My Uncle Del is a Pentecostal missionary in Zimbabwe." Someone will say, "Sure, I was born right here in Christian America."

The Evangelical view is different. We believe that no one is born into the world as a Christian. A conscious decision must be made to become a Christian. We call this the "born again" experience (see John 3). There is a true church of the first born consisting of all who have been redeemed, regardless of religious affiliation.

If, however, you accept the idea that a church member is a Christian, then Hitler was a Christian. Most people in the world would say that a church member is a Christian. The idea is popular in Christian circles, and most certainly the general view among the 4.5 billion non-Christians of the world.

It is understandable that many Jewish people view the Holocaust, perpetrated by "Christian" Hitler in Christian Germany, land of the Reformation, as a Christian phenomenon. Our task is to demonstrate to Israel and the Jewish people that this concept simply is not true. Thank God for the many Evangelicals who protested what Hitler was doing.

GAEBELEIN'S WITNESS

One who protested was an American clergyman, Arno C. Gaebelein, an outstanding Evangelical writer and preacher during the early part of this century. He became aware of the Nazi threat, and long before Hitler's worst side had been seen by others he was warning the world of the dangers inherent in Nazism. This is pointed out by Herman Voss and David Rausch in their book *Protestantism — Its Modern Meaning.* In 1930 Gaebelein described Hitler as being "an outspoken enemy of the Jews . . . one of the most fanatical anti-Semites of Europe."

Voss and Rausch describe Gaebelein's thought in some detail:

> An avid reader with contacts around the world, including Germany and Russia, Gaebelein underscored the growing power of fascism in Europe in the 1920s and in *Our Hope* (August 1932) remarked, "Especially threatening is it in Germany. Adolf Hitler, the clever fascist leader who is winning out in Germany and holds the power in his hands, is a rabid anti-Semite." When Hitler became chancellor in 1933, Gaebelein saw this as a serious "setback" for the German people, and he detailed Nazi boycotts of Jewish department stores and limitation of Jewish rights. To Gaebelein, fascism meant "the political conditions of the entire world are breaking up." It appeared as though the Great Tribulation was near.

And yet Gaebelein had no patience with those who tried to pin-point or date prophetic events or who would try to guess who the Antichrist might be. His philosophy was well-illustrated when he wrote in *Our Hope* (November 1933), "The editor has no use for day-and-year-setters, nor has he any use for figuring out the duration of the times of the Gentiles, nor has he any sympathy with men who prophesy that Mussolini, Hitler, Feisal, or any other person is the Antichrist. It is a morbid condition which seems to suit certain minds."

Gaebelein continued to write about atrocities against the Jewish people and the rise of German Teutonic paganism. An article on the Nazis in February 1936 was entitled "The Devil Marches on in Germany." When Adolf Hitler used the 1936 Olympic Games as a great propaganda play and tried to hide the persecution of the Jewish people from journalists, tourists, and government officials, Gaebelein was appalled that even David Lloyd George (1863-1945), the British statesman, was misled.[1]

EVANGELICALS IN NAZI GERMANY

Many evangelicals wrongly assume that the Evangelical church in Germany must have despised Hitler and rejected his leadership. That is not the case, however. There were few who stood up against him. I have personally met Evangelical and Charismatic preachers who were once in the Nazi party in Germany. Since their conversion to Jesus Christ most have repudiated Nazism and Hitler's actions. However, a few are still defensive of Hitler and the Nazi regime.

One preacher criticized me for mentioning the Holocaust. "Let the past be in the past," he said. "Don't keep digging it up. Besides, Hitler was not all bad. He was against the Communists. He built the autobahn (superhighway) and promoted the Volkswagen. He reversed the economic woes of Germany. He loved little children. He was kind to animals, and besides, he made the trains run on time."

It is impossible to treat such words with anything but the utter contempt of which they are worthy. Suppose someone would say to you, "Yes, Joe Smith raped and killed my wife, murdered the rest of my family, and was the mass murderer of 27 other people. But he wasn't all bad, after all he ran a nice ice cream parlor and was a faithful church member and always gave to the American Red Cross Foundation."

One could only say, "How disgusting! You have a sick mind."

A GODLY PASTOR'S TRAGIC MISTAKE

The sorry fact is that the German church leaders in general, including the Evangelicals, did nothing to resist Hitler. In fact many of them favored him. Voss and Rausch cite the late Dr. Oswald J. Smith, pastor of the great Evangelical People's Church of Toronto, Ontario, Canada, in this regard. Evidently, Rev. Oswald Smith was completely fooled by Hitler. We honor Smith for his great contribution to the Evangelical world, but nevertheless relate the following.

Yet, Smith's article, "My Visit to Germany," shows how effective Adolf Hitler was in his Olympic cleanup campaign and in his brainwashing of good, decent Protestants. The 46-year-old Smith was taken in by the fervent testimony of "true Christians" he visited in Germany during the Olympic Games. "What, you ask, is the real attitude of the German people toward Hitler?" Smith wrote. "There is but one answer. They love him. . . . Every true Christian is for Hitler." They also impressed upon Smith that "the Bolsheviks [Communists] were prepared to take over the country" and that "Hitler has saved Germany." Smith listened "spellbound" to the contented, happy Protestants, joyously writing that "all girls are trained to be mothers," makeup and lipstick had been eliminated, and mass immorality was being eradicated.

"Before Hitler's days, spiritism flourished." Smith rejoiced, "now occultism of every description is banned." In addition, Smith was more than thrilled that Russellism (Jehovah's Witnesses) was banned as dangerous to the nation. He suggested that the "United States and Canada could learn a valuable lesson in this regard." In actuality, both Smith and the German Protestants were to learn that when one person's religious freedom is violated, all religious freedom is on the chopping block.

Smith was so completely deceived by the propaganda that he referred to the "spiritual awakening that is coming to the German people." The Dom Cathedral in Berlin was full, with a minister who "preaches the old-fashioned Gospel. He spares no one. And none interferes with him. He deals openly with sin and salvation."

The "true Christian" Protestants of Germany had convinced Smith that they were on the brink of religious revival. "France I do not trust. France is Red, immoral and godless," Smith concluded. "Germany is Protestant. It was from Germany that Luther came." [2]

Dr. Smith recognized the mistake he had made and on several occasions publicly apologized.

HART, A MAN WITH A HEART

Gerald Winrod, who died in 1957, quoted Smith extensively, and published his articles in his *Defender Magazine*. (*Defender* has since been taken over and retitled by a pro-Israel Pentecostal, Dr. Hart Armstrong). Actually Winrod had been a defender of the Jews in the 1920s, but by 1935 he was justifying Hitler and had turned against the Jews. Gaebelein was to identify Winrod as a "secret follower of Hitler." It is startling to discover that Winrod, a strong biblical Zionist could turn about-face and persecute the Jews through his writings.

Yet, we see the same thing happening today in certain Evangelical and Charismatic camps. May God deliver us from this spiritual treachery. May God deliver us from this spiritual insanity. Currently Rev. Gordon Winrod, a Fundamentalist, is carrying on his father's tradition of Christian anti-Semitism. His anti-Semitic literature is published under the auspices of a church he pastors in Gainesville, Missouri.

Gerald Winrod was a great believer in the spurious *Protocols of the Learned Elders of Zion*, and he distributed copies widely. The *Protocols* purport to be an outline of a Jew-Zionist plot to rule the world. American Evangelical leaders like Arno Gaebelein, Harry Ironside, Keith Brooks, and many others signed Dr. Donald Gray Barnhouse's petition denouncing the *Protocols* as an anti-Semitic forgery.[3] At the same time, most German Evangelicals were silent, or even supportive, of Hitler.

EVANGELICALS WHO SAW THE LIGHT

The news is not all bad. It is encouraging to discover that many Canadian and American Evangelicals did actually denounce Hitler. Pentecostal preachers were almost universally clear in their anti-Nazi declarations. Voss and Rausch state: "During Hitler's 'final solution' to the Jewish problem, Fundamentalist-Evangelicals believed that the Jewish people were being exterminated by the millions, while liberal Christian periodicals, such as *The Christian Century*, were labeling the reports of atrocity as propaganda. Gaebelein's *Our Hope* magazine gave factual reports of atrocities against the Jewish people during the 1930s and 1940s. The fundamentalist and evangelical world view lent itself very well to such convictions, even when they seemed beyond the realm of belief and left the premillennialists in shock."[4]

The good news today is that there are many Evangelicals who are in tune with biblical truth in relation to Israel and the Jewish people. How I thank God for those who refuse to be intimidated, who rise above the general apathy that attends this subject. Not willing to be part of a silent majority, they will not yield to the coercive manipulation of either liberal church hierarchies nor of the biased media. They will not be cowed by fear tactics. We refuse to join today's conspiracy of silence on Israel's case in the Middle East struggle.

SOME OMINOUS TRENDS

We must not smugly take comfort in the fact that many American Evangelicals did resist Hitler from afar, while condemning our German colleagues. It is easy to be self-congratulatory when surrounded by our agreeing brethren.

However, looking at the current North American Evangelical scene, especially in certain quarters of the Charismatic and Pentecostal movements, we see a shift away from biblical literalism. It reminds one of the kind of reversal made by Gerald Winrod on the Israel/Jewish issue. I am distressed to see certain pastors and leaders who once took a strong biblical stance on God's promises to national Israel, today are hobnobbing with the Kingdom Now and Dominion crowd. A few have openly embraced anti-Israel doctrine. The silence of others, formerly so outspoken, is significant.

If Charismatics are going to fellowship with our Kingdom Now brethren, they should take every opportunity to correct them on their unscriptural attitude toward Israel. For the most part I do not see this happening. In fact, some are going even further astray and are changing their theological stance on truly critical issues. There are notable exceptions. Rev. John Hagee, pastor of Cornerstone Church in San Antonio, Texas, does not hesitate to go into Charismatic churches and conferences and speak strong corrective words.

Many have been silenced for the sake of "unity." But what kind of unity is it that calls for silence on major issues? What kind of unity is it that denies us the right to speak out on vital issues? What kind of unity is it when a few brethren, with strange new doctrines, set the agenda for us all? What kind of unity is it that causes Kingdom Now friends to accuse those of us who are friends of Israel of being satanic, inspired by the devil, deceived, and guilty of preaching heresy? I am told that I should either change my views concerning Israel, or if I cannot do that, then I should be silent for the sake of unity. What unity is there in this?

TRUE UNITY

My view is that, regardless of disagreements, I am united with all born-again believers. We have one head, Jesus Christ (see 1 Cor. 12). If we are saved through the blood of Jesus we are united, whether you like me or not, or agree with me or not. I am willing to let God decide who is saved and who is not. That is not my task. There is damaging division in the Church, but the Church of born-again persons is spiritually united in the body of Christ. Perhaps the final and total realization or manifestation of that unity awaits the time of His coming.

We certainly need a more visible manifestation of that unity, but the neo-modernist Evangelicals and Pentecostals are not promoting that kind of unity. They are promoting a coercive unity, promoted by soul force and psychological manipulation.

Unity we have, but truth is elusive and must be pursued with vigor. Regardless of what you may hear or think to the contrary, the devil's principle end-time tactic is not to cause division, but to promote deception. Indeed division is deplorable, and Satan will use it, but deception is worse and can hinder the kingdom of God, and in the extreme can even damn souls.

I cannot stop telling you that what is being preached in certain quarters today is exactly the same replacement theology that both Protestant and Roman Catholic pastors and teachers were promoting in pre-Nazi Germany. We had better be alert to these alarming trends.

Don't ever say, "It cannot happen here." I hear from some of my brethren that God no longer has any use for natural Israel. The Church has taken the place of Israel in God's economy. That is called the doctrine of replacement. Secondly, there is the doctrine of contempt. Simply stated it claims that since the Jews killed Christ they are worthy of any punishment that falls upon them. The Holocaust? Good enough for them.

In the light of this strange philosophy how should one view the slaughter of Christian martyrs under the old Roman Empire and more recently under the Communists? Good enough for them? You cannot have it both ways.

Many replacement theologians are promoting the same anti-Semitic theology that the churchmen of Hitler's day were preaching. Hitler's henchmen actually quoted pastors and church leaders in justifying their heinous acts against the Jews.

SCAPEGOAT SYNDROME

Let a major depression hit the world. Let really hard times come to this country. Let another Hitler arise, this time in our own midst. (It can't happen here. Oh?) Some of the modernistic Evangelicals I have described will be among the first to follow him. They may not light the gas furnaces in the death camps, but like the German churchmen, they will provide the fuel and build the boxcars.

Replacement theologians sit in ivory towers and write their books denouncing those of us who are biblical lovers of Zion. They are erudite gentlemen, skillful crafters of words and weavers of ideas. But below their ivory towers the front line volunteer troops pick up the gauntlet and carry on the attack against Zion in a cruder fashion.

How can a Christian be anti-Semitic? To be anti-Semitic is to cooperate and agree with the devil. It is Satan's desire to destroy the nation of Israel and nullify the promises of God.

THE WAY OF THE FUHRER

Hitler grew up in Austria, and in 1914 moved to Munich, Germany. He enlisted in the German army during the First World War, served as a corporal, and in August 1918 was injured by poison gas. Germany was defeated. After the war was over Hitler moved back to Munich where he got involved with the National Socialist German Worker's Party (NSDAP). He soon gained control of the party. In November 1923 his radical party tried to take over the Bavarian government. This failed effort is remembered as the "Beer Hall Putsch." During his nine-month interment at Landsberg Fortress Prison, Hitler wrote his infamous book *Mein Kampf* (My Struggle). It is his autobiography, philosophy, and endless rant against the subhuman, diabolical Jews. A great deal of the book consists of his attacks against the Jews. He finally concluded that the Jews were not real human beings at all.

Hitler campaigned against the Communists, promised to make the economy recover and to restore the fallen glory of Germany. He became the leader of the Nazi Party and led his nation into the Second World War. Here are a few samplings of Hitler's hateful words against the Jews:

Wherever I went, I began to see Jews, and the more I saw, the more sharply they became distinguished in my eyes from the rest of humanity.

Was there any form of filth or profligacy, particularly in cultural life, without at least one Jew involved in it? If you cut even cautiously into such an abscess, you found, like a maggot in a rotting body, often dazzled by the sudden light — a kike!

I didn't know what to be more amazed at: the agility of their tongues or their virtuosity at lying. Gradually I began to hate them.

For me this was the time of the greatest spiritual upheaval I have ever had to go through. I had ceased to be a weak-kneed cosmopolitan and became an anti-Semite. . . . Eternal nature inexorably avenges the infringement of her commands. Hence today I believe that I am acting in accordance with the will of the Almighty Creator: *By defending myself against the Jew, I am fighting for the work of the Lord.*[5]

HITLER'S HOLY WAR

In Hitler's mind he was fighting a holy war. Islam calls it a *jihad*. Hitler's war was indeed a spiritual war, but it was not a holy war. It was an unholy war. The god he served was Satan, the god of this world, the enemy of the Almighty God and His people (see 2 Cor. 4:4). Matthew 6:23 says that "if your eye is bad your whole body will be filled with darkness. If therefore the light that is in you is darkness, how great is the darkness."[6]

How deep and how malevolent the darkness out of which Hitler proclaimed, "The Jews are a race, but not the image of God. They are an image of the devil."[7]

Systematically these black parasites of the nation [Jews] defile our inexperienced young blond girls and thereby destroy something which can no longer be replaced in this world. . . . The folkish-minded man, in particular, has the sacred duty, each in his own denomination, of making *people stop just talking superficially of God's will, and actually fulfill God's will, and not let God's word be desecrated.*[8]

Hitler proclaimed that in persecuting the Jews he was doing the work of the Lord. The link between Hitler and the professing Church is clear to see. First of all, he was a lifelong member of the Roman Catholic Church. Secondly both Roman and Protestant theologians had laid the groundwork of his hatred and destruction of the Jews.

MARTIN LUTHER

Alexis Rubin comments:

> Sadly, Luther's hateful diatribes against Jews, coming from the highly respected founder of Germany's major Protestant religion, had a great impact on later generations of Germans. They influenced Germany's nineteenth century anti-Semitic movement and gave its advocates an air of legitimacy. Numerous books and pamphlets appeared in print detailing Martin Luther's "heroic" struggles against the Jews. In the 1930s and 1940s Hitler's Nazi propagandists borrowed heavily from the earlier German anti-Semites and from Luther's urging "not to suffer them, or bear with them any longer."[9]

ZHIRINOVSKY

Friend, we would be naive to think that there are no potential Hitlers in the world today. The second most powerful politician in Russia at this moment certainly qualifies. If he would become president of Russia/C.I.S. in a future election, Vladimar Zhirinovsky, self-proclaimed anti-Semite, has declared his willingness to invade Europe, "seize Alaska, carve up Poland, and reconquer Finland." He declares his intention to re-invent the Soviet Union. His expansionist views for Mother Russia extend all the way to the Mediterranean. In a previous presidential election he placed third, and "next time he is likely to do better."[10]

TOO LATE FOR HALF MEASURES

Christians, it is time to stop playing church. Take these issues seriously. Get involved in advancing the plan and purpose of God. Spend time in prayer and in learning from the Holy Spirit as you read the Bible. Break out of your four walls and find out what is going on in your world.

Pastors, I urge you to get involved in these important issues facing the Church today.

CARGAS, A CATHOLIC, ACCUSES

No one puts it better than Professor Harry James Cargas:

> Adolf Hitler, a baptized Catholic, who was never excommunicated by Rome, implemented a policy of total destruction because, and only because, *he was able to.* Only because people willingly cooperated in individual and mass murders. Who, for example, were the architects who designed the ovens into which people were delivered for cremation? Who meticulously executed the plans for the efficient gas chambers into which naked men, women, and children were herded to die? Who originated the design for the camps, those models of economical, technological destruction? Which firms bid on the contracts to build the camps, the gas chambers, the ovens?
>
> Which doctors performed experiments on Jewish victims? Who shaved their heads, and all bodily hairs to gain materials for cloth and rugs? We've heard of lampshades made from Jewish skin, of soap made from Jewish bodies, of "enforcers" throwing Jewish victims — most of them dead, but not all — into huge pits, of brutal guards crushing Jewish babies' skulls with rifle butts, and shooting aged and unhealthy Jews who couldn't keep up on the forced marches, and forcing naked Jews to stand for hours in freezing weather for either convenience or amusement. Who were these tormentors?
>
> What of the train engineers who guided the cattle cars packed with starving, dying, dead Jews to their locales of internment? And what of the ordinary citizens of many European nations who, as the death trains passed through their communities, would throw bits of bread into the cattle cars to be entertained by watching famished Jews fight over the food in an agonizing display of attempt at survival?
>
> So who were all of the people who cooperated with Hitler's master plan? They were in the thousands, perhaps in the millions. How many people does it take to exterminate 12,000,000 human beings, half of them Jews, half of them non-Jews? . . . We are not here concerned with something that Nazi Germany did alone,

rather of that cosmic catastrophe performed in *Christian Europe.* [11]

Indeed, who were these people? Were they so different from you and your neighbors? Were they not ordinary people caught up in a tidal wave of hate under which flowed a riptide of apathy?

BUT, IT'S NOT MY FAULT

Christians may protest, "I wasn't in Germany. I did nothing to the Jews. It isn't my fault." No one wants to accept responsibility, but we must. The prophets of Israel confessed the sins of the nation as if they had committed the sins themselves. Niemoller believed that all Christians should repent of their guilt and lack of involvement so that never again would such monstrous horrors go unprotested by believers in Jesus Christ.

MUTUAL INTEREST

Evangelicals ought to know that we have a vested interest in being protective of our Jewish friends. The same anti-God forces that have always wanted to destroy the Jews also want to destroy us. I appeal to my Evangelical brethren who are into a denial of literal interpretation and the resultant replacement theology to rethink their doctrine and return to a Biblical standard before it is too late.

Notes

[1]David A. Rausch and Carl Herman Voss *Protestantism — Its Modern Meaning* (Philadelphia, PA: Fortress Press, 1987), p. 150.

[2]Rausch and Voss, *Protestantism — Its Modern Meaning,* p. 151.

[3]Rausch and Voss, *Protestantism — Its Modern Meaning,* p. 152-153.

[4]Rausch and Voss, *Protestantism — Its Modern Meaning,* p. 153.

[5]Adolph Hitler, translated by Ralph Manheim, *Mein Kampf* (Boston, MA: Houghton Mifflin, 1971), p.56, 57, 63-65.

[6]Bob Rosio, *Hitler and the New Age* (Lafayette, LA; Huntington House, 1993), p. 52.

[7]Joachim Fest, *Adolph Hitler* (New York, NY: Harcourt, Brace, Jovanovich, 1973), p. 232.

[8]Hitler, *Mein Kampf,* p. 562

[9]Alexis P. Rubin, editor, *Scattered Among the Nations* (Dayton, OH: Wall and Emerson, 1993), p.103.

[10]Carroll Bogert and Dorinda Elliot, "The Laughing Fascist," *Newsweek,* December 27, 1993, p. 26, 30.

[11]Harry James Cargas, *A Christian Response to the Holocaust* (Denver, CO: Stonehenge Books, 1981), p. 3-5.

7

THE TEN LOST TRIBES

Robbing Israel of Her Identity and Heritage

> *Satan's attempts to destroy the Jewish people have taken various forms in history, from the days of Antiochus Epiphanes to the murderous plan of Hitler. Now the evil one is promoting the lie that the Jews are not truly the Jews, thus robbing Israel of its promises and covenants and transferring them to the Anglo-Saxon race!* — William Varner[1]
>
> *Who are Israelites; to whom pertaineth the adoption, and the glory, and the covenants, and the giving of the law, and the service of God, and the promises* (Rom. 9:4).

One way of robbing modern day Israel is to deny that they are the true Israel of the Bible. Some do this by transferring all the promises made to Israel in the Old Testament to the Church with the claim that the Church displaces Israel in the economy of God. How strange that the allegorists (who claim that the Scripture is not literal in reference to Israel) want the Bible to be very literal when it suits their purposes.

All the Scripture concerning redemption is to be taken literally. But when it comes to Israel, they want us to see Israel as the Church.

How strange that some are very happy to transfer all the blessings promised to Israel for obedience to the Church, but are just as willing for the curses pronounced in the Old Testament upon the disobedient, to be visited upon the heads of the Jewish people of today. There is an inconsistency here! The problem with allegorizing the Scripture is that it introduces an anarchy of interpretation. Every person becomes a law unto himself or herself. What is to prevent you from taking any passage and saying, "This is not literal," and then attaching any prejudiced meaning you wish?

TEN LOST TRIBES?

Another novel theory is that the Jewish people are not representative of all the 12 tribes, but only Judah and Benjamin. The 10 northern tribes allegedly wandered off and became the ancestors of Europeans and Americans. The theory is commonly called British Israelism or Destiny of America. The anti-Semitic Christian Fundamentalist "Identity" movement capitalizes on this theory.

In this scheme of interpretation England becomes Ephraim and the United States is Manasseh. It is a puzzle to me how crossing the Atlantic transformed members of the tribe of Ephraim to members of the tribe of Manasseh. That is not the only difficulty the British Israelites face, however. The fact is that there is no basis in history or Scripture for the claims of the British Israel adherents.

William Varner observes that the identity robbers hold the view that "Anglo Saxons are thus the Israel of the Bible. Therefore, according to this view, the present-day Jews are from the tribe of Judah, are under a divine curse, and are not to be identified with Israel at all. Furthermore, the Anglo-Saxon peoples, including the British (i.e. Ephraim) and America (i.e. Manasseh) are the inheritors of the covenants and promises of the Old Testament."[2]

DIVISION OF ISRAEL

After the reign of King Solomon the 10 northern tribes seceded from the two southern tribes, Judah and Benjamin. The rupture took place in 930 B.C. Jeroboam ruled the northern tribes from his capital in Samaria. Rehoboam ruled the southern two-tribe coalition from Jerusalem. For one account of this carefully read 1 Kings 11:43-12:33:

> And Solomon slept with his fathers, and was buried

in the city of David his father: and Rehoboam his son reigned in his stead. And Rehoboam went to Shechem: for all Israel were come to Shechem to make him king. And it came to pass, when Jeroboam the son of Nebat, who was yet in Egypt, heard of it, (for he was fled from the presence of king Solomon, and Jeroboam dwelt in Egypt;) That they sent and called him. And Jeroboam and all the congregation of Israel came, and spake unto Rehoboam, saying, Thy father made our yoke grievous: now therefore make thou the grievous service of thy father, and his heavy yoke which he put upon us, lighter, and we will serve thee. And he said unto them, Depart yet for three days, then come again to me. And the people departed. And king Rehoboam consulted with the old men, that stood before Solomon his father while he yet lived, and said, How do ye advise that I may answer this people? And they spake unto him, saying, If thou wilt be a servant unto this people this day, and wilt serve them, and answer them, and speak good words to them, then they will be thy servants for ever.

But he forsook the counsel of the old men, which they had given him, and consulted with the young men that were grown up with him, and which stood before him: And he said unto them, What counsel give ye that we may answer this people, who have spoken to me, saying, Make the yoke which thy father did put upon us lighter? And the young men that were grown up with him spake unto him, saying, Thus shalt thou speak unto this people that spake unto thee, saying, Thy father made our yoke heavy, but make thou it lighter unto us; thus shalt thou say unto them, My little finger shall be thicker than my father's loins. And now whereas my father did lade you with a heavy yoke, I will add to your yoke: my father hath chastised you with whips, but I will chastise you with scorpions.

So Jeroboam and all the people came to Rehoboam the third day, as the king had appointed, saying, Come to me again the third day. And the king answered the people roughly, and forsook the old men's counsel that they gave him; And spake to them after the counsel of the young men, saying, My father made your yoke heavy, and I will add to your yoke: my father also chastised you with whips, but I will chastise you with scorpions.

Wherefore the king hearkened not unto the people; for the cause was from the Lord, that he might perform his saying, which the Lord spake by Ahijah the Shilonite unto Jeroboam the son of Nebat. So when all Israel saw that the king hearkened not unto them, the people answered the king, saying, What portion have we in David? neither have we inheritance in the son of Jesse: to your tents, O Israel: now see to thine own house, David. So Israel departed unto their tents. But as for the children of Israel which dwelt in the cities of Judah, Rehoboam reigned over them.

Then king Rehoboam sent Adoram, who was over the tribute; and all Israel stoned him with stones, that he died. Therefore king Rehoboam made speed to get him up to his chariot, to flee to Jerusalem. So Israel rebelled against the house of David unto this day. And it came to pass, when all Israel heard that Jeroboam was come again, that they sent and called him unto the congregation, and made him king over all Israel: there was none that followed the house of David, but the tribe of Judah only.

And when Rehoboam was come to Jerusalem, he assembled all the house of Judah, with the tribe of Benjamin, an hundred and fourscore thousand chosen men, which were warriors, to fight against the house of Israel, to bring the kingdom again to Rehoboam the son of Solomon.

But the word of God came unto Shemaiah the man of God, saying, Speak unto Rehoboam, the son of Solomon, king of Judah, and unto all the house of Judah and Benjamin, and to the remnant of the people, saying, Thus saith the Lord, Ye shall not go up, nor fight against your brethren the children of Israel: return every man to his house; for this thing is from me. They hearkened therefore to the word of the Lord, and returned to depart, according to the word of the Lord.

Then Jeroboam built Shechem in mount Ephraim, and dwelt therein; and went out from thence, and built Penuel. And Jeroboam said in his heart, Now shall the kingdom return to the house of David: If this people go up to do sacrifice in the house of the Lord at Jerusalem, then shall the heart of this people turn again unto their lord, even unto Rehoboam king of Judah, and they shall kill me, and go again to Rehoboam king of Judah.

Whereupon the king took counsel, and made two calves of gold, and said unto them, It is too much for you to go up to Jerusalem: behold thy gods, O Israel, which brought thee up out of the land of Egypt. And he set the one in Beth-el, and the other put he in Dan. And this thing became a sin: for the people went to worship before the one, even unto Dan. And he made an house of high places, and made priests of the lowest of the people, which were not of the sons of Levi.

And Jeroboam ordained a feast in the eighth month, on the fifteenth day of the month, like unto the feast that is in Judah, and he offered upon the altar. So did he in Beth-el, sacrificing unto the calves that he had made: and he placed in Beth-el the priests of the high places which he had made. So he offered upon the altar which he had made in Beth-el the fifteenth day of the eighth month, even in the month which he had devised of his own heart; and ordained a feast unto the children of Israel: and he offered upon the altar, and burnt incense (1 Kings 11:43-12:33).

Many northern Israelis were horrified when King Jeroboam set up a rival religion with golden calf worship at Bethel and Dan.

NORTHERNERS MOVE SOUTH

Dissatisfied with the apostasy of Jeroboam and the false priests at Bethel and Dan, many true believers in Jehovah moved south to Jerusalem. They knew that according to the writing of Moses the only place where the Passover and the sacrifices would be acceptable to God was at the Temple on Mt. Moriah in Jerusalem (see Deut. 12:5-7; 16:2-6; Isa. 18:7). In the Isaiah reference Zion refers to Jerusalem.

Shortly, all the 12 tribes were represented in the south. Obviously the number of people who immigrated was significant. God even addresses the 12 tribes in the south: "Speak unto Rehoboam the son of Solomon, king of Judah, and to *all Israel in Judah and Benjamin*" (2 Chron. 11:3). (Emphasis added.)

The Levites, whose priesthood had been rejected by Jeroboam, led the way and were followed by the other godly folk in the north. Of course some came for political and other reasons, but no matter, that only strengthens the case.

"For the Levites left their suburbs and their possession, and came to Judah and Jerusalem: for Jeroboam and his sons had cast them off from executing the priest's office unto the Lord: And he ordained him priests for the high places, and for the devils, and for the calves which he had made. And after them *out of all the tribes of Israel* such as set their hearts to seek the Lord God of Israel came to Jerusalem, to sacrifice unto the Lord God of their fathers" (2 Chron. 11:14-16). (Emphasis added.)

ANOTHER MIGRATION

Later, when Asa reigned king in the south, another great company came from the north. This is found in 2 Chronicles 15:9: "And he gathered all Judah and Benjamin, and the strangers with them out of Ephraim and Manasseh, and out of Simeon; for *they fell to him out of Israel in abundance*, when they saw that the Lord his God was with him."

We are left with no doubt that by the time of the captivity of the northern tribes, all the 12 tribes of Israel were well represented in the south. Therefore when the northern tribes went into the Assyrian captivity in 722 B.C., many members of the 10 tribes were left in the southern kingdom of Judah. Much later (586 B.C.) when the Babylonians took Judah into captivity, members of *all the tribes of Israel* went into the Babylonian captivity, because of these earlier migrations from the north to the south.

THE PROPHET ISAIAH

Isaiah lived in Jerusalem and prophesied to Judah, the southern kingdom. Decades after the fall of the north (722 B.C.), Isaiah wrote, "Here ye this, O house of Jacob, which are called by the name of Israel, and which are come forth out of the waters of Judah . . ." (Isa. 48:1). This was written about 690 B.C. Also note verses 12-14. It is in this monumental chapter that God promises not to make a full end of Israel. This refutes the British Israel idea that only the north was called Israel after the dividing of the nation following Solomon's death.

CAPTIVITY OF THE TEN NORTHERN TRIBES

King Hoshea was the last ruler of the northern (10 tribe) kingdom. Shalmaneser, King of Assyria came against him in a war that the

Assyrians won. The final fall of Israel took place in 722 B.C. Hoshea had reigned from 732 B.C. until the fall of the northern kingdom. Many, but not all, of the citizens of Israel were taken into slavery in Assyria.

Later the succeeding Babylonian empire conquered the lands controlled by the Assyrians and hence inherited the descendants of the 10 (never lost) tribes of northern Israel that had been deported by Shalmaneser.

SLAVES ARE VALUABLE

The Assyrians were a powerful and clever people. The Israelite slaves were a great prize. It is hard to think that they were allowed to go wandering off into Europe. In the shameful days of slavery in America many stories were told of how escaped slaves were relentlessly pursued and recaptured at all costs, if possible. Slaves were valuable property. They brought a high price on the auction block. It is not likely that the Assyrians were any less careful with their slave property.

NOT ALL NORTH ISRAELITES DEPORTED

Indeed a passage such as 2 Kings 17 might, upon superficial examination indicate that all of the 10 tribes of north Israel went into captivity. This must be understood contextually and by comparison with many other Scriptures which bear upon the subject. Indeed, years after the fall of the north to Assyria, King Hezekiah of Judah issued a call to all Israel to come and worship in Jerusalem, and to celebrate the Passover there.

> So they established a decree to make proclamation through all Israel, from Beersheba [extreme southland] even to Dan [the far north] that they should come to keep the Passover unto the Lord God of Israel at Jerusalem. . . . So the posts went with the letter from the king and his princes throughout *all Israel, and Judah* . . . saying, Ye Children of Israel, turn again unto the Lord God of Abraham, Isaac, and Israel, and he will return to the remnant of you, that are escaped out of the hand of the kings of Assyria (2 Chron. 30:5-6).
>
> So the posts passed from city to city through the country of Ephraim and Manasseh even unto Zebulun . . . divers of Asher and Manasseh and of Zebulun humbled themselves and came to Jerusalem (2 Chron. 30:10-11).

And the children of Israel that were present at Jerusalem kept the feast of unleavened bread. . . ." (2 Chron. 30:21).

For further insight please read all of 2 Chronicles 30. Varner notes:

> Not all of the northern tribes went into captivity in 721 B.C. Archaeology has confirmed this fact which is so clearly taught in Chronicles. Excavations have revealed that the population of Judah rapidly increased after the fall of the northern kingdom as a result of the many refugees mentioned in 2 Chronicles 11:14-16. Furthermore, archaeologists have uncovered the annals of the Assyrian Sargon, in which he tells that he carried away only 27,290 people and fifty chariots (*Biblical Archaeologist*, VI, 1943, p.58).
>
> Since estimates of the population of the northern kingdom at that time range from 400,000 to 500,000, clearly less than one-twentieth of the population was deported, primarily the leaders from the area around Samaria. The 10 tribes, therefore, were never lost because they were never deported! Their kingdom was destroyed and ceased to exist, but most of them stayed, with some around Samaria intermingling with the new immigrants to form the Samaritans (2 Kings 17:24-41).[3]

Over 80 years passed by after Hezekiah's revival and reform movement, then during the time of King Josiah of Judah the same condition is described. The call goes out from the king and the response for an offering for the temple comes back from "Manasseh and Ephraim and of all the remnant of Israel, and of all Judah and Benjamin . . ." (2 Chron. 34:9). All of this takes place at the time the British Israelite theoreticians would have us believe the 10 "lost" tribes were wandering all over Europe.

JEW AND ISRAELITE USED INTERCHANGEABLY

The division of north and south of Israel ended with Babylonian captivity. After the return from Babylon the terms Jew and Israelite are used interchangeably. Ezra calls the returning remnant Jews 8 times, and as Israel 40 times. Nehemiah speaks of the Jews 11 times. The same people are called Israel 22 times in the Book of Nehemiah. Later we will note the same usage in the New Testament.

BABYLONIAN CAPTIVITY

The Babylonians, under Nebuchadnezzar, conquered the southern kingdom of Judah. The final fall of Judah took place in 586 B.C. When the Judeans (and all Israel in their midst) were taken to Babylon, they found descendants of the northern kingdom living in the expanded Babylonian empire, which had conquered Assyria. Not so many generations had gone by that these people had forgotten who they were. Just like you compare genealogical notes when you meet a relative you have not known before, you can be sure that these genealogy-conscious Israelites recounted many a family tree. Many happy family reunions took place.

RETURN TO THE LAND OF ISRAEL

After the 70 years of the desolation of Jerusalem, many captives, freed by Cyrus the Persian, conqueror of Babylon, went back to the land of Israel to rebuild the temple and ultimately the city walls of Jerusalem. While many Israelites were assimilated into the heathen cultures of Assyria and Babylon, many retained their identity and returned to the land of their fathers, preserving all 12 tribes of Israel in the Holy Land.

THE WITNESS OF EZRA AND NEHEMIAH

Over and over the Book of Ezra refers to "all Israel" returning to the land and occupying it. (See Ezra 2:70; 3:11; 8:35; 10:25, etc.) Ezra speaks of a "sin offering for all Israel, twelve he goats, according to the number of the tribes of Israel" (Ezra 6:17).

The Book of Nehemiah bears witness, long after the return, in similar fashion to the presence of all 12 tribes being back in the land, not scattered out over Europe. "And all Israel in the days of Zerubbabel and Nehemiah . . ." (Neh. 12:47).

How can the adherents of British Israelism make the claim that the 10 tribes were "lost"?

TRIBAL IDENTITY

There never were 12 races of Israel. There were 12 tribes and only one nation of Israel, up until the reign of Solomon.

Tribal identity was based on male descent. For example, if a young woman from the tribe of Asher married a young man from the tribe of Judah, she became a member of Judah and their male children carried on the lineage of Judah. The matter of tribal identity was important for inheritance rights. The tribes were allowed to and, as a matter of fact, did freely intermarry.

PROMISES TO ISRAEL

The British Israel theory came to its zenith at a time when the British Empire held sway in much of the world, "The empire upon which the sun never sets." Theologians were puzzled as to what the prophecies of blessing and regathering to Israel in the last days meant. Some Bible scholars taught they were literal; that the Jewish people would one day return to Palestine and establish a new nation in fulfillment of God's plan revealed in prophecy. Time has shown these literalists to be right.

WORDS, WORDS, WORDS

British Israel writers made much of the similarity of such terms as Anglo-Saxons compared to Isaac's sons. Of course, the actual Hebrew words have no similarity at all. Isaac is Yitzhak and son is Ben, in Hebrew. One incredible theory now claims that the real Jerusalem was not in the Middle East at any time. It was Edinburgh, Scotland. "And they shall turn away their ears from the truth, and shall be turned unto fables" (2 Tim. 4:4).

The trail of the wandering tribe of Dan is supposed to be marked by Danmark, the river Danube, DarDanelles, etc. One might as well try to trace the descendants of Ham, son of Noah to Hamburg, Germany, or BirmingHam, Alabama. Both are equally ridiculous.

Yes, Jews have been dispersed throughout the world. They have wandered far, but the uniqueness of the Jewish-Israelite people is that they never lost their identity.

This is not to say that some did not assimilate, and lose their identity, but on the whole the identity is preserved. This is why the prophecy of the Bible is so marvelous. It has been absolutely unerring in its accuracy. The existence of the Jewish people as a unique people is the strongest proof of that. To deny this is not only to rob modern Israel, and thus aid and abet the cause of the anti-Semites (Jew haters), but it also robs the Church of the strong authority of the infallible Word of Almighty God.

DIASPORA

It is true that not all the Israelites returned from the captivities. Many were scattered abroad, but not lost. God said that He would "sift the house of Israel among all the nations," not just Europe (Amos 9:9). They retained their Jewish-Israelite identity. Thus, as Peter preached to the crowd on the day of Pentecost there were Jews from the dispersion present; they were visiting from all parts of the known world. (See Acts 2.) Most Jews today do not know their tribal identity. But the identity exists, based on male descendency. God knows the genealogy of every human on earth. He knows the tribal identity of every person who is a Jew.

Intermarriage has taken place, but no matter how thin the bloodline, God knows where each descendent of Jacob is.

ONE HUNDRED AND FORTY-FOUR THOUSAND

When it is time for the seventh chapter of Revelation to be fulfilled and for the sealing of the 144,000 — 12,000 of every tribe of Israel — it is God who makes the selection, not man. These are the sealed servants of the Almighty. Servants? They must render service to Him by declaring the message of His truth, and as a consequence a multitude of people from every tribe and nation and tongue, hence, many Gentiles will be redeemed. (See Rev. 7.)

TRIBES OR DENOMINATIONS?

In our introduction to this chapter we mentioned the theory that the church is Israel. The seventh chapter of Revelation is a real embarrassment to anyone believing this. Certainly the 12 tribes are not 12 denominations of the church! It is much more satisfying to simply believe the Word in a simple, literal fashion. It really makes sense that way. Anything less reduces the noble ideas of God to nonsense.

The great Presbyterian pastor and Bible expositor, Donald Grey Barnhouse, concurred with this literal view of the 144,000 in Revelation chapter seven. He wrote, "The 12 tribes then must be taken as literal Israel and not as the Church. At the time of the division of the kingdoms, the faithful of the northern tribes obeyed the Word of the Lord and went to Jerusalem in sufficient numbers to guarantee the succession of all the 12 tribes. . . . This, of course, destroys the claims of those who have looked upon Britain and America as being the 10 lost tribes, who have imagined that there is a difference between the Jews and Israel. They are the same and most definitely all the tribes are now seen in Judah."[4]

NEW TESTAMENT WITNESS

A godly Israelite, Anna knew her tribal identity in the time of Jesus. She was of the tribe of Asher (see Luke 2:30).

The apostle Paul was of the tribe of Benjamin. He bears witness to that fact himself. He said, "I am a Jew." Paul also says, "I also am an Israelite" (Rom. 11:1).

The terms "Jew" and "Israelite" were used interchangeably after the return from Babylon, and that condition prevailed into New Testament times. The New Testament speaks of Israel 75 times and uses the word "Jew" 174 times. (For examples, see Acts 21:39; 22:3; Rom. 11:1; 2 Cor. 11:22; Phil. 3:5.)

THE MISSION OF JESUS

Jesus claimed, "I am not sent but unto the lost sheep of the house of Israel" (Matt. 15:24). Since Jesus only ministered in the region of Israel it would seem that all Israel was present and represented there, notwithstanding the fact that many were dispersed in other nations, all the time retaining full knowledge that they were Jewish.

Jesus commissioned His followers with these words, "Go rather to the lost sheep of the house of Israel" (Matt. 10:6). This was early in His ministry and the disciples knew nothing at this time of a great world commission which was to come later. For now they were restricted to Israelites, who were present in the land at that time.

ON THE DAY OF PENTECOST

In the great sermon on the Day of Pentecost Peter cries, "Ye men of Judea" and "ye men of Israel...." Peter calls his listeners Jews and of the house of Israel. He says to them, "Let all the house of Israel know assuredly that God hath made that same Jesus both Lord and Christ...." All of the references in this paragraph are from the second chapter of Acts.

THE THRONE OF DAVID

The royal throne of England is purported to be the very throne of King David. One British Israelite writes, "Elizabeth II actually sits on the throne of King David of Israel. She is a direct descendant, continuing David's dynasty. It is the very throne on which Christ will sit after His return."

The same theory states that the throne was taken from Judah (the Jews) and given to the 10 tribes. Jesus is said not to have been a Jew.

How could Jesus be of the house of David and not be a Jew (of the tribe of Judah)? David himself was of the tribe of Judah. British Israelites insist on this strange teaching to support their theory that a curse rests on the Jews for crucifying Jesus and that the curse does not apply to the descendants of the 10 "lost" tribes. Possibly all British Israelites are not anti-Semites, but their ideas are certainly seized by the haters of Israel as potent weapons against the chosen of the Lord.

British Israelites frequently try to engage me in argument, and it

is my observation that most of them harbor real anti-Semitic sentiments. It would not be fair to say that all British Israelites hate the
Jewish people, but the attitude is so common that it makes me
uncomfortable. The theory of British Israel is by nature anti-Semitic,
because it denies the Jewish people of their proper place in the plan of
God.

That the throne of David is in England, resting place of the 10 lost
tribes becomes a silly notion when one reads, "And the Lord rejected
the seed of Israel and afflicted them . . . he rent Israel from the house
of David . . . so Israel was carried away out of their own land to Assyria
. . ." (2 Kings 17:20-23).

FULFILLED PROPHECY

How can we overlook the fact that through the centuries there
have been godly expositors and Bible teachers who have called for a
literal interpretation of the Scriptures, including the scores of passages that speak of a return of the Jewish people to what was
previously called Palestine? How can we scorn the simple observation that what these faithful teachers have spoken and written, based
on God's infallible Word, has actually come to pass in our times? It
is no wonder that the very existence of the modern nation of Israel is
such an embarrassment to the British Israelites and all other replacement theologians!

"Therefore say unto the house of Israel . . . I will take you from
among the heathen, and gather you out of all countries, and will bring
you into your own land . . . ye shall dwell in the land that I gave to your
fathers . . . the desolate land shall be tilled . . . and ruined cities are
inhabited" (selected passages from Ezek. 36). Ezekiel also declares
after the "dry bones" vision that Judah (Jews) and Israel (10 tribes)
shall be one and will be joined together in the regathering. Read
Ezekiel chapter 37, note verses 16-17. Verse 22 says that they will be
one nation "they shall no more be two nations." This is the condition
that prevails in Israel today.

GREAT FUTURE FOR ISRAEL

Some object that the nation of Israel is a secular society and that
most of the Jewish people do not even practice their own religion. Is
it some great problem that God is not a liar? This is precisely what the
Lord said would happen in the last days. First the Jewish people
regather as a secular nation, mostly in unbelief, then there will be a
great spiritual awakening in the sovereign timing of God. Do you have

the patience to allow God to have His way? It is no problem to me that the prophecy of God is accurate. It would be disturbing if it were any other way.

WHERE DO YOU STAND?

Many readers of this book already agree with our conclusions. This chapter will supply you with a few Bible answers to the false teachers who deny Israel her rightful place.

But is it enough just to believe right? Is it not true, as James writes, that faith without works is dead? He counsels us to "be ye doers of the word and not hearers only" (James 1:22). When you stand before the Lord one day you want to hear Him say, "Well done (not well thought out) thou good and faithful servant. . . ." Prophecy is for more than intellectual stimulation. It is a call to action, to implementation of the plan of Almighty God. God wants participants, not mere spectators in the end-time drama of the ages.

It is not enough to just believe that Israel is a fulfillment of prophecy. You are called to do something about it, to be supportive of God's called and chosen nation. No matter what Israel herself thinks of His plan at this time. No matter what mistakes Israel makes. You are called to cooperate with that plan of God for the present season.

Some make a great deal out of the fact that the words Hebrew, Jew, and Israelite have specific, technical meanings. That is true, but by New Testament times the terms were used interchangeably as proven by the fact that the apostle Paul on various occasions said, "I am a Jew . . . I am a Hebrew . . . I am an Israelite . . . I am of the tribe of Benjamin."

Jesus clearly was a Jew, being of the lineage of David of the tribe of Judah. Some make the wild claim that Jesus was an Aryan, and not Jewish at all.

Friend, Jesus was a Jew. The Jew is coming back. The Book of Revelation calls Him the Lion of Judah! Are you ready to face Him and give account of how you have treated His Word and His brethren?

Anglo Israelism is based on a distorted interpretation of a false reporting of historical and non-historical events. It is not based on, nor is it consistent with, the Word of God.

If you are a Jew-hater or if you have embraced any of the doctrines that deny Israel's place in God's plan, then you have every right to be nervous right now.

God has determined: Israel will survive. We also determine, with the Almighty One, Israel will survive.

Notes

[1]Willaim Varner, *Jacob's Dozen, A Prophetic Look at the Tribes of Israel* (Bellmawr, NJ: Friends of Israel Gospel Ministry, 1987), p. 99.

[2]Varner, *Jacob's Dozen,* p. 94.

[3]Varner, *Jacob's Dozen,* p. 96-97.

[4]Donald Grey Barnhouse, *Revelation, An Expository Commentary* (Grand Rapids, MI: Zondervan Publishing, 1971), p. 146-147.

8

THE KHAZARS

Are The Jews Really Jews?

Awake, sleepers, from your sleep, and ye who are sunk in slumber rouse yourselves and examine your actions. Repent and remember your Creator, ye who forget the truth because of transient vanities, who go astray all year after idle and useless things which cannot deliver. Look to your souls, amend your ways and deeds, and let every one of you forsake his impure thoughts. — Maimonides, Yad: Teshuba 1180,2.2

Awake, awake, Deborah: awake, awake, utter a song: arise, Barak, and lead thy captivity captive, thou son of Abinoam (Judg. 5:12).

Buy the truth, and sell it not; also wisdom, and instruction, and understanding (Prov. 23:23).

Awake thou that sleepest, and arise from the dead, and Christ shall give thee light (Eph. 5:14).

Despisers of Zion rummage through musty tomes of history for any tattered scrap of information that can be used against the Jews of today. One bizarre theory that is popular in anti-Semitic circles is that the Jews have no relationship to Abraham. They are descendants of the Khazars, of an ancient Russian kingdom.

Theodore Winston Pike claims, "The greatest source of pride for Jews is their belief that they are the blood descendants of Abraham. Out of that conviction has come not only identity for Jews, but deep comfort through the ages. Modern scholarship, however, has begun to question whether all who consider themselves Jews are in fact Jews at all. There is mounting evidence that the great majority of Jews today (the Ashkenazim or Eastern European Jews) are not the offspring of Abraham but descendants of the ancient Central European nation of Khazaria, converted to Judaism in A.D. 740."

Pike adds, "There are many aspects of the darker side of Judaism which Jews do not mind knowing as long as Gentiles are not in on the secret. The ghost of Khazaria is not one of them. The Khazar origin of most Jews today is one secret in a religion of secrets which even they cannot entertain."[1]

In spite of what Pike claims about the Jews trying to keep it a secret, most of his alleged documentation comes from Jewish sources! The Khazar idea is one which is fascinating to many Jewish scholars.

Stan Rittenhouse, author of *For Fear of the Jews,* dwells on the Khazar theme, claiming that "Yiddish is the mother-tongue of the Khazars or self-styled 'Jews,' originally from Eastern Europe."[2]

Perhaps we are not surprised when Gentile anti-Zionists deviously twist the obscurities of history to build a house of deceit in our minds. But Arthur Koestler is a Jew. He supports the most radical view of the Khazar theory in his book *The Thirteenth Tribe.*[3]

Why would a Jew undertake such a damaging endeavor? It has been observed that there is no one any more anti-Semitic than an anti-Semitic Jew, as noted by Sander Gilman in *Jewish Self-Hatred.*[4]

Koestler has the distinction of being a Jew, widely quoted by a motley assortment of anti-Semites. On the other hand, Koestler is said to be a self-loathing Jew who would like to deny his ancestral identity. He has been described by a fellow Jew as, "nothing more than a typical, old-fashioned self-hating assimilationist, in love with Gentile culture, and hoping to become absorbed in a blue-eyed and fair-haired paradise, where 'the Jews' will only be a bad memory of a people who insisted on bringing trouble on themselves by being different for no good reason."[5]

What shall we make of this? Beyond all the rhetoric, what are the facts?

THE EMPIRE

Between the seventh and tenth centuries A.D. a powerful empire existed in the regions of the Crimea, the Volga, and the Caucasus, areas that lie between the Black Sea and Caspian Sea (also known as the Sea of the Khazars). At one time Khazaria spanned west to the Danube River and occupied Kiev around A.D. 862.

The origin of the Khazar people is obscure. *Encyclopedia Judaica* says, "The Khazars, a Turkic stock, originally nomadic . . . may have belonged to the empire of the Huns (fifth century C.E.) as the Akitzirs, mentioned by Priscus. . . . The Khazars probably belonged to the West Turkish Empire (from 552 C.E.) . . . also called Turks and Huns."[6]

In the latter part of the eighth century King Bulan, ruler of the Khazars, became a Jew. Bulan arranged for a debate to take place between Muslim, Christian, and Jewish scholars. After listening to the three sides he decided to accept the religion of the Jews. Later Khazaria's King Obadiah "built synagogues and schools and introduced the Khazars to Torah, Mishnah, Talmud, and liturgy."[7]

Historical references to the Khazars are scant and not all agree. We know rulers, nobles, and some of the lower classes converted to Judaism, but whether any large numbers were involved is open to question. After the defeat of Khazaria at the hands of the Russians, most reverted to other religions, some converted to Christianity, and some just abandoned religion altogether. Why be Jewish in a land where the Russians were constantly persecuting the Jews?

Raphael Posner says, "However, the extent of the Khazars' observance of Jewish law is somewhat questionable. Some sources indicate that their adherence to Judaism was imperfect since they retained a number of pagan customs dating back to their Turkic origins."[8]

One must note that there were millions of Jews in the world when the King of Khazaria converted to Judaism. Did they suddenly disappear off the face of the earth? Are none of their descendants alive in the world today?

In the areas conquered by the Khazars, "Jews had been living there from at least as early as the sixth century, and Eldad Hadam provides a detailed account of them."[9] A Jewish population co-existed with the Khazars. Some of the Khazar leadership and nobility, including the king, converted to Judaism. Some of the population converted to Judaism. No doubt intermarriage took place.

In addition, considerable numbers of Jews living in the Diaspora, wishing to escape persecution, moved to Khazaria when the leadership of the Khazars converted to the Jewish religion.

The Jews have never been a race. They are a people. Abraham is the patriarch. His son Isaac and grandson Jacob were the chosen seed. Jacob's 12 sons headed the 12 tribes of Israel. The tribes freely intermarried, and tribal identity was carried on through the male descendants. Gentiles who converted to Judaism became a part of the lineage, their children traceable to Abraham. The Jews today could be traced to Abraham, Isaac, and Jacob/Israel, if records existed. The record does exist in the mind of God. When He determines to select 12,000 of each tribe of Israel to do His service He will have no problem finding them. They are not lost. (See Revelation 7.)

A LETTER FROM PROFESSOR CHAIM RABIN

I became seriously interested in the Khazar theory in the summer of 1978. I wrote a letter to Benjamin Jaffe in Jerusalem, expressing my deep concern for the growing popularity of the anti-Semitic Khazar fantasy. I asked him if he knew of any Israeli scholar who could give me some basic facts. Benjamin, an historian and author of great acclaim, turned my letter over to Professor Chaim Rabin who wrote the following letter to Jaffe:

Dear Mr. Jaffe,

Thank you for showing me David Lewis' letter. I have read it with some dismay. We Jews have suffered enough from racialism, it has cost us six million of our people — and now the racialist argument raises its ugly head in another form!

The answer to the racialist contention is, of course, twofold. Its first component is the question whether the Jews are a pure race, every Jew being a descendant of Abraham, Isaac, and Jacob. Now, it is clear that there are no pure races in the world. The Jews are not only a people, but also a religion, and over the centuries the Jewish religion has always attracted a thin trickle of converts.

At one time only there seem to have been a large number of converts: those were the Greek and Roman "Judaizers" of the period before and after the beginning of Christianity. However, research has shown that such people were not admitted into the Jewish community, and therefore also did not intermarry with Jews, unless they were willing to keep all Jewish laws, which most of them found too difficult. Thus only very few actually joined, and it appears that the majority were absorbed into the Christian community. There were also at all times Jews who married non-Jewish women after they had joined the Jewish community. The most outstanding example is Ruth, the ancestress of King David (and thus also of Jesus).

Clearly, the small additions thus made cannot possibly be interpreted as implying that racially the Jews of today are not the Jews of biblical times. I am not a statistician, but it should be possible to work out what percentage of non-Jewish ancestors the average Jew of today would have if the foreign influx were to be estimated even as high as one percent in each generation (I think 0.001 percent would be closer). Besides, any Christian should agree that a person who has properly converted to Judaism is a Jew to all purposes, including the purpose of racial statistics, and indeed this very principle is expressed by the custom of giving converts the ritual patronymic "son of Abraham."

The second component is the Khazars. It is complete nonsense to argue that the present-day Jews derive from the Khazars. For one, only the Russian Jews, if any, could possibly derive from the Khazars, not the Polish, Lithuanian, Bohemian, or Hungarian Jews, because we know nothing of a migration of Jews out of Russia into the west after the Khazar episode about 800. All Jewish movements after that time, until the nineteenth century, were into Russia, not out of it.

But even in the nineteenth century, the vast majority of Jews lived outside Russia, and therefore could not derive from the Khazars, and the Jews which settled in Palestine were mostly other than Russian.

But if there is any Khazar blood in Russian Jewry, it is so little as to be practically negligible. Only the king and some of the nobles became Jews. Most of the people did not become Jews, and were no doubt absorbed by other Turkish tribes after the dynasty fell, in the tenth century. In fact, after the eleventh century the Khazars are mentioned in Arabic sources as Muslims.

A Jewish historian in Spain, Ibn Da'ud, says that in the early twelfth century there were some Jewish scholars of Khazar origin in Toledo. If this is true, then it shows where the remnants of the Jewish Khazar aristocracy went after the Russians had destroyed their state. The Russians would hardly have permitted the descendants of their arch-enemies to go on living in their country and to set up communities. The language of the Khazars is described as being related to Bulgarian, which means the Turkish dialect the Bulgars spoke before they adopted a Slav language in their new Balkan home.

There are no Jews whatsoever in Russia who speak or spoke a Turkish dialect. The only group close to Jews who speak a form of Turkish are the Karaites of Russia and Poland, but the Karaites separated from the main body of Jews in the eighth century, and did not intermarry with them — and in any event the Karaites speak not Khazar Turkish but Crimea Turkish, and have nothing to do with the Khazars.

All other Jews of Russia spoke Yiddish, which is a form of German originally spoken in the area of the Middle Rhine and the Main, around Frankfurt, and their customs and culture are those of medieval German Jews. If there had been a considerable population of Jews of Khazar origin, it is quite unimaginable that they would have accepted the language and habits of Jewish immigrants from Central Europe, since the Khazars were converted by Jews from the Arab countries, and therefore had links with Sephardi Jewry (which explains why they went to Spain), and it is a well-known fact that Sephardi Jews resisted, even in small groups, absorption by the German-Ashkenazi Jewish communities with whom they happened to come in contact.

There is thus not a shred of evidence that there is a Khazar factor of any meaningful size in present-day Jewry. Arthur Koestler is a great writer, but his attitude to Jewish matters has always been irrational: first he became an enthusiastic advocate of violence of Jews against their opponents in Palestine (*Thieves in the*

Night), later he became a Communist, and after being disappointed with Communism, tried his hand at Asian mysticism, and then "made his account" with his own Jewish origins by declaring himself a Khazar Turk! We have no objection to Mr. Koestler considering himself whatever he wishes — but it seems a bit unjust that because his fancy is to be a relative of Attila and Gengis-Khan, all Jews must become Turks."

Yours sincerely,
Professor Chaim Rabin
1 September, 1978[10]

KHAZARIA DEFEATED AND SCATTERED

The fortunes of Khazaria began to wane. Defeat after defeat came from the Russians and other invaders. They fled in large numbers fearing the wrath of the fierce Russians. The work of S. M. Dubnow was translated from the Russian into English by I. Friedlaender. Dubnow enlightens us with this:

Concerning the Russians, with whom the King was at war, and who were ready to "destroy the whole land of the Ishmaelites as far as Bagdad," were speedily realized. A few years later the Slavonian tribes, who had in the meantime been united under the leadership of Russian princes, not only threw off the yoke of the Khazars, whose vassals they were, but also succeeded in invading and finally destroying their center at the mouth of the Volga. Price Svyatoslav of Kiev devastated the Khazar territories on the Ityl, and, penetrating to the heart of the country, dislodged the Khazars from the Caspian region (966-969). The Khazars withdrew to their possessions on the Black Sea, and established themselves in particular on the Crimean Peninsula, which for a long time retained the name Khazaria.

The greatly reduced Khazar kingdom in Taurus, the survival of a mighty empire, was able to hold its own for nearly half a century, until in the eleventh century it fell prey to the Russians and Byzantines (1016). The relatives of the last Khagan fled, according to tradition, to their co-religionists in Spain.

The Khazar nation was scattered, and was subsequently lost among other nations. The remnants of the Khazars in Crimea who professed Judaism were in all likelihood merged with the native Jews, consisting partly of the Rabbinates and partly of Karaites."[11]

DAVID DOLAN, CHRISTIAN JOURNALIST

David Dolan is a Jerusalem based journalist reporting for CBS. An Evangelical, Dolan has written a book worthy of being read by every Christian. If you want to know the truth about the Middle East, this is the book for you. It is well-documented, yet written in a style that is easy for anyone to understand. Here you will find answers to the hard questions the critics ask about Israel.

One thing that makes the book enjoyable as well as informative is that Dolan writes his personal testimony, along with his fascinating revelations. He delves into some hard questions like the battle for Deir Yassin, the bombing of the King David Hotel, the demographics of how many Arabs and Jews actually lived in Palestine before Israel became a nation, and what would be fair for all concerned today?

Dolan's book *Holy War for the Promised Land* is written for lay persons and scholars alike. It tackles some of the tough questions about Israel and the Middle East, including the Khazar question. He meets head-on with the anti-Semitic claim that the Jews are not descendants of Abraham, but are instead the descendants of the Russian Khazar tribes. Dolan points out that the end result of this kind of thinking is that since the Jews are not really Jews, they have no claim to the land of Israel.

Some people fall for this nonsense, and even those who refuse to believe it have little information to refute the Khazar theory. Here are a few words David Dolan shares in a footnote to Chapter 10.

It has become popular among Mideast Arabs in recent years, along with neo-Nazis and others, to maintain that East European and Russian Jews are not descendants of ancient Jews at all. Therefore, they have no right to live in the Holy Land. This case was made in a Saudi Arabian-sponsored ad printed in October 1988 in major American newspapers.

The ad stated, "In A.D. 740 a large kingdom of Europeans, located in modern day Russia, converted to Judaism. This group had no biological connection with any of the original Jews." Therefore most of the Jews in

Israel are not biological Jews, but descendants of European converts, also known as "Ashkenazi" or "White Jews" who can "make no biblical claim to the Arab lands in Palestine, including Jerusalem."

This argument is based on the conversion to Judaism in the eighth century of leaders of the Khazar's kingdom located in south central Asia. Subsequently many Khazars converted to Judaism and were dispersed when the Russians destroyed the kingdom in the eleventh century.

But it is also known that at least some Jews from the West moved to Khazaria to escape persecution. More importantly, it is well documented that many West European Jews moved east to Poland, Lithuania, etc., during the Middle Ages, after they were forced out of France, Germany, Austria, etc. (This is why Yiddish, a German-Hebrew mixture was the main language of such East European Jews).

Certainly Khazar's Jewish converts, as converts elsewhere, mixed over the years with known physical descendants of Abraham, but it is historically absurd to maintain that "European White Jews" have no ancient Jewish ancestry. Such widely believed myths, propounded by a leading "moderate" Arab state, illustrate the deeply held Arab prejudice against Israel.[12]

A good summation of the matter was sent to me in a letter by Dr. Mike Nangle of Edmonton, Alberta, Canada. He wrote, "Another false claim is that most, about 80 percent, of modern or East European (Ashkenaz) descent are actually not true *Jews,* but are allegedly Khazars (Kuzarim in Hebrew)."

To this claim Dr. Nangle replies, "Yes, from the 700s to about 1250, some of the Turkic tribes in Russia did "convert" to a form of Judaism. The historic evidence, however, is that the *rulers* became *true* converts and married into the community of Israel. Most of the Khazars observed some outward forms such as circumcision and keeping of festivals. Essentially though, they were warlike nomads and moved on into history, becoming assimilated into other cultures — in practical terms they became *extinct*. They were lost to the historical record.[13]

THE SUPREME CONSIDERATION

The final question is not, who were, nor where are the Khazars, but, can God keep His word to Abraham? And, has God kept His word to Abraham? Genesis 12 records the unilateral, unconditional covenant which God initiated with Abraham. In Genesis 26:4 the covenant is restated: "And I will make thy seed to multiply as the stars ... of heaven, and will give unto thy seed all these countries; and in thy seed shall all the nations of the earth be blessed."

Note the declaration of Deuteronomy 1:10: "The Lord your God hath multiplied you, and, behold, ye are this day as the stars of heaven for multitude."

The non-literal interpreters of the Bible scoff at us for being "simple minded" enough to believe this verse in a plain sense. After all there are billions of stars in the universe. But in Abraham's and Moses' sky there were, as today, only around 4,000 visible stars. With no telescopes with which to probe further, these words were, in their eyes fulfilled.

We all know of Israel's disobedience and subsequent punishment, being scattered among the nations. Now, under great duress, having passed through the fires of the Holocaust, the final regathering to the land has begun. We rejoice with Israel to see her promises being fulfilled. We look forward to the golden day when it will be complete.

Christian, I would not want to have to stand before the judgment seat of Christ and have to explain any British Israel, or Khazar denials of the true Israel's identity, for these ideas are idle words.

Israel will survive, Christian, but will your works survive in the day of your evaluation? (See 1 Corinthians 3.)

Notes

[1]Theodore Winston Pike, *Israel Our Duty — Our Dilemma* (Oregon City, OR: Big Sky Press, First ed., 1984), p. 297, 303.

[2]Stan Rittenhouse, *For Fear of the Jews* (Vienna, VA: The Exhorters, 1983), p. 67.

[3]Arthur Koestler, *The Thirteenth Tribe* (New York, NY: Popular Library, 1976).

[4]Sander L. Gilman, *Jewish Self-Hatred* (Baltimore, MD: The Johns Hopkins University Press, 1986), p. 333-336.

[5]*Midstream*, March 1977, p. 40.

[6]*Encyclopedia Judaica* (Jerusalem, Israel: Keter Publishing House, 1972), Vol. 10, p.944.

[7]Raphael Posner, editor, *My Jewish World* (Jerusalem, Israel: Keter Publishing House, 1975), Vol. 4, p.18.

[8]Posner, *My Jewish World.*

[9]Arkady Lvov, "Shades of Forgotten Ancestors," *Midstream,* February, 1983, p. 50.

[10]A private correspondence. The late Benjamin Jaffe was the head of the Department of External Affairs for the World Zionist Organization in Jerusalem. He authored a major book on the history of the modern state of Israel.

[11]S.M. Dubnow, *History of the Jews in Russia and Poland From the Earliest Times Until the Present Day,* (Philadelphia, PA: The Jewish Publication Society of America, 1916), Vol. 1, p. 28.

[12]David Dolan, *Holy War for the Promised Land* (Nashville, TN: Thomas Nelson Publishers, 1991), p.240-241.

[13]Mike Nangle, *A Very Relevant Issue* (Edmonton, Alberta: private correspondence, undated).

9

ISRAEL — DUTIES AND DILEMMAS

Response to Evangelical Anti-Semitism

> *Since the Deicide, the Jews have been delivered into the hands of the demons . . . they are only fit to be butchered . . . their behavior is no better than that of swine and oxen in their gross lewdness. . . . The synagogue is a brothel, a cave of brigands, a den of ferocious animals.*
> — Saint John Chrysostom
>
> *Anti-Semitism is a noxious weed that should be cut out.* — U.S. President William Howard Taft
>
> *Their heart cried unto the Lord, O wall of the daughter of Zion, let tears run down like a river day and night: give thyself no rest; let not the apple of thine eye cease* (Lam. 2:18).

We do not normally respond to every piece of anti-Semitic literature that arrives at our research center. Usually such items are just added to our already bulging files. When a book or paper proclaiming itself as representative of the Evangelical churches projects an anti-Semitic stance we pay closer attention. That item goes in a special file, for special examination. Since we cannot refute everything that comes our way, we have selected one book for special attention and comment.

When the book *Israel: Our Duty — Our Dilemma* by Theodore Winston Pike came to us in the mail in 1984 we paid it special attention, noting that it was a strange example of Evangelical anti-Semitism. Whereas it is not unusual for amillennialists, post-millennialist, and allegorical interpreters in general to be theologically anti-Semitic, this book is different. Pike, the author, claims to be a premillennial, biblical literalist. While Pike claims to have a new approach to the subject of Israel and prophecy, actually he offers nothing but a rehash of old arguments against the Jews, and Israel.

WE MUST RESPOND

Pike's book demands a response. A concerted effort is being made to use this book to subvert normal Evangelical support for Israel and empathy for the Jewish people. Pike boasted that over 18,000 copies of this book have been sent out, free of charge, to pastors and Christian leaders. Obviously there is big money behind this effort. The book sells for $9.95. Even calculating a wholesale cost of the books, adding the cost of packaging, handling, and postage, we are looking at an expensive and ambitious project. We want to know, who

is putting up the money? What is the motivation? What is the purpose of this book and what ends are to be gained by the sponsors?

We are responding because the author sent out a letter asking for response. He challenges any and all to refute what he has to say.

MISUSE OF TALMUDIC REFERENCES

The book *Israel: Our Duty — Our Dilemma* critically quotes the Jewish *Talmud* to support his vi-

This is the book making waves in the Evangelical world.

cious accusations against the Jews. The *Talmud* is a large set of books consisting of biblical commentary, explanation of Jewish religious life, philosophy, etc.

It is no secret that the *Talmud* attempts to refute the claims of Christianity, just like Christian commentaries refute each other on numerous points of difference.

Pike quotes various contemporary rabbinical teachers, linking this with the *Talmud* to allege that Jews in general approve of incest, pederasty, bestiality, and a host of other crimes and sins. Pike completely ignores the high moral tone of the writings of Jews in general, and the *Talmud* specifically.

Oh, yes, there are Jews today in the pornography industry and in the perverted Hollywood film industry — Jews along with a host of Gentiles. Yes, there are Jews involved in secular-humanistic activities, along with a host of Gentiles. And there are rabbis who soundly condemn their own scoundrels. Why single out the Jews as a target and indict Jews in general for what only some Jews are doing? Why not use the same standard on the Gentiles?

For us there is no dilemma. We know our duty, and it is to comfort Zion and not add to her sorrows, and in a forthcoming issue of the *Jerusalem Courier* we will comment at length on Theodore Pike's book.

THE RABBI'S DISTRESS

The rabbi said to me, "David, I am spending most of my time telling my Jewish colleagues that Evangelical Christians are our best friends and allies. Now this comes along and creates a climate of doubt, making my friends think I have fantasized

Like Christian clergy, Jewish rabbis represent a wide range of views. Why does Pike never show pictures like this? When 14,000 Christians marched in Washington, DC, to protest abortion there were many Jews and rabbis among them.

everything I have been telling them."

Rabbi Yechiel Eckstein, author of *What Christians Should Know about Jews and Judaism,*[1] was referring to the book *Israel: Our Duty — Our Dilemma* by Theodore Winston Pike.

NOT AN ANTI-SEMITE, PIKE CLAIMS

In a letter to his followers Pike pointed out that it is amazing how the logic and documentation of *Israel: Our Duty — Our Dilemma* silences criticism. Pike added, "I am still waiting for someone to even call me an anti-Semite." He must not be listening to the people I am hearing. I have heard him called an anti-Semite by both Christians and Jews. Only Mr. Pike himself can answer to the question of whether or not he is an anti-Semite. Even if you are not familiar with his book, reading this chapter will acquaint you with some of the major questions Christians who love Israel are facing today.

We are responding to Mr. Pike for three reasons: First, he puts forward arguments against the Jews that few people are equipped to evaluate, much less refute. How many of your friends have all 18 volumes of the Soncino *Talmud*, so they can check the accuracy of Pike's attacks?

Secondly, I am concerned that our silence would be perceived as an admission that Theodore Winston Pike and others of his ilk are right and cannot be answered.

Third, and this is the most serious reason, we clearly understand that Israel has not been a high priority item on the Church's agenda and there is little awareness of the real issues involved. Even where a vague sympathy for Israel exists in the churches there has been little biblical education on the subject.

ABOUT RABBINICAL JUDAISM

Pike states a premise in his introduction to the book that seems to set the stage for his whole argument. He says, "We know astonishingly little about Rabbinic Judaism. . . . Christians know next to nothing concerning Jewish history during the 1,800 years following the destruction of Jerusalem in A.D. 70." I certainly have no argument with the truth of that statement. It could also be pointed out that the average Christian knows abysmally little about the history of the Church. So what does that prove?

Pike continues, "Yet that period is of equal significance with the Old Testament toward an understanding of what rabbinic Judaism is all about."[2]

Our Christian task is not primarily to discover Rabbinic Judaism, but to discover what the Bible teaches about the destiny of Israel and how we should be involved. Pike makes the outrageous claim that Jews don't want Gentiles to read the *Talmud.* Quite the opposite is true. I own a complete set of the Soncino translation of the *Talmud.* It was given to me by a Jewish family in Chicago. Rabbis hold classes to teach non-Jews the *Talmud.* Not many respond, but some have an interest. The new *Steinsaltz Edition* of the *Talmud* might, with its modern English, attract more Gentile readers, and it is widely advertised for sale.

EXAMINING PIKE'S EVIDENCE: BESTIALITY

The *Talmud* often presents many possible answers to a question. You will see how Pike uses only a partial passage to allegedly prove his point, and even in this case the passage he cites is not saying what he claims. Pike writes:

> Although the *Talmud* condemns bestiality in general terms, as might be expected, there are exceptions. As we have seen, the Pharisees rationalized that when the Bible condemns those who lie "carnally" with a beast, it is referring to those who do so in a "normal" or "carnal" manner, not in a perverted manner, which is exempt. A woman's intercourse with a dog, the Pharisees held was sufficiently normal to make it perverted, and thus subject to punishment, while the sex act of a man upon an animal was sufficiently perverted to make it free from punishment.
>
> Pike "quotes" the *Talmud*: "The reference is to bestiality. If a woman allows herself to be made the subject thereof, whether naturally or not, she is guilty. But if a man commits bestiality, he is liable only for a connection in a natural manner, but not otherwise." (Footnote to Sanhedrin. 55a.) Cited by Pike.[3]

Actually the passage both in Sanhedrin 55 and in the complete footnote demands punishment for this sin. The sin is never condoned. Also in the footnote: "The meaning according to the interpretation of Tosafoth is clear. Yet R. Papa's objection is not made in order to prove that unnatural incest is not liable, which in fact it is, but that if a distinction is to be drawn, unnatural bestiality is far more likely to be liable than unnatural incest. On Rashi's interpretation, R.

Papa's objection is explained thus: Since a woman is naturally the passive object of sexual intercourse, it follows that she should be punished for bestiality only when the connection is carried out in a natural way. But as man is the natural offender in an unnatural crime he should be punished for unnatural connection."[4]

Pike might accuse me of also taking a passage out of context, since this is a relatively brief quotation. But, no, I have attempted to restore the context, although to be sure of accuracy one should read the many, many pages in *Sanhedrin* dealing with these sins. You will find that the sins are frankly discussed. There are various points of view as to the nature of the sins, including pederasty, adultery, incest, homosexuality, etc., and there is discussion as to appropriate punishment. But *never are these sins condoned nor excused.*

THE BASIS FOR TRUTH AND UNDERSTANDING

As an evangelical believer I must have a clear understanding for the reason why I believe what I believe. The foundation of all Christian truth is the Bible, the Word of God, not an understanding of history or anyone's philosophy, nor the *Talmud*. Pike uses more interpretations of history and the *Talmud* than interpretation of Scripture in his work.

Any idea that is to be expressed as Christian doctrine must be capable of being proven *from the Scripture alone.* If this cannot be done we cannot accept it. Only after establishing a biblical case can I legitimately examine history and philosophy, in the light of what the Scripture has revealed. The Bible is the model by which we view reality. Can Pike confirm his theories by the Word of God? I tell you no, he cannot. His argument rises or falls on his presentation of such data as the *Talmud*, what some Jews are doing today in the realm of politics, entertainment, the media, etc. I contend that his understanding of this data is flawed, though not totally inaccurate, as we will point out. His final conclusions are therefore unacceptable, regardless of how much seemingly supportive evidence from non-biblical sources he marshals.

OUR REAL DUTY

Our task is not to figure out what rabbinical Judaism is all about. It is to cooperate with and implement the plan and purpose of God, knowing that "faith without works is dead." No, Mr. Pike, there is no dilemma; we have no difficulty identifying our task in relation to Israel. The Word of God alone is our mandate. For many years we have shared scriptural premises with our readers in our publications, books, and pamphlets. Readers of these materials are among the strongest friends of Israel and the Jewish people.

TORAH OR TALMUD?

Theodore Pike claims that Orthodox Jews revere the *Talmud* above the Torah (the Old Testament, especially the five books of Moses). I categorically deny that this is true. I have asked many rabbis exactly where their priority rests in the matter of authority. Without exception I have been told that the Torah is the supreme authority. Certainly there is high regard and reverence for the *Talmud*, but without the Torah there would be no *Talmud*, for the *Talmud* is a commentary on the Torah.

Rabbi Yechiel Eckstein states, "The Torah (the Hebrew Bible, the Old Testament) is not only God's revealed word to man, but it has also been passed on to us from generation to generation without error. This doctrine of inerrancy underlies the traditional Jewish hermeneutic." *Hermeneutic* means method of interpretation.

Eckstein continues, "Every word in the Torah as we have it today is divine, without error, and consequently, imparted to man for an express purpose." This orthodox rabbi explains, "Everything there is to know about life can be derived from the Torah." Eckstein explains the importance of the *Talmud* to the Jewish people but makes it clear that Torah is supreme in authority.[5]

DELVING DEEPLY

Pike suggests that our need is to delve deeply into the *Talmud* to find out the hidden truth about the Jews he views as being so evil.

I wonder if Pike would accept that to understand Christianity one should delve deeply into the ante-Nicene church fathers, or the edicts of the Council of Trent, or the writings of Christian teachers both good and heretical?

Most Evangelicals would contend that to understand Christianity one should study the Old and New Testaments. All other auxiliary studies of history and philosophy would be of possible, but not primary, value for the determination of Christian truth.

WHAT IS THE TALMUD?

Put into its simplest terms the *Talmud* consists, largely, of extensive rabbinical commentaries on the Hebrew Scriptures, which Christians call the Old Testament.

Pike seems to make a damaging case against the Jews by quoting very selectively from the *Talmud.* He quotes anything that seems to make the Jews look bad or immoral. He fails to mention that several arguments are stated in the *Talmud* on certain subjects, presenting various points of view, *some of which are rejected.* Some subjects have various arguments presented without any conclusion being drawn. Never does he point out the loftier or more noble aspect of the *Talmud.*

OUT OF CONTEXT

He pulls some statements entirely out of context and thus a distorted meaning is projected. Several pages of the *Talmud* (Soncino edition, English translation) are reproduced in the Appendix of the book. On page 310 of the first edition of Pike's book (there are changes in the arrangement of the later editions) a portion of Sanhedrin 55a is reproduced. Pike comments in his own words at the bottom of the page: "Sanhedrin 55a — Unnatural incest and bestiality permitted."

Careful examination of the page photographically reproduced reflects nothing of this nature, but rather that there are varying degrees of punishment to be meted out for variations of these sins, which are clearly labeled as sins.

When it says in the *Talmud* that when a man has sex with a girl under the age of three, "it is nothing," the larger context of the passage shows condemnation to the perpetrator of this abuse. "It is nothing," protects the rights and innocence of the child, holding her guiltless.

JEWISH VIEW OF THE TALMUD

It is very helpful to examine a modern Jewish evaluation of the *Talmud.* Nathan Ausubel, a Jewish scholar, has written many books on Jewish subjects. He has an international reputation as an authority on Jewish culture and history. He is the author of *The Book of Jewish Knowledge,* distributed by Crown Publishers. In his article on the *Talmud* he says:

> The *Talmud* is the literary reservoir of Rabbinic
> Judaism that was created during the Hellenistic Age in
> Jewish history: It is not just one book — as is commonly
> taken for granted — but a collection of many books.[6]

This is a very important observation on the nature of the *Talmud* and we will expand your understanding of a little known subject by further quoting Ausubel:

In addition, the *Talmud* contains opinions, discussions and debates, and moralistic aphorisms and biographic exempla of the Rabbinic Sages. These are presented to the devout in order to inspire emulation in wisdom and ethical conduct.

The Protestant biblical scholar of the nineteenth century, Franz Delitzsch, once defined the vast scope of the *Talmud* 'as an immense public assembly in which thousands, even tens of thousands, of voices of at least five centuries are heard to rise and commingle.[7]

As you read the following statement you easily recognize that one could take statements from the *Talmud* out of context and present a meaning exactly opposite of the *Talmud*'s final conclusions.

We do not infer that Christians should study the *Talmud* for spiritual guidance, but on the other hand they should not misrepresent what it says to the detriment of the Jewish people. Their *Talmud* is not to be used as a weapon against them. I am simply showing why we disagree with Pike's claims about what the *Talmud* means. (Note: In the following, Mishnah is part of the *Talmud*.)

Ausubel writes:

> Definitely, the Mishnah is not a legal code in the accepted modern sense. It is not a code in which every sentence, every clause, every word, and even every comma of a stated law has strict validity. The Mishnah was intended to be not a dogmatic but a flexible instrument of extra-biblical jurisprudence. Its laws stemmed from Rabbinical opinions that on many matters were often divergent but not binding. Where there was no disagreement about a particular law among the authorities, it was stated simply and with finality. But where there was dissent among the Sages, the opinion of any one of them was weighed with equal detachment against the opinions of the others. . . .
>
> Taking this into consideration, much of the time it is not only inexact but also quite meaningless to say: 'The *Talmud* states . . .' when in reality it frequently is only the opinion of one particular Rabbi presented there.[8]

The *Talmud* contains the opinions and arguments of many

scholars who disagreed with each other. Quote these statements out of context and you can prove about anything. It seems to me that Mr. Pike has done some quoting out of context. I do not profess to be a specialist in the *Talmud*, but we are uncovering some interesting flaws in Pike's approach to the Jews via the *Talmud*.

Ausubel speaks of "heated religious-legal debates between the rival Rabbinic schools of Hillel and Shammai in Jerusalem toward the end of the first century B.C.E."

If you think one can take any statement out of the *Talmud* and say, "This is what the Jews believe," consider Asubel's observation:

> Like the Greek philosophers, they too forged their ideas and moral values in the smithy of free discussion and sharpened them in the thrust and parry of controversy with their opponents. In the final analysis, the continuing debates over the religious laws and traditions between Hillel and Shammai (and, after they had died, between their disputatious disciples for centuries after) supplied the materials that make up the *Talmud*. There were times, though, when these fraternal wranglings were more fierce than exalted in spirit.
>
> For more than two centuries, the rival Rabbinic schools of Hillel and Shammai contended with each other in public discussions over religious doctrine, legal principles, moral ideas, ritual practices, and social ethics. The *Talmud* records 316 such debates. By all indications, these debates were not always conducted with decorum and amiability; they were, often, acrimonious. In fact, on a number of occasions they even grew lamentably violent.[9]

Theodore Winston Pike delights in finding any *Talmudic* passage he can to show a seeming bias toward a low moral philosophy in Judaism. He fails to note the nature of the *Talmud* as we are describing it to you. One wonders why he fails to note the high moral tone set in most of the writings of the *Talmud*. Why does Pike only look for the dark side?

Ausubel shares the following from the *Talmud*, listing some of the wise, pious, moralistic sayings of various contributors to the *Talmud*:

Yoseh, the son of Yochanan of Jerusalem, said:

"Let your house be opened wide, let the poor be members of your household."

Shemaiah said: "Love work, hate power, and do not try to be on intimate terms with those who rule."

He [Hillel the Elder] used to say: "If I am not for myself, who will be for me? And if I am only for myself, what am I? And if not now — when? And, 'The more flesh, the more worms; the more possession, the more anxiety.' "

Shammai said: "Say little and do much, and receive all men with a cheerful face."

Simeon [ben Gamaliel] said: "Not (Torah) learning but doing is the chief thing. By three things is the world preserved: by truth, by justice and by peace."

Eliezer said "Let the honor of your fellow man be as dear to you as your own."

Joshua said: "The Evil Eye, the Evil Inclination, and hatred of his fellow men can drive a man out of the world."[10]

We are quoting these citations used by author Nathan Ausubel extensively for good reason: It is very important that you understand the nature of the *Talmud* if you are to skillfully analyze the charges against the Jews leveled by such authors as Pike.

The Gemara is the Rabbinic commentary on the Mishnah code. The text of the latter left itself open to further free discussion of its laws, opinions, and traditions by the simple act of juxtaposing many of the majority opinions of the Tannaim with the rejected dissenting absence of unanimity in these decisions posed a challenge — in fact, almost an invitation — to the later Rabbinic teacher, the Amoraim or Expounders, following the codification of the Oral Laws (about 200 C.E.), to explore those disagreements; either to reconcile them or to agree upon more satisfactory decisions. . . .

The *Talmud* abounds in discussion and comment on a wide array of subjects on every conceivable situation, relationship, and value imaginable in the life, religion, and culture of the Jews during the Rabbinic Age. It dwells with earnestness and poetic feeling on the problems of faith, repentance, sin, and piety; on prayer and Torah-study; on medicine and hygiene; on mathematics and astronomy; on marriage and divorce; on ethics — especially on the just and benevolent treatment of the poor, the worker, the needy, the weak, the Gentile stranger, and the slave. It provides the scrupulous person with a chart of guidance for righteous conduct along every step of his way and for the regulation of just relationships in society, whether between parents and children, husband and wife, borrower and lender, loser and finder, judge and accused, a man and his community, Israel and the nations, and, not least upright intercourse between Jews and Gentiles. In no other body of the religious literature of mankind can there be found such an abundance of commentary on the moral imperative for world peace and on the arts of peace, on brotherhood, and the practices of humanity.[11]

THE BIBLE IS THE SUPREME AUTHORITY

Although Mr. Pike charges that the Jews put the *Talmud* above the Bible in authority, Ausubel comments:

> With the single exception of the Bible, which supersedes it in authority, the *Talmud* in all its divisions remains the exhaustive storehouse of knowledge and illumination about Judaism, Jewish life, laws, mores, and culture.[12]

The great Jewish sage Maimonides was deeply upset by some in his day who distorted the meaning of the *Talmud* by concentrating only on certain out-of-context statements.

Ausubel explains:

> The great rabbinical exegete-poet-humanist of Toledo, Abraham ibn Ezra (1093-1167), was thus able to write a detached evaluation of the allegories, parables, and legends in the Gemara and Midrash: "Some of them are fine silks, but others are heavy sackcloth." Being painfully aware of the latter, Maimonides complained bitterly that there were certain scholars who, motivated by a cynical disregard for the truth, were trying to bring the great literature of the *Talmud* into disrepute by one-sidedly concentrating their critical attention not on the

"fine silks," but only on the "heavy sackcloth." By the process of arbitrary selection, he charged, they endeavored to cull from its numerous tractates every item of absurd reasoning, every superstition and hairsplitting exercise in logical futility. This — so they said — was the *Talmud*; therefore it was unworthy of the intelligent man's interest.

However, as is well known to the informed, the childish notions, the trivia, and incongruities which mar the *Talmud* may also be found in the religious and philosophical writings of the Greeks and the Romans, of the church fathers and the medieval Christian schoolmen, [as well as some modern commentators].

The *Talmud* — if the intention is to weigh it in the balance scales of culture — should be considered as a giant literary storehouse that is stocked with a great number of different intellectual elements which, when taken together, constitute the Jewish religious civilization of the Rabbinic age. Generally, it is of a very high order — wise, gentle, humane, ethical, and enlightened. It always sounds the overtones of a love for people and a spiritual exaltation that is rarely met with in other than Jewish religious writings. Notwithstanding this, it also contains a large assortment of pointless naiveté, taboos, superstitions, demonic lore, myths, legalistic interpretations, numerological calculations, and absurd argumentation. The sublime and the ridiculous, the profound and the superficial, are often found in it in an uncomfortable and hard-to-reconcile proximity, unless one keeps in mind that these polarities represent different cultural levels among the Jews of antiquity.[13]

Pike claims that to understand modern Judaism and the state of Israel we must delve into "some of the darker aspects" of the *Talmud* and the Zohar. He calls us to reconsider Israel's role in the light of "history [listed first], Scripture, and rabbinic literature, the aspirations and attitudes of Israel." This is the only way, he claims, that we can comprehend Israel's role in God's plan. I claim on the contrary that we discover modern Israel's role *in the light of the Scriptures alone*. All other data can then be evaluated in the light of sound biblical conclusions.

THE CHRISTIAN TALMUD

There is no Christian *Talmud* and we can be thankful for that. Just imagine some panel of churchmen getting together to compile all the arguments and disputations of Christian scholars of the ages. Include the writing and thinking of Roman Catholics, old line Protestants, Evangelicals, Fundamentalists, and Pentecostals. Mix in the ponderings of "Christian" atheists, agnostics, and "Christian" New Agers. Throw in the resolution recently passed in favor of lesbianism by an "evangelical" women's group.

Compile a Christian *Talmud* including the Pulpit Commentary, the writings of Teilhard de Chardin, the late Bishop James Pike, Dan Betzer, Jeanne Dixon, Billy Graham, Oral Roberts, Kenneth Copeland, J. Dwight Pentecost, C.M. Ward, Dr. John Walvoord, every pope of Rome, Robert Tilton, Paul Crouch, Rush Limbaugh, Augustine, Origen, all the anti-Nicene church fathers, Harry Emerson Fosdick, Martin Luther, Bultman, Tillich, John Calvin, C.I. Schofield, Barth, Hal Lindsey, Gary North, David Hunt, Earl Paulk, J. Narver Gortner, Jimmy Swaggart, Constance Cumby, Pat Robertson, John Wannanmacher, Jim Bakker, Norman Vincent Peal, J. Wallace Hamilton, Finis Dake, John Hagee, and a few thousand more. What a mixture! Good and evil. You can use it to prove anything. It would really prove nothing. Now hold all "Christians" of today (we use the term "Christian" here in the generic sense, as is understood by modern society) accountable for this Christian *Talmud*.

Does Pike want to examine all the sins of the Jews? Then to be fair let's drag all the skeletons out of the Church's closet. Don't think for a moment that the cupboard is bare. Our history is loaded with scandal. Let's re-examine the inquisitions, the bloody crusades, and countless deeds of treachery and war all done in the name of Christ.

One thing the Jews can't match western Christian civilization on — and that is the Holocaust. Of course Pike blames the Jews for the Holocaust, but I cannot really take that seriously. He says the Jews need persecution to survive. I guess they are mimicking churchmen who claim, "The blood of the martyrs is the seed of the Church." We have all heard that saying a few hundred times. How easy it is to measure by a double standard!

Have there been Jews who hated Gentiles and Christians? Indeed there have been. Shall we now examine all the hateful anti-Semitic sayings of our own church fathers, so carefully preserved for us until this day? Read *Legacy of Hatred* by David Rausch, a brilliant

Christian, Evangelical theologian. Dr. Rausch chronicles the sad saga of "Christian" persecution of the Jews from centuries past until the present.[14] Reading the dark side of Church history is a discomforting thing.

To be completely fair, let's muck around in the Church's past history of meanness and murder. Watch a Jewish wife and a daughter being raped repeatedly in the presence of husband and father, in the church, in the name of Christ. That was the Inquisition. Behold the Christian knights of the Crusades sweeping across Europe on their way to the Holy Land, killing entire Jewish communities on their way. You say, "But I am not responsible for those heinous deeds." How interesting. Yet the Jews are responsible for the past. Again, why the double standard?

WHERE IS THE INDICTMENT?

After all the alleged dirt of the past is dug up from questionable sources and paraded in Mr. Pike's book, and after every indictment is in, let me ask for one thing: Show me the writings of the living, modern rabbis who advocate bestiality, pederasty, or any of the host of crimes Pike chronicles, allegedly from the teaching of the *Talmud*.

No need to point out that there are Jewish pornographers, or drug pushers. I will simply demand that the use of the double standard be stopped. There are a multitude of criminals and pornographers who have nominal church membership. Again, such charges do not prove anything one way or the other. Most Mafia bosses are known to be church members. Mafia Dons are notorious for their support of the Church. Should you be judged or held accountable because of that?

IF IT WERE SO ...

What if every charge Pike makes against the Jews was accurate? What if they were the most evil people on the face of the earth? The fact is they are not. My observation is that Jews are like anyone else. In every culture there are good and bad and those representing the entire range in between. Jews are no better or no worse than any other people on earth. But what if all of Pike's worst charges against them were true? Would this shake my faith in the Word of God? No, it would not.

LIKE THE BIBLE SAYS

Ezekiel 36 and 37 foretell a return of the Jews to the land. They will come back in a state of unbelief. Most Jews of Israel today, about 80 percent, are not religious, even in the light of Judaism. This is no problem to the believer in Scripture, *for that is exactly what the Bible says would happen.* There are many godly, believing Jews in Israel and throughout the world today, and in His time, God will put a new heart within them all (see Ezek. 36:26; 37:14).

Zechariah speaks of the coming of Messiah (see Zech. 12:9-10). The Lord declares that He will "remove the iniquity of that land in one day" (see Zech. 3:9; Rom. 11:25-27.) Pike has a problem with the religious condition of the people in Israel. It should be no problem to see that the Bible is right and not wrong in what it prophesied. I also have a problem with the religious condition — not just of the Jews, but of all humanity. For all of the heated debate, Israel will survive. It is the sovereign will of God.

THE "MISSIONARY" LAW

Pike betrays a misunderstanding of the laws of Israel when he claims that Israel has an anti-missionary law that prohibits Christians from giving away a Bible outside of church walls. He claims that anyone who offends in this manner faces up to a five-year jail sentence.

Friends, that simply is not true. Bibles are given away every day of the week, including the Christian New Testament Scriptures. Christian bookstores can be found in the old city of Jerusalem as well as in Jewish districts in the new part of Jerusalem. One of the largest Jewish (not Christian) bookstores in Jerusalem has New Testaments for sale. Bible societies operate openly. Evangelical churches operate with open doors. Books by Billy Graham and other Christians are for sale in Jewish bookstores in Israel.

True, the Jewish people are not responsive to any large degree to this Christian activity. True, the orthodox have tried to outlaw these activities, but without success. While the Israeli government does not issue visas to Christians who want to come into the country as missionaries (with the exception of missionaries to the Arab peoples), the country allows the local people religious freedom. There is a clergy visa status granted to some foreigners who are resident in the land. Certainly there is a higher degree of freedom here than in most parts of the world, including most of the Islamic countries neighboring Israel.

NO BRIBES

There is a law that applies to the religious community that has been misinterpreted as an anti-missionary law. The law is that no one may bribe (with money or material goods such as food or clothing) another person to change from one religion to another. Some unscrupulous missionaries have, unfortunately, been guilty of this type of bribery. A poor Jewish man might be approached with an offer of money, food, clothes, and shoes for his children if the family will convert and be baptized. It makes good copy for the fund-raising newsletter to have a few recent "converts." I think that such dishonest missionaries are in the minority. Yes, in spite of visa prohibition there are hundreds of Christian missionaries working in Israel. Further note that although some orthodox people have brought bribery charges against certain missionaries, my inquiries indicate that no one has been successfully prosecuted under this law against bribery.

UNCONDITIONAL SUPPORT OF ISRAEL?

We are charged with the sin of giving "unconditional moral and military support" to Israel. Christians are questioned whether they should "provide the nation of Israel with the horrific and maiming weapons of war." Frankly I thought it was the secular governments of the world that were in the arms trade, not the Church. Have I missed something? Furthermore, none of my colleagues give any semblance of unconditional support or agreement to every decision of the Israeli government. We give our unconditional consent to the idea that according to the Word of God and its prophecies Israel has a right to exist in the land promised to her.

SHELTERING THE JEWS

Various Christian ministries who disagree with our approach to the Scripture and to Israel have accused us of "sheltering the Jews from the judgment of God."

I am ruefully laughing. How can such a statement be made seriously? Is God so impotent that David Lewis could shelter someone from His divine wrath? If God has determined to punish *anyone,* I am quite sure He will do it without my permission or approval.

On the other hand, I am determined to shelter the Jewish people from the wrath of man. If only more Christians had spoken out against Hitler and his henchmen, the Holocaust could have been prevented or diminished in its effect. I am interested in sheltering my Jewish friends from the wrath of Christian anti-Semites who would again provide the philosophical fuel for the gas furnaces of Auschwitz and Buchenwald. The churches in Germany had preached for centuries that the Jews were replaced by the Church and that any punishment that came upon them was well deserved. No, the Church did not light the fires of Moloch, but they supplied the fuel. Hitler's henchmen quoted German theologians in justifying their horrific deeds.

I don't even agree with everything my own government does, but I am a loyal, patriotic American citizen. I speak for the right of our sovereign nation to exist with an independent government. We may not agree with everything Israel does, but as Bible-believing citizens of the kingdom of God we hold for her right to exist.

THE QUESTION OF RACE

Pike speaks of Israel as a "Unique Race." He then expounds his reasons for believing that the true Israel is the church. Curiously, however, he later speaks of the Sephardic Jews as the true Israel that will fulfill a role in God's future plans on this earth. Mr. Pike betrays a strange racial bias by saying, "As heirs to Christian and occidental values, we in the West have difficulty comprehending any persons or system so ruthless as to sacrifice even a few of its own people in order to archive an objective. We cannot really understand an Oriental bent of mind which values cunning, trickery, and expedience more than honest principle." He adds a strange illustration, "That is why the West was so vulnerable to the feigned moderation of Tito in Yugoslavia."[15]

I truly do not know what to make of such comments. Indeed Slavic people will be deeply offended by this, to say nothing of the Jews. For all the current troubles going on in the former Yugoslavia, I cannot even relate this broad characterization to the many dear Slavic friends I know to be honest, loving, and generous people.

I don't know if Pike is personally acquainted with many Jewish people, either. I have a wide acquaintance among the Jewish communities of America and Israel. While there are bad people in every group in the world, these descriptions do not fit the hundreds of Jewish friends I know so well. I suppose Mr. Pike and I live in two different worlds. I just wish he could get to know my Jewish and, yes, my Arab friends, as well. We could write many chapters and tell many true stories about this matter, but that is for a later time.

JEWS ARE COMMUNISTS

This was Hitler's theme song. He rode into power on his platform of anti-Jewish, anti-communism.

Let one thing be clearly understood. I am totally anti-Communist. Also, I know there are Jewish Communists. This is a source of distress to many Jewish leaders. There is no accounting for the actions of some people, Jew or Gentile.

Si Frumkin's article, "The Jewish General Who Trains the PLO" appeared in *Israel Today Magazine*. Frumkin is a contributing editor to the publication, and former director of the Southern California Council for Soviet Jews. He wrote:

> I have recently come across a document that was captured by the Israeli forces when they took a PLO strong point in Lebanon.
>
> The document is a copy of a graduation certificate for an Arab terrorist who successfully completed a commanders' course at a military training center near Moscow. There is really nothing surprising in the Soviet training of terrorists — it has been going on for quite a while.
>
> What is surprising and sickening is the name of the commandant of this training center for PLO officers who had signed this graduation certificate. It is General David Dragunsky, one of the very few (or maybe the only one) Jewish generals still on active duty in the Soviet army.
>
> General Dragunsky is always proudly trotted out by the Soviets whenever they need a Jew to show to their critics. Dragunsky is a member of the Jewish Anti-Zionist Committee, he signs all the letters in which the Soviet Jews deplore Zionism and pledge loyalty to their Soviet Motherland. In spite, or because of all this, I feel that the Soviets went too far, even for them, in appointing General Dragunsky to command a school that trains men and women how to kill Jews.
>
> The decision to use a superannuated Jewish officer could only have been taken in order to humiliate, to show contempt, to prove that this man, this Jew, this soldier is no more than a dog who has forgotten how to growl, and will keep on licking his owner's hand.
>
> But then, the Soviets have tried to purposely perpetuate the myth of the Jewish coward and the Jewish draft dodger. When after World War II Soviet historians published lists of the Hero of the Soviet Union medal winners, broken down by nationalities, every national-

ity, except the Jewish one, was represented. The list included 10 Komis, 9 Udmurts, 8 Latvians, 8 Lithuanians, 6 Karels — but no Jews! Not until 1963 was it learned from a Polish publication that the Jews had earned 108 Hero of the Soviet Union medals, and that the Jews were fourth in the number of decorations while being the eleventh in size of population.

The proportion of Jews in the Red Army was much greater than their proportion in the population, and it was probably even greater than officially known; Jewish officers were encouraged by their superiors to change their names to more Russian sounding ones in order to get more cooperation from their soldiers. Leaders of guerrilla units and commandos hid their Jewishness, and General Dovator, a famed commander of a crack Cossack regiment that operated on horseback behind German lines, concealed his Jewishness from his troops, the traditionally anti-Semitic Cossacks.

Still, the myth grew and became accepted that the Jews did not fight and that the Jewish soldiers had bought their medals on the black market in Tashkent, far from the enemy lines. In 1945, a much decorated Jewish officer returned to Kiev. He was attacked on a street by several thugs who tried to rip the medals from his uniform. The officer pulled out his gun and shot one of the attackers. This caused a city-wide pogrom during which 16 Jews were killed. The attackers were never tried, but the officer was court-martialed, reduced in rank, and transferred to another unit.

It was probably this officially sanctioned belief in Jewish weakness that caused such consternation among the Soviet officials, and such joy and pride among Soviet Jews, when Israel handily defeated the Soviets' Arab clients again and again. The fact of a Jew-warrior, Jew-hero is unacceptable and humiliating to the Soviet anti-Semites and I feel that they tried to relieve what they consider their own humiliation by the Jews through humiliating the Jewish General Dragunsky.[16]

WHY RUSSIA HATES ISRAEL

To the comments of Mr. Frumkin I will add words written by an

Israeli, Perez Tura, who lives in Rehovot, Israel.

There is quite a lot of antagonism — to put it mildly — between Moscow and Jerusalem, initiated and instigated by the former. What is the real, underlying cause for that phenomenon, especially when looking at the unusual disproportion in territory and in population? It almost seems that Israel — in the eyes of the USSR — is either an obstacle or maybe even — a competitor?

After the War of Independence Israel fought successfully against one or more Arab states in 1956, 1967, and 1973. These successes on the battlefield — without military help from the outside — benefited also the West, indirectly, by thwarting Soviet designs regarding the Middle East. The West is, and was, quite reluctant to admit this; more than once it forced concessions and retreats, not on the aggressor, but on the successful defender. The USSR broke relations with Israel not once, but twice, both in 1956 and 1967.

Without going too much into the details of the facts and occurrences described above, one question at least seems worthwhile answering: Why the new anti-Semitism — now called anti-Zionism — by Moscow?

If we want to understand that antagonism properly and not superficially, we ought to perceive that there exists a conflict between two competing conceptions: the socialist world revolution, and the reign of universal peace, morals and justice as envisaged a long time ago by the prophets of Israel. The Return to Zion — also foretold by the prophets — is just part of that redemption. Only very few of the participants in that drama are fully aware of this, but it seems to be a feasible explanation. The Return to Zion — and all that it implies, is not a purely rational affair — even if it has created a new reality.

Here, a look at the timetable of history might prove enlightening. The forerunners of modern political Zionism, notably Z. H. Kalischer, and the writer Moses Hess (Rome and Jerusalem) published their ideas and writings at about the same time as the *Communist Manifesto* by Karl Marx — namely about the middle of the 19th century. The Balfour Declaration, and the October Revolution — i.e. the beginnings of the Jewish National Home, and of the USSR — were practically simultaneous events! Toleration and competition (even involuntarily) cannot co-exist easily. Against this background — or underground — the struggle between the Jews in the USSR wishing to return to the ancestral homeland, and the Soviet state, acquires a special significance.[17]

RABBI BUTMAN'S PERCEPTION OF THE JEWISH EXPERIENCE IN RUSSIA

Rabbi Shmuel M. Butman is a regular writer for *The Jewish Press.* Here is his point of view relating to the Jewish experience in Russia and why some Jews became communists:

> As a result of the economic upheaval, population dislocation and general chaos of World War I and its aftermath, the Torah-education system of pre-war Russia had collapsed. Young people were drawn towards the political movements, particularly the Bolsheviks, often at first simply as a means of self-defense against the pillaging "White" bands who massacred Jews mercilessly. Soon the Yevsektzia (Jewish section of the Communist party) began systematically wiping out all the vestiges of Judaism. The masses of Russian Jews, who had been strictly Torah-observant, just stood back in despair as they saw their world collapse around them. There seemed nothing anyone could do.[18]

Rabbi Butman goes on to tell the story of a great orthodox (Chassidic) leader, Rabbi Yosef Yitzchok Schneersohn, who refused to give up. He led a campaign to restore Jews to their faith.

> Their successful nationwide accomplishments couldn't go unnoticed for long. In 1927, the Rebbe was arrested. First condemned to death, then to ten years hard labor in the frozen north, then to three years exile in the Urals, he was finally released on 12 Tammuz, (his 47th birthday) as a result of worldwide protests (including Heads of State of the United States, France, and Germany). After several months he was forced to leave

the USSR. But he couldn't forget Soviet Jewry. He traveled to the United States to raise money to help them.[19]

Why do we quote these Jewish sources? In answering Theodore Pike we take note of his extensive use of alleged quotes from Jewish *Talmudic* and other sources. This material should show you that there is another mode of Jewish attitude and thinking quite different from the picture that Mr. Pike paints.

AND SO FORTH ...

We cannot examine every point of Theodore Winston Pike's thesis in *Israel: Our Duty — Our Dilemma,* a book of 346 pages.

Maybe it is a good thing that the Church is being challenged in this fashion. Most Evangelicals have coasted along with a glossed-over view of Israel, harboring a vague sympathy for her, but without any real substantial knowledge of God's Word on the subject other than a nodding acquaintance with a few favorite texts. Now you are going to be forced to examine why you believe what you believe. Pastors who have placed Israel at the bottom priority slot of their church's agenda are going to be forced to take a better look at the issues, and go back to the Word of God for answers.

We have not spoken to Pike's ideas relating to the Khazar theory, that the Jews will rule the world under Antichrist, that the Antichrist will be a Jew, that Judaism/Israel/Jerusalem are Babylon, and we have not answered to his interpretation of Israel's participation in the Lebanon war. (For this last item see my book *Magog 1982: Canceled — Did Israel Prevent the Third World War?*[20]

THE LAST STRAW

In spite of all the bad things he has written against the Jews, Mr. Pike says that he is not an anti-Semite. You will have to judge that for yourself. I find it interesting that Mr. Pike seems to suggest the destruction of the State of Israel.

He says, "In the light of the coming desolation of Israel by Antichrist, *the Bible's advice to Israel today could not help but be that the whole experiment should be disbanded until God is behind it.* (Emphasis Pike's). It is no exaggeration to say that the agony and humiliation of dissolving the present Jewish nation in Palestine would be infinitesimal compared to the consequences for the Jews of perpetuating it until a full two-thirds of world Jewry will die under the judgment of both God and the Antichrist."[21]

There are a lot of people who would like to see such a wish fulfilled. Israel will never willingly abandon the land. How could the removal of the Jews be accomplished? It could only be achieved by violent war against the Jews. Does the book *Israel: Our Duty — Our Dilemma* contribute to such a cause? That is for you to decide.

Notes

[1]Yechiel Eckstein, *What Christians Should Know about Jews and Judaism* (Waco, TX: Word Books, 1984).

[2]Theodore Winston Pike, *Israel: Our Duty — Our Dilemma* (Oregon City, OR: Big Sky Press, first ed., 1984), p. 1.

[3]Pike, *Israel: Our Duty — Our Dilemma*, p. 31.

[4]Rabbi I. Epstein, translator, *The Soncino Talmud* (London, England: Soncino Press; Seder Nezikin vol. 4 Sanhedrin 55a, 1935), p. 372.

[5]Eckstein, *The Soncino Talmud*, p. 29.

[6]Nathan Ausubel, *The Book of Jewish Knowledge* (New York, NY: Crown Publishers, 1964), p. 442.

[7]Ausubel, *The Book of Jewish Knowledge*, p. 442-443.

[8]Ausubel, *The Book of Jewish Knowledge*, p. 445.

[9]Ausubel, *The Book of Jewish Knowledge*, p. 446-447.

[10]Ausubel, *The Book of Jewish Knowledge*, p. 448.

[11]Ausubel, *The Book of Jewish Knowledge*, p. 449-450.

[12]Ausubel, *The Book of Jewish Knowledge*, p. 450.

[13]Ausubel, *The Book of Jewish Knowledge*, p. 452-453.

[14]David A. Rausch, *A Legacy of Hatred* (Chicago, IL: Moody Press, 1984).

[15]Pike, *Israel: Our Duty — Our Dilemma*, p. 5-14, 155, 306.

[16]Si Frumkin, "Israel Today," *Jerusalem Post*, May 30, 1986, p. 5.

[17]*Jewish Press*, July 25, 1986, Brooklyn, NY, p. 5.

[18]Shmuel M. Butman, *Jewish Press* July 18, 1986, Brooklyn, NY, p. 10.

[19]Butman, *Jewish Press*.

[20]David A. Lewis, *Magog 1982 — Canceled* (Green Forest, AR: New Leaf Press, 1982).

[21]Pike, *Israel: Our Duty — Our Dilemma*, p. 287

10

BIBLICAL ZIONISM

Toward a Christian Understanding of Zion

> *Support of Israel means the support of biblical Zionism, which is the conviction that God made an everlasting covenant with Abraham that his seed through Isaac and Jacob would have a biblical mandate to possess the land of Israel forever.* — Pastor John Hagee
>
> *Sing, O daughter of Zion; shout, O Israel; be glad and rejoice with all the heart, O daughter of Jerusalem* (Zeph. 3:14).

Who has a right to the land of Israel? Biblical Zionists believe that the Jewish people have a right to the land. Lay aside the Bible and we have no more to offer than the vain philosophers who so easily switch from one side to the other on this much debated issue that demands the attention of all the world. We have no such option. Our stand for Israel is firm.

Christians who take the Bible literally believe that the aliyah (return) of the Jews is a fulfillment of God's Word for our times. They also believe in a coming kingdom of God on this earth, a Messianic age. The Church knew no other doctrine for the first 200 years of its history. Chiliasm, a belief in the literal thousand year visible kingdom, the Millennium, was the common belief for the first two centuries of the Church. Only when scholars began to allegorize the Bible, ceasing to take it literally did the alternate view of amillennialism gain acceptance.

Messiah will reign from the re-established throne of David in Jerusalem. Resurrected, King David will be co-regent with Christ. Israel will occupy a position of glory and rulership over the nations of this world. Born-again Christians will join with Messiah and the leaders of Israel in administering the kingdom of God on earth. We are marching to Zion!

IT WAS THE WORST OF TIMES

New Age gurus plot a cleansing of humanity and dream of the elimination of those of us they deem to have "low vibratory rates." Neo-Nazis scream epitaphs of age-old hatreds towards non-Aryans. Evidence linking Hitler to the New Age philosophy of H. P. Blavatsky emerges.

Serbs launch the latest genocide against the Bosnians. South Africa is about to explode. Lebanon lies in ruins. Somalia is a field of tragedies. Ireland is in flames. Haiti, ridden with corrupt politics and voodoo, is a disaster area. The proliferation of nuclear weapons seems to be unchecked. We are helpless as North Korea and Iran join the nuclear club. Iraq has rebuilt her military strength equal to the time of Gulf War I.

Economic analysts warn of impending disaster. The media beats the doomsday drum daily.

> A noise shall come even to the ends of the earth; for the Lord hath a controversy with the nations, he will plead with all flesh; he will give them that are wicked to the sword. . . . Behold, evil shall go forth from nation to nation, and a great whirlwind shall be raised up from the coasts of the earth. And the peaceable habitations are cut down (Jer. 25:31-37).

As ever, the forces of evil are unleashed against the nation of Israel. A dangerous and risky peace plan threatens her very existence. Malevolent spirits which infest the United Nations, attempt to revive the disgraceful idea that "Zionism is racism." In 1975 the United Nations voted in favor of a resolution stating that Zionism is a form of racism. It is not — it is the Jewish national liberation movement.

Although the UN resolution was finally rescinded recently, there are those who would like to see some such resolution reinstated in the UN.

ISRAEL, GOD'S ZION

If Zionism is racism then God is a racist because He is the author of Zionism. His favor of Israel is sung in the Psalms: "The Lord doth build up Jerusalem: he gathereth together the outcasts of Israel. . . . Praise the Lord, O Jerusalem; praise thy God, O Zion. . . . *He hath not dealt so with any nation*: and as for his judgments, they have not known them. Praise ye the Lord" (Ps. 147:2,12,20).

Zionism did not come into existence in 1897 when Theodore Herzl convened the first Zionist Congress in Basel, Switzerland. It begins in the opening pages of your Bible, in the twelfth chapter of Genesis. Moses recorded the unconditional promise of God in which the land is promised to the seed of Abraham forever. Later the promise is repeated to Jacob (Israel) as the promised seed (see Gen. 35:12).

The very integrity of God and His Word is at stake. God is not asleep. His Word is being, and shall be, fulfilled. He sees the activities of people today. As individuals and as a nation we should bless Israel, for the Almighty promises to "bless those who bless and curse those who curse" the promised seed of Abraham through Isaac and Jacob (Israel).

Foolish people argue whether the Jews are actually the seed of Abraham. What? Do you think God is incapable of fulfilling His Word to Abraham? God means what He says. Israel is not a race, but a people, an ethnic group, a nation. That nation has descended from Abraham, Isaac, and Jacob (Israel). That nation is alive in the world today and will never be destroyed. We will examine the matter of the identity of the Jewish people further in this book.

"Oh that the salvation of Israel were come out of Zion! When God bringeth back the captivity of his people, Jacob shall rejoice, and Israel shall be glad" (Ps. 53:6).

THE MEANING OF ZION TO CHRISTIANS

To Christians who agree with literal interpretation of the Bible, the words Zion and Zionist have special meaning. Zion, in Scripture, first meant the city of Jerusalem. Later it was expanded to include the Temple Mountain, then the expanded city of Jerusalem, finally the whole land of Israel (in some passages). Christians become a part of Zion by the new birth; that is, we become a part of the commonwealth of Israel. This is not replacement theology. It is rather participation theology. The Church never replaces Israel, but our spirits are bonded to the spirit of Israel. We pray and work for her well-being. We pray for her ultimate redemption.

In the Jewish world there are many Zionist organizations. They come in all political flavors, but they have one thing in common and that is the idea that Israel is a national home for the Jewish people, as is stated hundreds of times in the Bible. We agree with this basic concept of Zionism.

Christian Zionists may or may not participate in the political process of Zionism in any of its forms, but they believe in the basic Zionist ideal. They believe it because it is taught in the Word of God. "Let them all be confounded and turned back that hate Zion" (Ps. 129:5). "For the Lord hath chosen Zion; he hath desired it for his habitation" (Ps. 132:13).

USE THE WORD ZIONISM

Some Christians shy away from calling themselves Zionists because of the negative press the word has gotten. I think we should use the word. We should not hesitate to tell our friends, "I am a Christian Zionist." This will raise eyebrows, prompt questions, start dialogue, and in many cases provide you with a platform from which to address your concepts of how to participate in the plan of God for Israel and the Church. You could make

Christian Zionist open air meeting in Tel Aviv. Over 2,000 Christians participated.

good use of the seven-point statement on the Christians United for Israel membership card, mentioned elsewhere in this book.

God commands us to "Pray for the peace of Jerusalem" (Ps. 122:6). This necessitates that we pray for the peace of the nations around Jerusalem and for a normalization of relations between Israel and her neighbors. The end of the age will come in due season, but as long as the believers are here, our mandate is to pray and believe for peace in Jerusalem.

SUPPORT ISRAEL

True believers should be supportive of Israel. The Jews have returned to the land a second time (Isa. 11:11) and they will not be driven out of the land again (Amos 9:13-15). This is the divine plan. We are not merely spectators, but we are called to end-time involvement in that plan of the Almighty. How shall we be involved?

INTERCESSION

Prayer is the greatest force available to us. "Pray for the peace of Jerusalem, they shall prosper that love thee" (Ps. 122:6). Pray for the leaders of Israel. Pray for the Arabs and their leaders. Pray for the leaders of our own nation, that their decisions relating to Israel shall be divinely inspired. God does hear and answer prayer.

A few years ago while leading a tour group in the Holy Land, we had a powerful prayer meeting at Megiddo, overlooking the Armageddon Valley. We were led to pray for the release of hostages held in the B'nai B'rith building in Washington, DC. They were captives of the Hanafi Moslems. While in prayer, God led me to cry out, "I command the Hanafi Moslems, by the authority of Jesus Christ, to loose those captives and set them free." The next morning our Israeli tour guide came into the dining room at Kibbutz Hagoshrim with the excited announcement, "Rev. Lewis, the prayer is answered, the hostages have been turned loose." This was no mere coincidence.

There is a God who hears and answers prayer. God is not reluctant to answer. He will intervene in human affairs when we invite Him to do so.[1]

"The ministry of the church," said the late Watchman Nee, "includes the bringing down to earth of the will that is in heaven. This is to be done by diligent application in prayer, through the power of God the Holy Spirit and in the name of God the Son, pressing importunately for the victorious goal of all true prayer. Thy will be done in earth, as it is in heaven."[2] We pray, "Do good in thy good pleasure unto Zion: build thou the walls of Jerusalem" (Ps. 51:18).

FAITH AND GOOD WORKS

"Faith without works is dead" (James 2:20). Some things we can do nothing about — we must leave it in the hands of God. When there is something you can do, put legs to your prayers. Write the president and your congressman. Tell them of our biblical view that the USA should not make demands of that nation that are suicidal. Address the current situation in the Middle East. God will bless and honor you for doing this. Reward will accrue to your account in eternity's ledgers.[3]

When Christians say that they are biblical Zionists it says some important things about their faith. God is sovereign and can give any portion of the world to whomsoever He wills. He has ordained that the seed of Abraham through Isaac and Jacob (Israel) shall possess that tiny spot of land called Israel in perpetuity. This is based on a unilateral covenant made with Abraham. The covenant is unconditional. Our faith in God and His Word demands this belief. A biblical Zionist experiences a great love for Israel and the Jewish people, and will undertake legitimate action to protect Israel and to combat anti-Semitism wherever it is manifested.

We know many Arabs living in Israel and other parts of the world who privately describe themselves as Christians who love and support Israel. In some cases they even say they are Zionists!

Dr. Anis Shorrosh, a born-again Palestinian Christian writes glowingly of Israel's prophetic destiny in his remarkable book *Jesus, Prophecy and the Middle East*.[4]

Widad Van der Hoeven, an Arab Christian testifies strongly in Israel's behalf:

> As an Arab Christian girl, I was taught to hate the Jews. But the Lord made it clear to me that I could not love Him and hate His people. We often refuse to remember that Jesus himself was a Jew and that the Bible clearly teaches that God gave the land of Israel to the Jews.
>
> I call Ishmael (meaning "God heareth") the son of impatience. Because Abraham and Sarah could not wait for the birth of Isaac whom God had promised them, Ishmael was born. Ishmael's jealousy of his brother began with the birth of Isaac. The seed of bitterness continues to this day. Islam teaches that Ishmael, not

Isaac, was the son of promise whom God asked Abraham to offer on Mount Moriah. It is true that Ishmael was to be the father of twelve princes (Gen. 17:20) and his descendants would be innumerable (Gen. 16:10), but the Arabs are not satisfied with this.

The birth of the state of Israel revived the enmity of the Islamic Arab world and gave the "jihad" (holy war) new incentive. Arab rulers tried to unite their people through hatred of Israel. Arab Christians cannot be freed from the dark power of Islam as long as they consider themselves Arabs first and Christians second. They make a terrible mistake! Psalm 83 shows that God's anger is upon the nations that are against Israel.

I want my people, the Arabs, to be blessed. This is why I stand by God's people, the Jews, who I believe should return to the land of Israel. God wants to open the eyes of the Arabs to His blessings for them. But first, we Arabs must be humbled before Him and come to the end of our abilities — of our oil.

Arabs should not feel threatened nor inferior to Jews, because in Christ we have access to God's blessings.[5]

It may surprise you to know that while Israel does not draft

Bashara Shahin, an Israeli Arab who serves in Israel's army.

Palestinian Arabs into the Israeli defense forces, a number of Arabs choose to join. "Bashara Shahin and Geris Maroun from the Golani Brigade, and Romon Mata of the Artillery swore allegiance to the State of Israel on the 'New Testament' according to their belief. More Arab soldiers — Christian and Moslem — are joining the Tsahal [army] ranks and are all sent to fighting units."[6]

Mary Shahin, mother of Bashara, has spoken to thousands at the Christian Celebration of the Feast of Tabernacles in Jerusalem. The evening meetings of the feast are held in the Binyanei Ha'Ooma Convention Center, Jerusalem's largest auditorium. She speaks approvingly of her son's army involvement. We know the Shahin family personally and note their Bible-based love and concern for Israel.

The *Jerusalem Courier* featured an interview with Henry Hinn, an Israeli Arab of Palestinian ancestry. He spoke with great favor toward Israel and even defended Israel's actions in the 1982 Lebanon War.[7]

PROTECTORS OF ZION

We are called to be protectors of God's Zion. We oppose anti-Semitism wherever it rears its ugly head. We believe the Bible in its most literal sense. We believe that Israel exists by the will and decree of God. There is simply no other explanation. No other nation has been driven from its homeland, endured a 19-century Diaspora, and still maintained an ethnic and national identity. The Jews have been subjected to continual pogroms and persecution and still they have survived.

No other nation has returned to its homeland after being absent for hundreds of years. The Hebrew language is the only "dead" language to be brought to life again. One cannot believe in coincidence of this magnitude. It is the work of God and the fulfillment of His Word.

Call it a fulfillment of prophecy or call it a manifestation of the sovereign will of God, one must recognize that God has an ongoing plan and purpose for the Nation of Israel. We are Christian Zionists. We are not political Zionists, although we recognize that God uses human instrumentality to bring His purposes to pass. We are biblical Zionists. "That I may shew forth all thy praise in the gates of the daughter of Zion: I will rejoice in thy salvation" (Ps. 9:14).

IS THIS HERESY?

For our faith in God's Word, I and my colleagues are charged from pulpits, in print, on radio and television, with "vicious heresy." We are called blasphemers and anti-Christ by other Christian ministers who disagree with us about Zion. Charges like this have been leveled against us over and over through the years. This is a severe charge laid to our account, for by all biblical evidence an heretic is a damned soul. We should never call our Christian opponents heretics, even though we believe they are teaching error. We leave the state of their salvation in the hands of God.

ISRAEL, MAJOR ISSUE IN THE CHURCH

I was in a major leadership conference some time ago. A Charismatic leader asserted, "The identity of Israel is the major issue facing the Church today." His idea is that the Church has totally replaced Israel and that national Israel has no more role to play in God's economy. He strongly objects to my teaching. Although a delegate among equals, I was denied a voice in this interdenominational conference. Although the "unstructured" meeting was advertised to be an open exchange of ideas among Christian leaders, my colleagues and I were effectively silenced. Those who have opposed us in their publications, specifically because of our stance on Israel, prophecy and the Kingdom, were given ample time to express their views. No effective rebuttal was allowed. We requested time to answer. We were denied. We protested this unchristian treatment. Still and finally we were denied.

Yes, the hottest issue confronting the Church today regards the identity of Israel. This is highlighted by the fact that the tired old doctrine of replacement is being loudly proclaimed in certain Christian circles.

Pastors and other Christian leaders are being told that whether or not national Israel has a place in the end-time plan of God is a low priority item on the churches agenda. For the sake of unity among Evangelicals, Charismatics, and Pentecostals, we are told that we really ought to be quiet about the matter.

RADICAL ACCUSATIONS

Neo-kingdom and Dominion teachers continue to shout their theologically anti-Semitic views from the housetops, but my friends and I are ordered to leave the subject alone, lest we be the cause of division in the Church. But the sword they wield cuts two ways. Their's is a double standard. They seek not unity but subordination to their world view.

Some churchmen are expressing strong, anti-Israel views in widely circulated books and newsletters.

Rousas John Rushdoony, creator of the Chalcedon Foundation and grandfather of the Dominionist movement says that Christians who are supportive of Israel and the Jewish People are heretical.

In his book *Thy Kingdom Come*, in addition to calling our view of prophecy a "millennial pipe dream," and the Rapture teaching a manifestation of "pagan salvation," Rushdoony says:

> Premillennial and amillennial interpretations are tainted with the background of Manichaean heresy with its surrender of matter to darkness. A further heresy clouds premillennial interpretations of Scripture - their exaltation of racism into a divine principle. Every attempt to bring the Jew back into prophecy as a Jew is to give race and works (for racial descent is a human work) a priority over grace and Christ's work and is nothing more or less than paganism. It is significant that premillennialism is almost invariably associated with Arminianism, i.e. the introduction of race into prophetic perspectives is accompanied by, and part and parcel of, the introductions of works into the order of salvation. This is the essence after all, of the pharisaism which crucified Christ and which masqueraded, as it still does, as the epitome of godliness.
>
> *There can be no compromise with this vicious heresy.* (Emphasis mine).[8]

Rushdoony uses strawman tactics here. Premillennialists do not see a surrender of matter to darkness. Rather, we believe in the triumphant return of Jesus Christ and the reclamation of the physical world. We see the end of this age looming. We do not believe Jesus is coming to destroy the world, but to deliver it. We anticipate not the end of the world, but a glorious new beginning, brought about by the return of Christ.

In a letter to his subscribers Gary North takes delight in the troubles currently plaguing Israel in that he believes it will discredit the premillennialist movement, claiming that "The state of Israel will become their theological millstone."[9]

David Chilton, another prominent reconstructionist, writes:

> The god of Judaism is the devil. . . . Christ himself

will force them [the Jews] to come and bow down at the Christian's feet. . . . Modern apostate Jews have absolutely no theological, and therefore no historical and legal right to the land of Palestine.

Christian Zionism is blasphemy. It is a heresy. . . . Christians have no theological stake whatsoever in the modern State of Israel. It is an anti-God and anti-Christ nation . . . to support the enemies of the Gospel is not the mark of a Gospel minister, but of an anti-Christ.[10]

However, we have it on good authority that this is not so: "Thus saith the Lord; I am returned unto Zion, and will dwell in the midst of Jerusalem: and Jerusalem shall be called a city of truth; and the mountain of the Lord of hosts the holy mountain" (Zech. 8:3).

How clearly the Bible forecasts a return of the Jews to the land of their fathers. "I will bring again the captivity of my people of Israel, and they shall build the waste places . . . I will plant them upon their land" (Amos 9:14-15).

"I scattered them among the heathen, and they were dispersed through the countries" (Ezek. 36:19).

"And say unto them, Thus saith the Lord God; Behold, I will take the children of Israel from among the heathen, whither they be gone, and will gather them on every side, and bring them into their own land: And David my servant shall be king over them; and they all shall have one shepherd: they shall also walk in my judgments, and observe my statutes, and do them" (Ezek. 37:21,24).

There are hundreds of passages like this in the Bible. The New Testament reaffirms the future restoration of the kingdom of Jacob (see Luke 1:33). The Bible never refers to the church as Jacob — that is a term reserved for national Israel. This was recognized and taught clearly by Jesus and the apostles. Paul declares the ultimate redemption of Jacob-Israel: "And so all Israel shall be saved: as it is written, There shall come out of Sion the Deliverer, and shall turn away ungodliness from Jacob" (Rom. 11:26). This future redemption will apply to all Israelites living at the time of the coming of Messiah. (See Zech. 3:9.)

THE CRUX OF THE MATTER

If one grants a literal interpretation of the Bible, the question is settled. Israel has an ongoing place in God's plans for the future. An excellent treatise on this subject is Dr. Robert Shank's book, *Until the Coming of Messiah and His Kingdom*.[11]

For an excellent work on Bible interpretation see Dr. Paul Lee Tan's book, *The Interpretation of Prophecy*.[12]

Here is the crux of the matter: How do we interpret the Scriptures? Do we follow a premise of literal interpretation or do we accept the allegorical method? This is no mere intellectual exercise. The consequences are serious.

WHO SHALL PROTECT THE JEWS FROM A NEW HITLER?

Theologians in pre-Nazi Germany were teaching the anti-Semitic doctrines of replacement and contempt.

Hitler's henchmen actually quoted both Roman and Protestant churchmen in justifying their heinous acts against the Jews.

My colleagues and I are frequently accused of "sheltering the Jews from the wrath of God." It is alleged that we are the real anti-Semites, for if we allowed God's wrath to come upon them, it would drive the Jews to Christ.

This is a strange and twisted form of illogical thinking. In the first place, we should not imagine that any person or group of people could stop God from pouring out His wrath on any nation, should He so desire! Secondly, while we are not interested in interfering with the sovereign acts of God, we are determined to protect the Jewish people, God's chosen, from the wrath of man, and from any present or future "Hitlers." Thirdly, that the wrath of man dumped on the Jews would bring them to Christ, has not proven to be correct as witnessed by long centuries of "Christian" anti-Semitism. Certainly the Holocaust in "Christian" Germany, led by Hitler, who was a church member until the day he died, did not bring the Jews into the fold of the Church.

A PROBLEM FOR SOME

Some maintain that since Jewish people resist the gospel of Jesus, we should not favor them. They are quick to point out that many in Israel are secular, not even practicing Judaism.

It is no problem to the Bible literalist, however, that the Bible is right and not wrong in this regard. Ezekiel predicts that the Jewish people will regather in unbelief, and hardness of heart. First comes the national restoration, then the spiritual restoration (see Ezek. 36-37). Zechariah describes a glorious Messianic time when God declares that "I will remove the iniquity of that land in one day" (Zech. 3:9). This concurs with Paul's statement that when "the fullness of the Gentiles be come in . . . all Israel shall be saved; as it is written, There shall come out of Zion the Deliverer, and shall turn away ungodliness from Jacob" (Rom. 11:25-27).

It has not been our purpose here to address the question of missions. That has been the subject of a thousand books and tens of thousands of essays written throughout the centuries. The sole premise we are declaring here is that Israel exists by divine mandate. By no means does this imply that Israel is perfect, nor that we agree with all of her policies. I don't even agree with all the policies of my own country, yet I am a loyal citizen. We support Israel because of the revelation of God's Word.

Israel has a right to a secure place among the nations. Christians should intelligently cooperate with the plan of God and not give comfort to those who are the enemies of Israel. Your prophecy charts may all be in order, but when you stand before the Lord you will want to hear Him say, "Well done [not thought about] good and faithful servant" (Matt. 25:21;NIV).

While we know a brief time of unprecedented trouble is coming on all the world, it is not our business to promote it. It will come in its time. God has decreed the survival of the Jewish people in spite of all the troubles that will beset the world in the end-time transitional period. In the light of this we determine to cooperate with the known plan of God for His chosen people and nation of Israel.

"The people shall dwell in Zion at Jerusalem: thou shalt weep no more: he will be very gracious unto thee at the voice of thy cry: when he shall hear it, he will answer thee" (Isa. 30:19). "Comfort ye, comfort ye my people, saith your God. Speak ye comfortably to Jerusalem" (Isa. 40:1-2).

BIBLICAL ZIONISM DEFINED

The premise of biblical Zionism can be simply stated as follows: "The earth is the Lord's and the fullness thereof; the world, and they that dwell therein. For he hath founded it . . ." (Ps. 24:1-2). God is sovereign and can give any part of the world to whomever He wills. God has decreed that the Jewish people shall possess the land promised to Abraham, Isaac, and Jacob (Israel). (See Gen. 12:1-3; Deut. 1:8, 4:31, 30:4-5, 32:8,52; Isa. 14:1; Jer. 30:3,10-11; 31:8; 32:37; Ezek. 20:42; Amos 9:11-15; and hundreds of other biblical references.)

The community of nations should be content to allow the Jewish people to dwell in that small area comprising less than 1 percent of what today is known as the Middle East.

Our Christian faith further mandates that we be involved in the purposes of the Almighty, for as James writes, "But be ye doers of the word, and not hearers only, deceiving your own selves" (James 1:22).

There is a very special wall near the United Nations which was, ironically, donated by the former USSR. It is the Isaiah Wall which bears the inscription: "They shall beat their swords into plowshares and their spears into pruning hooks." This a quotation from a biblical Zionist, Isaiah, who further declares the intention of the Lord to return His scattered people to the land of their fathers (see Isa. 43:5,6).

Isaiah speaks of a regathering of the scattered Israelites from the four corners of the earth, a prophecy that saw no fulfillment until this era we live in. The assurance of this regathering to the land is not even based on Israel's integrity or faithfulness; it is based on God's sovereign will and integrity.

"For my name's sake will I defer mine anger, and for my praise will I refrain for thee, that I cut thee not off. Behold, I have refined thee, but not with silver; I have chosen thee in the furnace of affliction. For mine own sake, even for mine own sake, will I do it: for how should my name be polluted? and I will not give my glory unto another. Hearken unto me, O Jacob and Israel, my called; I am he; I am the first, I also am the last" (Isa. 48:9-12).

GOD, FATE, AND ISRAEL

The existence of Israel is a testimony to the miracle-working power of God. Anyone who helps to insure the continued existence of Israel cooperates with the divine plan.

The children of Israel are God's chosen people (see Deut. 7:6; Ps. 33:12; Isa. 46:1), and the whole history from Abraham to the very end of time, is foretold by prophets — history written in advance.

Israel is called the everlasting nation — a bold thing to say of any people. Throughout their long history they have been threatened with extinction. They have been crushed and humbled, massacred by the millions, banished from their homeland, scattered in all countries, yet have never lost their identity. They cannot be rooted out. Some of the most powerful nations have conquered and enslaved them. The conquerors have ceased to exist, the conquered live and thrive. Even now we watch them renewing their youth and seeking to regain their homeland which they had lost two thousand years ago — a nation whose very existence is a miracle.

Read the story of Israel, leaving God out of the

account, and their history resolves itself into a riddle, an enigma, insoluble by ordinary laws which govern the lives of nations. When we study it in the light of God's plan and purpose, it is seen to be a most marvelous romance, of which God is the Author. A nation which, after endless vicissitudes and judgments, emerges and will take its place in the world's history as faithful servants of an all-conquering God, and who obey His will for the benefit and blessing of the human race. He hath not dealt so with any nation.[13]

THY WILL BE DONE

One could take a fatalistic attitude and say, "Well, if it's God's will for Israel to exist then it will exist." This is true. God's will shall ultimately be done. However, there are many ways the human race can follow in arriving at that final fulfillment of His kingdom. One day we will stand before God, as believers for our evaluation (see 1 Cor. 3). Our works will be tried by fire. Don't you want to stand before the Saviour as one who worked to implement His will? We never work to thwart His will. We strive to comprehend and then cooperate with the divine will.

Normally, in this present world, God's will is not done. A perennial question is, "If God is all powerful and loving, then why does He not stop wars and suffering?" Actually, the terrible agony of our world is a manifestation of humanity's rejection of the will of God. God's will toward man is good. Satan is the prince of death (see John 10:10). Satan is the destroyer. That is why the prayers and good works of God's people are so important.

For this cause we pray, "Thy will be done in earth as it is in heaven." God ever seeks a person who will intercede for the nation so that destruction may be averted. Ezekiel shares the lament of God, "I sought for a man among them that should make up the hedge and stand in the gap before me for the land" (Ezek. 22:30). In that dark and bitter hour of Israel's history there was no one to stand in the gap. Calamity fell upon the land. What will it be in our day? Will the believers cry out to God? Will our nation bless Israel and thus receive blessing from the Almighty? These are important choices for you to consider.

"Their heart cried unto the Lord, O wall of the daughter of Zion, let tears run down like a river day and night: give thyself no rest; let not the apple of thine eye cease. Arise, cry out in the night: in the beginning of the watches pour out thine heart like water before the face of the

Lord: lift up thy hands toward him for the life of thy young children, that faint for hunger in the top of every street" (Lam. 2:18-19).

"Cry out and shout, thou inhabitant of Zion: for great is the Holy One of Israel in the midst of thee" (Isa. 12:6).

BIBLE REFERENCES TO ZION

Here is a list of every biblical reference to Zion. You may find this to be a convenient resource for further research.

Zion:

2 Samuel 5:7	Psalm 137:1,3
I Kings 8:1	Psalm 146:10
2 Kings 19:21	Psalm 147:12
2 Kings 19:31	Psalm 149:2
I Chronicles 11:5	Song of Solomon 3:11
2 Chronicles 5:2	Isaiah 1:8,27
Psalm 2:6	Isaiah 2:3
Psalm 9:11,14	Isaiah 3:16,17
Psalm 14:7	Isaiah 4:3,4,5
Psalm 20:2	Isaiah 8:18
Psalm 48:2,11-12	Isaiah 10:12,24,32
Psalm 50:2	Isaiah 12:6
Psalm 51:18	Isaiah 14:32
Psalm 53:6	Isaiah 16:1
Psalm 69:35	Isaiah 18:7
Psalm 74:2	Isaiah 24:23
Psalm 76:2	Isaiah 28:16
Psalm 78:68	Isaiah 29:8
Psalm 84:7	Isaiah 30:19
Psalm 87:2,5	Isaiah 31:4,9
Psalm 97:8	Isaiah 33:5,14,20
Psalm 99:2	Isaiah 34:8
Psalm 102:13,16,21	Isaiah 35:10
Psalm 110:2	Isaiah 37:22,32
Psalm 125:1	Isaiah 40:9
Psalm 126:1	Isaiah 41:27
Psalm 128:5	Isaiah 46:13
Psalm 129:5	Isaiah 49:14
Psalm 132:13	Isaiah 51:3,11,16
Psalm 133:3	Isaiah 52:1,2,7-8
Psalm 134:3	Isaiah 59:20
Psalm 135:21	Isaiah 60:14

Isaiah 61:3
Isaiah 62:11
Isaiah 64:10
Isaiah 66:8
Jeremiah 4:6,31
Jeremiah 6:2,23
Jeremiah 8:19
Jeremiah 9:19
Jeremiah 14:19
Jeremiah 26:18
Jeremiah 30:17
Jeremiah 31:6,12
Jeremiah 50:5,28
Jeremiah 51:10,24,35
Lamentations 1:4,6,17
Lamentations 2:1,4,6,8
    10,13,18

Lamentations 4:2,11,22
Lamentations 5:11,18
Joel 2:1,15,23,32
Joel 3:16-17,21
Amos 1:2
Amos 6:1
Obadiah 17,21
Micah 1:13
Micah 3:10,12
Micah 4:2,7,10
Zephaniah 3:14,16
Zechariah 1:14,17
Zechariah 2:7,10
Zechariah 8:2-3
Zechariah 9:9,13

Zion's:
Isaiah 62:1

The Word Sion is the same as Zion in the Old Testament. In the New Testament (KJV), Sion is the Greek equivalent to Zion. The KJV has one other reference translated Sion which is a different Hebrew word and refers to the peak of Mt. Hermon. It has no relationship to all the other references to Zion/Sion. The passage referred to is Deuteronomy 4:48.

Sion:
Psalm 65:1
Matthew 21:5
John 12:15
Romans 9:33

Romans 11:26
Hebrews 12:22
1 Peter 2:6
Revelation 14:1

These references may be integrated into a study of each Bible passage that has to do with the promises and covenants to Israel, and to the prophecies relating to Israel. Many studies by competent evangelical scholars are available. An excellent textbook on this subject is *Israelology: The Missing Link in Systematic Theology* by Arnold Fruchtenbaum.[14]

Notes

[1]David Allen Lewis, *Smashing the Gates of Hell* (Green Forest, AR: New Leaf Press, 1993, 6th ed.), chapters 1,2,3,14.

[2]R. Arthur Mathews, *Born for Battle* (Kent England: STL Books 1978, 1987, 8th Ed), p. 106-107.

[3]Lewis, *Smashing the Gates of Hell,* chapter 8.

[4]Anis Shorrosh, *Jesus, Prophecy and the Middle East* (Mobile, AL: Anis Shorrosh Evangelistic Association, 1979).

[5]Widad Van der Hoeven, "A Christian Arab Speaks," *Jerusalem Courier,* Vol. 3, #2, 1983, p 1.

[6]Jacky Hoogy, "Arab Soldiers in Tsahal," *Jerusalem Courier,* Vol. 7, #2, 1988, p. 17.

[7]Henry Hinn, "A Palestinian Speaks Out," *Jerusalem Courier,* Vol. 3, #2, 1983, p. 1ff.

[8]Rousas John Rushdoony, *Thy Kingdom Come* (Fairfax, VA: Thoburn Press, 1978), p 134.

[9]Gary North, *Newsletter,* Feb. 1988 (Tyler, TX: Institute of Christian Economics).

[10]David Chilton, *Days of Vengeance* (Fort Worth, TX: Dominion Press, 1987), p. 127-128, 618-619.

[11]Robert Shank, *Until the Coming of Messiah and His Kingdom* (Springfield, MO: Westcott Publishers, 1982).

[12]Paul Lee Tan, *The Interpretation of Prophecy* (Rockville, MD: Assurance Publishers, 8th ed., 1988).

[13]Samuel Schor, *The Everlasting Nation and Their Coming King* (London, England: Marshall, Morgan & Scott, circa 1930s), p 6-7.

[14]Arnold G. Fruchtenbaum, *Israelology: The Missing Link in Systematic Theology* (Tustin, CA: Ariel Ministries Press, 1993).

11

MY JOURNEY

Testimony of a Christian Zionist

My personal journey into Zionism began when I was 11 years old. I found Israel in the pages of the Bible, when there was no actual nation of Israel. In 1943 there was only the Bible and faith. — D.A.L.

But upon mount Zion shall be deliverance, and there shall be holiness; and the house of Jacob shall possess their possessions (Obad. 1:17).

By sharing a personal testimony of my own experience, I hope to inspire some of my colleagues to join me in this incredible journey. "We are marching to Zion!" I have high hopes for the next generation of preachers, teachers, and lay leaders. Already our ranks are being swelled with bright young men and women who have caught this holy vision for Zion. We elders in the cause rejoice in each of these welcome and honored colleagues.

At our 1985 United Nations press conference on Zionism and racism, I declared myself to be a Christian Zionist. Here is part of my statement, given to the press and others present at the conference. These words were followed with a demand that the UN abolish their scandalous resolution (1975) which equated Zionism with racism:

I have no Jewish ancestry, but I am a Zionist.

I am not formally affiliated with the political heirs of either Herzl nor Jabotinsky, but I am a Zionist.

Some of my Christian brethren, even those who agree with my supportiveness of Israel and war against anti-Semitism, would rather that I did not use the term. Nevertheless, I am a Zionist.

Some of my Jewish friends take exception to a Christian appropriating this term, but nevertheless, in the manner that a Christian can be a Zionist, I am a Zionist.

My definition of Christian Zionism is embodied in the creed of Christians United for Israel. Here is our seven-point statement:

1. The Bible is the Word of God.

2. God owns the whole world.

3. God can give any portion of the world to whom-ever He wills.

4. God has given the land of Israel to the Jewish people.

5. Christians should cooperate with the plan of God by praying for the peace of Jerusalem and acting in a

UN press conference held by Dr. Isaac Rottenberg (left) and Dr. David A. Lewis in 1985. The conference was to demand that the UN rescind the resolution equating Zionism with racism. This took place a short while later.

manner supportive of the nation of Israel, for its continued security and existence.

    6. Christians should actively oppose anti-Semitism.

    7. To be pro-Israel is not to be anti-Arab. Christians
express love and compassion for all people.

This platform does not imply that Christian Zionists agree with everything the Israeli government does.
It simply means that we believe the Word of God and
wish to cooperate with the Divine Plan. Membership in
Christians United for Israel is open to any Christian who
agrees to these seven statements.

THE LONG, LONG ROAD FROM SOUTH DAKOTA TO JERUSALEM

Let me share my testimony of how I became a Christian Zionist.
My personal journey into Zionism began when I was 11 years old. I
found Israel in the pages of the Bible, when there was no actual nation
of Israel. In 1943 there was only the Bible and faith. In 1944 Frederick
C. Painton, the Near East correspondent for the *Reader's Digest,*
wrote an article for the May issue, outlining the reasons why the Jews
would never have a homeland in Palestine. At that time the land was
under the British Mandate. Painton's final conclusion was the Jews
would never establish a nation principally because they were not
interested in having their own national homeland! "Then, if my
observations are correct, the Palestine problem will die out by sheer
lack of Jews who would give up their own homeland to plant
themselves anew in the sterile hills of Judea."[1] Not enough Jews
would ever want to take up residence there, thought Painton. But, at
the age of 11 years I was not reading Painton. I was reading the Bible.

A German evangelist had preached on prophecy, the Book of
Revelation, and the Jewish hope for 21 nights in the little Assembly
of God church in Britton, South Dakota. He said that the Jews would
return to Palestine and establish a nation. I listened with fascination.
I began to read the Bible, especially the Book of Revelation.

My Sunday school teacher, Alice Featherhuff, noted my keen
interest and encouraged me. She ordered a pocket-sized copy of
the Book of Revelation from a Bible society. It was my treasure.
I still have it, along with a Gospel of Matthew which she ordered
for me. It is even signed by her. Miss Featherhuff told me to read
Matthew 24 and 25, Jesus' Olivet discourse on the end times.
There I read the parable of the fig tree.

Yes, I found Israel in the pages of the Bible. Through biblical Israel I found the Jewish people. In my Bible I did not see a fossil people nor only historic characters. I saw a living nation with a hope and a future. There were no Jews in Britton, South Dakota, as far as I knew. But my soul was bonded to the soul of Israel nevertheless.

The sound Bible preaching of Bretschneider had sowed the seeds of Zionism in my young mind. I did not know it but I had become a biblical Zionist.

At the age of 15, on May 15, 1948, I was listening to the radio news. I heard that my president, Harry S. Truman, had just given de facto recognition to the new state of Israel which had declared its independence on the previous day, May 14, 1948. My mind staggered. My soul almost burst within me. My spirit was in ecstasy. "It's really happening, just like the preacher said it would. Just like I have read in my Bible. It is happening in my lifetime, before my very eyes." Bretschneider's biblical prediction had been fulfilled. Painton's rationalistic projections slink back into the silence of history like the gibbering of old foolish ghosts.

On that day I consciously became a Zionist. I knew that somehow my destiny was linked with that of the Jewish people.

Later, I attended Central Bible College in Springfield, Missouri, where I sat under the inspired teaching of Stanley Horton, Donald Johns, J. Robert Ashcroft, Calvin Holsinger, Frank M. Boyd, Ernest S. Williams, J. Roswell Flower, and others who further grounded my thinking in the Bible. By the time I was in my early twenties I was a committed theological Zionist.

In 1954 I was licensed as a clergyman in the Assemblies of God, and began my preaching ministry. I became a declared Zionist,

*My first tour group to Israel, in 1968. We met with
Deputy Mayor Dr. Andre Chouraque.*

preaching in the churches about the eschatological meaning and future of Israel. In 1956, after two years of itinerant ministry, I was ordained in the church.

In 1968 I made my first of 55 trips to Jerusalem. I became a Zionist activist at that time, realizing as St. James says that, "Faith without works is dead." On my very first trip to Israel I began meeting with the leadership of the nation.

On August 2, 1975, active participation shifted into high gear, when I organized a prayer demonstration for Israel in the nation's capital. With about 100 of my colleagues I stood in Lafayette Park across from the White House with a huge banner that read "Christians United for the Biblical Right of Israel to its Land." That month we launched Christians United for Israel. I serve today as the president of that organization.

CHRISTIAN ZIONIST ORGANIZATIONS

Following the meeting across from the White House a Jewish publication noted, "Itinerant Assemblies of God evangelist, David A. Lewis, and about 100 of his colleagues stood in front of the White House, in the first open demonstration of Christian love for the Jewish people in the history of the world." Ignore the historical inaccuracy of that statement. Concentrate on how few true demonstrations of unqualified love for the Jewish people had even been noted previously.

About 100 or more organizations like Christians United for Israel now exist. Many of the leaders of these groups got their fire kindled in one of our church conferences or in our annual prophecy conference in Springfield, Missouri. The movement is growing and advancing for the glory of God.

We go wherever God leads us. We depend on Him to open the

Pastors conferring with Dr. Chouraque. Left to right: Rev. Leland Gross, Dr. David Lewis, Dr. Chouraque, Rev. Gordon Churchill, Rev. Frank Mays.

Giving testimony at the Senate Foreign Relations Committee hearings.

Abba Eban spoke to the first meeting of NCLCI in 1978. Several congresspersons, a governor, and about 350 Christian leaders participated. David Lewis was one of the original five founders of NCLCI.

Each of these men has served as president of NCLCI. Left to right: Fr. Edward Flannery, Catholic; Bishop John Burt, Episcopal; David A. Lewis, Assemblies of God; and Franklin Little, Methodist.

doors of service He prefers for us. When I was called to give witness to the United States Senate Committee on Foreign Relations, on Israel, Jerusalem being the capitol, and the 1982 Lebanon war, He gave me the boldness to answer forthrightly to each of the senator's questions. Senator Percy held up a copy of my book about the Lebanon war, *Magog, 1982, Canceled.* He strongly challenged my conclusions and sources of documentation, but before I finished I had produced adequate documentation and presentation to turn the tide. I got letters from several senators thanking me profoundly for the material we had brought to their attention.

In 1978, it was my privilege to join hands with other Christian leaders to form the National Christian Leadership Conference for Israel, an organization that has widely impacted the Church world. The original founders also included: The Reverend Dr. William Harter, a Presbyterian pastor; Sister Rose Thering, a Roman Catholic nun; Dr. Franklin Littel, professor at Temple University and Methodist clergyman; and Dr. Arnold Olson, president emeritus of the Evangelical Free Church.

I have served a three-year term as president of NCLCI, and at present serve as the chairman of the board. At this moment our president is Bishop John Burt, an Episcopalian clergyman. In our leadership meetings *we have one theological ground* upon which we all stand in agreement. That is a commitment to Israel's continued

Sister Rose Thering, professor emeritus of Seton Hall University, serves as executive director of NCLCI and runs our New York office, which is in the America-Israel Friendship House. Bishop John Burt, president of NCLCI stands with Sister Rose.

secure existence and to opposing anti-Semitism. No doctrinal nor ecclesiastical compromise is encouraged nor demanded. Each participant retains the doctrinal commitment of the church with which he or she is affiliated.

Christian Zionism has a long and honorable history. There has not been a period of history when the Church did not have its literalists who realized God's ongoing intentions for, and relationship with Israel. Early in the history of the Church, due to the allegorical interpretive methods of men like Origen and Augustine, it seemed that the love of Zion would almost cease in the Church. But fortunately the flickering flame never was completely extinguished.

Dr. David Rausch has done a masterful work in his books *Zionism Within Early American Fundamentalism 1878-1918,* [2] and *A Legacy of Hatred.* [3] Rausch shows that there is a conflict in the church as relates to Zion. On one hand we observe the roots of anti-Semitism, and on the other hand the strongest expression of support for Israel and a determination to combat anti-Semitism.

In his diaries, Theodore Herzl, founder of the modern Zionist movement, refers to the Evangelical clergyman William Hechler more than to any other person. The Reverend Claude Duvernoy, a French Protestant Christian and citizen of Israel has written a masterful work about the relationship of Herzl and Hechler. In *The Prince and the Prophet* [4] Duvernoy recounts how Herzl, in times of great discouragement, received inspiration from Reverend Hechler, who was a dedicated Christian Zionist. Over and over Herzl refers to the encouragement Hechler was to him and to the Zionist cause.

NCLCI open air meeting in Lafayette Park, across from the White House in Washington, DC.

COMMITMENT

Rausch penetrates your heart with his challenge: "Without an understanding of the Holocaust, we would not question what our reaction might be while watching others being persecuted." He asks, "How much of your life would you risk for another racial or religious group? The study of the Holocaust cautions us against a quick answer. We see that often the jeopardizing of a career, a wife, children, or community set up circumstances made a clear-cut decision difficult. Good, decent citizens were conditioned or coerced to turn their backs on the plight of others; indeed, to promote the Nazi plan."[5]

After much heart searching the Christian Zionist will probably come to the Moses conclusion:

> And the Lord said unto Moses, I have seen . . . this stiffnecked people: Now therefore let me alone, that my wrath may wax hot against them, and that I may consume them: and I will make of thee a great nation.
>
> And Moses . . . said, Oh, this people have sinned a great sin, and have made them gods of gold. Yet now, if

Pastor John Hagee of San Antonio receives the annual Christian Leadership award from Christians United for Israel.

thou wilt *forgive their sin; and if not, blot me, I pray thee, out of thy book which thou hast written* (Exod. 32:9-10, 31-32, emphasis mine).

Moses said in essence, that if God was going to condemn and destroy Israel, then let his name also be blotted out of the Book of Life. The meaning of the Book of Life is revealed in the following Scriptures: Philippians 4:3; Revelation 3:5, 13:8, 17:8, 20:12, 20:15, and 22:19. "And there shall in no wise enter into it any thing that defileth, neither whatsoever worketh abomination, or maketh a lie: but they which are written in the Lamb's book of life" (Rev. 21:27).

How committed is the Christian Zionist movement? We are so committed that even if Israel did all the wrong things, even if the Jewish community began to attack us, we would never deny our commitment to biblical truth. Never will we abandon the action demanded by an acceptance of these truths. In short, my Jewish friends, like it or not, you are stuck with us. We have no other choice.

HOW TO STOP A CHRISTIAN BIBLICAL ZIONIST

Only one thing could stop me from being a Christian Zionist. Only one thing could quench this fire in my soul.

Persuade me that the Bible does not literally mean what it says.

Urge upon me the concept that the Bible is full of mythology, that its history is inaccurate.

Convince me that Israel has been replaced by the Church.

Prove to me that the prophecies relating to Israel are mere allegories.

Convince me that the existence of the modern nation of Israel is nothing more than an accident of history.

Persuade me that the Gospel of John, rather than being badly misinterpreted by theologians, actually is anti-Semitic.

Abandon the power and authority of the Bible and the Evangelical ceases to be an Evangelical. What you have then is an old-line liberal Christian who might support Israel and combat anti-Semitism for humanitarian reasons. But he might fall back into the predictable pagan patterns of old-line Christianity, manifesting hostility toward Israel, and apathy or negative attitudes toward the Jewish community.

Realizing that literal interpretation of the Bible logically leads to Christian Zionism, many neo-Evangelical Dominionists, Theonomists, Reconstructionists, and Kingdom Now advocates assail the bastions of literalism, deny Israel's ongoing place in the plan of God, and preach the twin doctrines of "Christian" anti-Semitism, to wit, replacement and contempt.

We are determined that Nazi persecution of the Jews shall not happen again. As long as there is an Evangelical church in the world we will sound the trumpet in our own ranks and command attention, regardless of the opposition we face. We will defy the neo-Evangelical anti-Semites. They must not gain ascendancy over the Church.

Notes

[1]Frederick C. Painton, "Report on Palestine," *Reader's Digest,* May 1944, p. 21-26.

[2]David A. Rausch, *Zionism Within Early American Fundamentalism, 1878-1918* (New York, NY: Edwin Mellen Press, 1979).

[3]David A. Rausch, *A Legacy of Hatred — Why Christians Must Not Forget the Holocaust* (Chicago, IL: Moody Press, 1984).

[4]Claude Duvernoy, *The Prince and the Prophet* (Jerusalem: Francis Naber & Duvernoy, 1966).

[5]Rausch, *A Legacy of Hatred,* p. 4.

12

LED BY THE SPIRIT

Evangelicals and Israel — the Bright Side

> Comfort ye, comfort ye my people, saith your God. Speak ye comfortably to Jerusalem (Isa. 40:1-2).
>
> Then he answered and spake unto me, saying, This is the word of the Lord unto Zerubbabel, saying, Not by might, nor by power, but by my spirit, saith the Lord of hosts (Zech. 4:6).
>
> About a decade ago, it dawned upon me that there is a deep reservoir of friendship for the Jewish people and the State of Israel within a large part of the vast evangelical community. — Rev. Frank Eiklor

Increase Mather was an American clergyman who became president of Harvard College. In 1669 Mather wrote a work titled *The Mystery of Israel's Salvation Explained and Applyed.* A Bible literalist, Mather said, "That after the Jews are brought into their own land again and there disturbed with Gog and Magog (Ezek. 38-39) who shall think with great fury to destroy the Israelites. . . . The Jews who have been trampled upon by all nations, shall become the most glorious nation in the whole world, and all other nations shall have them in great esteem and honor. Isaiah 60:1,3 . . . that the time will surely come, when the body of the twelve Tribes of Israel shall be brought out of their present condition of bondage and misery, into a glorious and wonderful state of salvation, not only spiritual but temporal."[1]

Rev. William Hechler, a British Evangelical pastor was the person most mentioned in the diaries of Theodore Herzl, who founded the modern Zionist movement in Basle, Switzerland in 1897. Hechler bonded his spirit to that of Herzl and dogged his footsteps all over Europe. The pastor had an uncanny ability to pry open doors that were closed to Herzl, getting him appointments with the Kaiser of Germany and other European leaders. When times of depression and thoughts of failure slowed the pace of Herzl, there was William Hechler buoying up his spirits with scriptural admonition and prophetic words.

There is a divinely appointed linkage between Evangelicals, Pentecostals, and Israel. Dr. David Rausch, professor at Ashland College, has written a monumental work, *Zionism Within Early American Fundamentalism, 1878-1918.*[2] Rausch brilliantly chronicles the fundamentalist and evangelical connection to a biblical Zionist dream.

OTHER EARLY CHRISTIAN ZIONISTS

We can only mention a few of the shining lights of Evangelical Zionism: Dr. Elhanan Winchester wrote in 1800 that "The return

Rev. William Hechler, a British Evangelical pastor who befriended Herzl and the Zionist cause.

of the Jews to their own land is certain." In 1852 a Reverend Bickersteth wrote *The Restoration of the Jews to their Own Land.* England's Balfour Declaration in 1917 had given hope to the Jews that they would be restored to the land. This was encouraged by Bible-believing Christians in Britain. In 1918 Dr. David Baron wrote in great detail about the coming return of the Jews to the land.

During the early 1900s Fundamentalists were conducting prophecy conferences in New York, Chicago, London, and other cities. There was always major emphasis on the Jewish nation.

I hope my colleagues in other churches will allow me to testify of my own church's stand on Israel. Truly, I do not feel that we are superior. But we all are unique and bring a particular point of view to this dialogue. This chapter was first written as an essay distributed at the General Council of the Assemblies of God in Minneapolis, in August of 1993. Our goal is to portray role-models out of our own history and experience for others to emulate. No doubt such a paper could be written for almost any church denomination.

THE PENTECOSTAL REVIVAL

When the Pentecostal revival started around 1901 there was an immediate affinity for the scattered Jewish people and a realization that Israel, as a nation, would live again in her ancient homeland. True, there were some anti-Semites in the ranks, largely people from old line denominations who brought their amillennial, replacement theology and anti-Jewish baggage with them, but they were a drastic minority. The Holy Spirit illuminated the prophetic word in the hearts of the majority who were obedient to His leading. The connection of the Pentecostals to Zion and Israel is not an insignificant consideration. The bonds are being strengthened each passing year. Even anti-Zionists are realigning their thinking as increasing sensitivity to the Holy Spirit's leading and revelation is manifested in the heart of this great fellowship.

Rev. C. F. Parham was founder and president of God's Bible College in Topeka, Kansas when the twentieth century Pentecostal revival in America began on January 1, 1901. In an all-night prayer meeting a student, Agnes N. Ozman, received the Holy Spirit and spoke in unknown tongues. It is interesting to note that Parham's daughter-in-law, Pauline Parham is both a Pentecostal and an ardent Zionist. She is a professor Emeritus at Christ For the Nations Bible College in Dallas, Texas. C. F. Parham's Pentecostal grand-daughter, Bobbi Hromas is the daughter of Pauline Parham. She is likewise a fervent Christian Zionist and heads up the American Christian Trust, one of the most significant prayer ministries in the world today. The Trust has its center a half-block from the Embassy of Israel in Washington, DC and from there prayer ascends 24 hours a day. Prayer is specially made for the USA and for Israel.

In 1917 the *Weekly Evangel* (which became the *Pentecostal Evangel*) declared that the Jews would return to the land, and chided leadership in the old line denominations, "The Christian leaders of today have utterly failed to grasp the import of what is likely to be one of the most significant and far-reaching events of this momentous period."[3]

GROWTH OF THE PENTECOSTAL MOVEMENT

The Pentecostal movement is the largest family of Protestants in the world according to statistics garnered from *Encyclopedia Britannica Yearbook* and *The International Bulletin of Missionary Research.* The I.B.M.R. claims that 54,000 new members are being added to the Pentecostal ranks daily. That reflects an increase of 19 million annually.

The statistics we have were compiled over four years ago, so the numbers are higher now. Pentecostals and Charismatics combined have a membership of 332 million in their congregations worldwide. They have the vast majority of the world's mega-churches (so called super churches). They have 66 percent of the Christian membership of Third World nations. Pentecostals and Charismatics give 34 billion dollars annually to Christian causes and missions. Of all the plans presently known for fulfilling the Great Commission, two-thirds of them are in the hands of the Pentecostals and Charismatics.

In statistical studies done by Burgess, McGee, and Alexander we are told that the Pentecostal churches (Assemblies of God, Church of God, Open Bible Standard, Foursquare

Pauline Parham and Bobbi Hromas.

Gospel, etc.) have 176 million members. Charismatics have 156 million adherents in the world. Thus there are 332 million Pentecostals and Charismatics, comprising 21 percent of all the Christians in the world.

THE ASSEMBLIES OF GOD

The Assemblies of God is the largest of the Pentecostal denominations. When E. N. Bell of Malvern, Arkansas, sent out his paper *Word and Witness* calling for Pentecostal ministers to come together to form a fellowship capable of bestowing recognizable credentials to ministers, to promote world missions, and to provide for a publishing house, many responded.

In 1914 they came to Hot Springs, Arkansas, for the first General Council. There the General Council of the Assemblies of God was born. The vast majority of the participants expressed a great love for the Jewish people, and most perceived that God had great plans for the nation of Israel, which was then not in existence.

The first General Council was meeting three years before the British Balfour Declaration, which stated, "His Majesty's government view with favour the establishment in Palestine of a national home for the Jewish people and will use their best endeavours to facilitate the achievement of this object, it being clearly understood that nothing shall be done which may prejudice the civil and religious rights of existing non-Jewish communities in Palestine, or the rights and political status enjoyed by Jews in any other country."

ISRAEL AND THE PENTECOSTAL CREED OF THE ASSEMBLIES OF GOD

The strength of the Assemblies of God has been its Statement of Fundamental Truths.[4] Each minister is asked to search his heart and mind each year and see if he still agrees with the statement of doctrine. The minister must sign a form indicating continuing agreement with the creedal statement of the church if his credentials are to be renewed. It is not a long statement. It is concise and deals with essentials, not a lot of potentially argumentative details. Basic to the Statement of Fundamental Truths is the fact that the Bible is the inspired Word of God.

THOMAS ZIMMERMAN, THE BIBLE AND ISRAEL

The late Rev. Thomas F. Zimmerman capably served the Assemblies of God as general superintendent for many years. I think that the greatest contribution Thomas Zimmerman brought to our movement was his constant emphasis on the Bible as the Word of God. I cannot recall ever hearing Brother Zimmerman speak without making some strong statement on the Word of God, and its absolute authority. I want to personally pay tribute to Thomas Zimmerman for his steadfast leadership in this realm. His contribution to the movement was multifaceted, but in my opinion this was his greatest gift to us. It is no wonder that he so strongly favored Israel, as revealed in things that he wrote.

In keeping with his steadfast regard for the Bible and its authority, in relation to Israel, Zimmerman wrote in the foreword of a book by Rev. Louis Hauff, "The author of *Israel in Bible Prophecy* has brought together in a single volume the history, prophecy, and biblical record of Israel. From the time of Christ until the present, the nation has played an increasingly important role in Bible prophecy."

Many writers have touched on the development of Israel from the viewpoint of Scripture, others from the historic and current day view, but few have combined the two areas as has this author. The research and source materials combine the work of many researchers, giving depth which one writer might not have obtained in a lifetime.

Because the volume covers the historic and prophetic, it is well suited for individual reading and study,

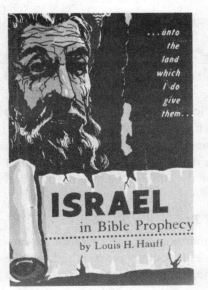

for research, and for classroom use. Of special interest to the Bible student will be the Scriptures related to Israel's prophecy, which the author has put together so as to form a complete picture of the past, present, and future.

A dynamic quality has been added to the volume in the introduction of dozens of great men who have helped to shape the destiny

Louis Hauff book — Dr. Tom Zimmerman wrote the foreword.

of Israel. The author weaves into the historic portions of the book the work of Dr. Chaim Weizmann, General Allenby, Theodore Herzl, Lloyd George, Premier Ben-Gurion, and others who in the modern history of Israel have had a hand in shaping its present, and whose shadows will fall across Israel's future.

Israel has been at the hub of the world for centuries. Yet, through fulfillment of biblical prophecy, God has steered the world around Israel and she has been left desolate. However, since the nation was partitioned in 1948, the world's eyes have again been focused on Israel. The author spotlights this focus and indicates how more and more the world will again begin to revolve around Israel and God's chosen people.

Ultimately, as Israel becomes the center of concentrated attention, it will play an even more important place in the closing days of our age. The author summarizes the prophecy on this in his closing chapter, pointing to the soon return of Christ for His own.[5]

THE CHURCH DIALOGUES, DISSENTS, DEBATES

There are many areas in which various members of the fellowship honestly disagree. We may have all kinds of disputes on externals, and many minor points of doctrine. As one who has spent his life researching and preaching on Bible prophecy, I have had plenty of opportunity to observe the latter!

But we do not disagree on the Statement of Fundamental Truths. If any disagree, how can they honestly renew their credentials and sign the statement each year? I would suggest that anyone who signs with "intellectual reservations" is handling the truth lightly and needs to repent. That person also needs to withdraw from the Assemblies of God. There are plenty of "liberal" fellowships where he or she can get credentials and minister.

Another alternative would be to offer revisionist amendments to the General Council and let the issue be debated on the council floor. Then, whatever is the decision of the church, that must be our mandate from that point on. We write this out of strong conviction and regard for the integrity of our fellowship.

Our great strength as a movement has been, that whatever else we may disagree on, we know there is a foundation on which all are required to stand in agreement, and that foundation is the Statement of Fundamental Truths. The Statement simply explains what we believe the Bible reveals about 16 areas of doctrine.

You will find Assembly of God churches that are formal, some that are very emotional. Some like intellectual preaching, some like old time camp-meeting preaching. Some like to sing from hymnals, others prefer Psalms, choruses, and an overhead projector. Some dance, some sit still. Some worship quietly, some are outgoing and fervent. But the glue that ideally holds us together, the one thing we all agree on, is the validity of the Statement of Fundamental Truths. There is a tiny minority of clergy persons who deceptively sign their annual renewal, with affirmation of agreement, but the vast majority are honest men and women who would not violate their conscience in this fashion.

Article No. 14 of the Statement of Fundamental Truths manifests what the Assemblies of God believes about the millennium and Israel:

THE MILLENNIAL REIGN OF CHRIST

"The second coming of Christ includes the rapture of the saints, which is our blessed hope followed by the visible return of Christ with His saints to reign on the earth for one thousand years (Zech. 14:5; Matt. 24:27,30; Rev. 1:7, 19:11-14, 20:1-6). This millennial reign will bring the salvation of NATIONAL ISRAEL (Ezek. 37:21-22; Zeph. 3:19-20; Rom. 11:26-27) and the establishment of universal peace" (Isa. 11:6-9; Ps. 72:3-8; Mic. 4:3-4). (Emphasis mine.)

Please note that "This millennial reign will bring the salvation of *National Israel. . . .*" This should be noted carefully. It demonstrates our conviction, that the clergy and members of the Assemblies of God believe that the nation of Israel has a future in the plan of God. Early editions of the *Pentecostal Evangel*, and its predecessor the *Weekly Evangel*, bear witness to this being a common view in our ranks from our very beginning.

THE 1927 GENERAL COUNCIL OF THE ASSEMBLIES — CROSSROADS OF DESTINY

In 1927 the Assemblies of God General Council met at the crossroads of destiny. While there have always been those who proclaimed these truths in the ranks of our church, it was not until 1927 that the Statement of Fundamental Truths was amended to add the sentence about Israel. Wayne Werner, church archivist, has been most helpful in forwarding my research in this area. The minutes of the 1927 council contain scant mention of the resolution which brought about the inclusion of the line about National Israel in item 14 of the Statement. A number of years ago Wayne gave me the phone number of an elderly minister, who he said had been present in every General Council, and has a nearly photographic memory.

I called the old saint and asked him questions about the 1927 General Council. He began by telling me who spoke the first night, what his text and topic were, then continued to tell me who led the morning devotions the following day, and continued thus through his recounting of the days of that historic council. I asked him about the resolution to include reference to National Israel in the doctrinal statement of the church. He said, "Brother Lewis, there was very little discussion and no dissent. It seemed good to us and the Holy Ghost to bring our church's constitution in line with the Word of God."

What an act of faith! There was no nation of Israel in existence in 1927. The few Jews in British Palestine were not faring well, suffering many reverses at the hands of the British. Now, if that line had been added at the General Council of 1949, it would merely be a fine bit of hindsight. But it was done in 1927 and shines forth as a magnificent act of faith. There are a few individual congregations in various denominations which have made strong statements on Israel, but as far as I can determine, the Assemblies of God is the only denomination that has a creedal statement indicating that God has an ongoing plan for the nation of Israel.

We seldom adjust the Statement of Fundamental Truths. Any changes that have been made were for clarification. Substantial change has not taken place. In formulating the Statement of Fundamental Truths, our early founders wisely avoided a lot of nit-picking arguments. They laid a basic foundation for us. That is our strength as a fellowship. Then in 1927, in the wisdom that God gave them, our church fathers again asserted that God has a continuing plan for National Israel. What a blessed heritage of faith and truth!

It is interesting to note that throughout 1927 the *Pentecostal Evangel* carried several articles favorable to the as yet non-existent Israel. In the February 5, 1927, edition *The Evangel* declared that the Jews would return, citing a Jewish Zionist leader, Dr. Sokolow, who said that the Messiah would come after the Jews had returned to their homeland.

God knew the struggle there would be with this concept in the last days. It is meaningful that these words are handed down to us by our church fathers. Remember this concept was amended to our constitution as an act of faith in God's Word in 1927 when no nation of Israel existed. The brethren in conference at the 1927 General Council knew exactly what their words "National Israel" implied. It meant nation of Israel.

Of course, our faith does not rest on individual church creeds, but rather on revealed truth recorded in the 66 books of the Bible. Further, when I speak of a plan for National Israel I am not referring to individual salvation. Individual salvation is personal, to be worked out, in the light of God's Word between the person and God. We simply believe that the nation of Israel is sovereignly chosen by God

The Rose City of Petra, a vast area surrounded by high red rock mountains. There is only one entrance, the Siq, a mile long crack in one of the mountains. The homes, temples, and tombs of Petra are carved inside the mountains surrounding the valley of Petra.

to fulfill a purpose, to ultimately bring glory to His name.

THE ROLE OF JORDAN IN PROPHECY

I have long taught that there would be a peace treaty between Jordan and Israel. Israel will find a place of shelter in Jordan during the Tribulation, at the lost city of Petra and perhaps elsewhere in the Hashamite Kingdom of Jordan. (See Dan. 11:41-45. Amman, Moab, and Edom are modern day Jordan.) The implication of this passage is that while the Antichrist will rule the whole world, there is one tiny nation, Jordan, that will escape his domination. This will be the result of divine intervention and protection. Here the Jewish people can flee for shelter in the time of the great global trauma.

I had a surprising conversation with a Moslem in Amman, Jordan, a number of years ago. Adnan told me that in his country there are some Moslems and Christians who have an unusual tradition. They say that when the world is under the thrall of a man of great evil (the Antichrist), he will defile the temple in Jerusalem. Then Jordan must provide shelter for the Jews who will come into her borders. He said that the Rose Red Lost City of Petra would be the principle refugee center. He told me that in its present state it could provide emergency housing for over 150,000 persons.

Baseem Rihani, director of archaeology for South Jordan and Petra told me that there is a lost city of Badir, almost unknown, and is connected by tunnels to Petra. I have visited Petra several times in past years. It is located in the area of the Edomites, who are descendants of Esau. I pondered, *Where did such a tradition come from?* Mr. Adnan Sawish could not tell me of its origin, simply that it existed.

If the statements of Adnan Sawish surprised me, I was literally astonished to learn recently that in World War II Jordan actually declared war on Germany!

"When World War II was breaking out, England, Australia, and France declared war on Germany. The date was September 3, 1939. Prince Abdullah of Trans-Jordan [now, the Hashamite Kingdom of Jordan] also declared war on Germany, but no record will be found of this in most history books. The reason for this tiny state's declaration of war was Germany's flagrant anti-Semitism. Both Arab and Jew are Semites. This prompted Hitler to make a public display of the issue. Standing with his aides before cameras and a map of the Mid-East, he asked where Jordan was. After being shown, he quipped that he would add a few Marks to the defense budget to cover the disturbance. About six German paratroopers were dispatched to Jordan. They were immediately captured and spent the remainder of the war as POWs."[6]

In July 1993, about eight weeks before the September 13 signing of the peace accord, we wrote in the *Jerusalem Courier,* "Our contacts tell us that ongoing secret negotiations between Jordanian and Israeli leaders may bring a peace treaty, in the next five years. May God grant it. Beh ezrat Hashem!"[7]

1933 — OM SALEEM

Let the scribe bring forth another of his treasures. Recently we learned of Om Saleem, a simple Arab housewife who was part of a

The **Pentecostal Evangel**

By My Spirit   HOLY BIBLE   The Whole Gospel to the Whole World   saith the Lord

Entered as second-class matter June 25, 1918, at post office at Springfield, Mo., under act of March 3, 1879. Accepted for mailing at special rate provided in Sec. 1103, of Oct. 3, 1917, authorized July 3, 1918.

Published weekly by The Gospel Publishing House, Springfield, Mo.

SPRINGFIELD, MO., JUNE 30, 1934
NUMBER 1055

$1.00 a year in U. S. A.
Single copies, 2 cents

The National Restoration of the Jews

By R. H. Boughton

ON this page there appears a photograph of the flag of Palestine which is seen flying from the all-Jewish manned trading schooner *Emmanuel.* The vessel is said to be the first vessel to sail under a Palestine flag for some 2,000 years. Has a new national flag of Palestine any significance to prophetic students today? We think it has.

Dispersed, but not Destroyed

For centuries now the Jews have been dispersed among the nations, but, like Jonah in the stomach of the whale, they remain unassimilated. The nations will never be comfortable—nor the Jews themselves, until they have been cast out from their unpleasant quarters on to the shores of their own native land; then the whale (the nations) will have peace, and Jonah (the Jews) will have prosperity in their God-given ministry.

Identity Preserved

For hundreds of years, the Jew has been without any corporate national existence, without a national center, a capital, government or flag; yet in spite of this, he has not lost his identity. A stroll through New York City provides an eloquent eulogy of the truth of the Scriptures regarding God's chosen people Israel, to whom was committed the sacred oracles, the testimony of Jehovah's unity, and in

whom was revealed the pattern of His redemptive plan for all mankind.

Their Land Desolated

At the time of the destruction of the Temple by Titus in A. D. 70 (within forty years of their cry regarding the crucifixion of their Messiah, "His blood be upon us and on our children"), 1,000,000 perished within Jerusalem; and in A.D. 135, another 580,000 of them were massacred by the Roman power. In this manner were they "rooted out of their land in anger and in wrath and in great indignation" (Deut. 29:28), and their cities laid waste. Their forests were ruined for the purposes of the siege (Isa. 6:11).

The Jewish national flag on the all-Jewish schooner, Emmanuel.

Suffering Divine Judgments

The Jewish prayer book contains the following prayer: "From then until now we have been killed, slaughtered, butchered; we have been left a small number, stepped upon, kicked and bitten and lonely, robbed and wounded, distressed and soiled with the dirt of earth, rejected and forsaken, torn by lions and bears, broken to pieces by ravenous beasts." They have found "no rest for the sole of their feet." Deut. 28:65. Banished from one country to another, buffeted hither and thither by the battering waves of natural hatred, and driven this way and that by the biting winds of blustering persecution; subjected to the fearful embrace of the "Iron Maiden" of the Spanish Inquisition (a hollow figure of a woman made of iron, and studded within w i t h spikes, in which the victims were enclosed, and embraced in its deadly arms till death intervened); the rack, burnings, unspeakable tortures and ignominies heaped upon them, fulfilling in a remarkable degree the judgments prophesied in D e u t. 28:15-68 (which read). This chapter contains a specific history of amazing detail and accuracy which has had a detailed fulfillment in the history of Israel through the years.

(Cont'd on Page Three)

Pentecostal Evangel, *June 30, 1934.*

Pentecostal fellowship in Jordan. In 1933 she prophesied under the power of the Holy Spirit that Israel would become a nation in 1948. The source of this information is Ron Banuk in California who is doing ongoing research on the things both orally declared and those written by Om Saleem, part of which record was kept by a Pentecostal missionary, Roy Whitman (1904-1992) who was the pastor of Om Saleem. Ron Banuk met and talked with Whitman on two occasions and thus learned of the visions and prophecies of Om Saleem.

In 1905, at the age of 12, Hannah Elias Aghaby, who later became known as Om Saleem, met a Methodist minister, General William Booth, founder of the Salvation Army, who led her to Christ. Later she married, and had a son named Saleem. She was thereafter commonly called Om Saleem (mother of Saleem) as his father was known as Abu Saleem.

PENTECOSTAL MISSIONS IN SALT AND AMMAN, JORDAN

In 1927, Assemblies of God missionaries, Laura Radford and Elizabeth Brown started a work in Salt, near Amman, Jordan. They were assisted by Roy Whitman, son of an American missionary in the Belgian Congo. Also an Egyptian Pentecostal evangelist, Barnaba Nos was used of God to bring revival to the congregation. Whitman opened a new work in Amman, and Om Saleem became a part of that congregation. The work was difficult, and there was no spirit of revival until 1933 when God gave marvelous visions to Om Saleem. This blessed the Assembly of God congregation and revival broke out in Amman. The Assemblies of God has a significant work there to this day.

Banuk deduces that the purpose of the visions were to provide the "indigenous spiritual infrastructure for a sanctuary the Jews would need during the Tribulation." Banuk cites a book *Signs and Wonders in Rabbath-Amman* by Pastor Roy Whitman for documentation. Whitman, who was a pastor of the mission in Amman, assisted Om Saleem in writing down her prophecies.

Banuk has access to photostats of these Arab language documents, and translation into English is taking place. Om Saleem also prophesied that the Jews would rebuild their temple in Jerusalem. There are some strange aspects to the Om Saleem story, and I think the prophecies are less than perfect, flawed in some details but as Banuk says, the whole saga is not yet known. There are areas where the predictions show great accuracy. Our vision of the future does not rest on such personal prophecies, but they are interesting and perhaps helpful if they do not in any way contradict the Bible.

JEWS OWN THE LAND

"The current controversy over territorial rights in Palestine is not new. This question has been disputed for over 3,000 years.

"In 1963 B.C. (Usher chronology) God appeared to Abraham . . . God said, "Unto thy seed will I give this land for an everlasting possession. . . ."[8]

The question of who rightfully owns the land of Israel is perennial. One who believes the Bible has no problem figuring it out that the Jewish people have a right to the land.

In 1967 Rev. Ralph M. Riggs, a former Assemblies of God General Superintendent, wrote an article *Who is the Rightful Owner of Palestine?*. The article was published in the *Pentecostal Evangel*. In this article he asserts the rightful Jewish ownership of the land of Israel.[9]

The *Pentecostal Evangel* for July 9, 1967, and August 20, 1967, expressed the belief that Israel's temple would be rebuilt in fulfillment of prophecy. Recent articles in the *Pentecostal Evangel* have indicated an ongoing interest and belief in the prophetic destiny of Israel.

OH! CANADA — HOW IT ALL BEGAN

Since ancient times we have witnessed Spirit-led men and women of God being in exactly the right place at the right moment to be used of God to bring His divine purposes to pass.

From out of the North came William Hull, a Canadian Pentecostal pastor, called of God to live in Jerusalem. The year was 1947. UNSCOP, (The United Nations Special

Ivan C. Rand, Canadian supreme court justice, who was a prime force in UNSCOP, bringing Israel into existence in 1948.

Committee on Palestine) was deliberating the partition plan which would provide for the division of British mandated Palestine into a state for the Jews and a state for the Arabs. I met William Hull, who was living in Victoria, Ontario in the years of his retirement. He told me the story of how God used him to influence Canadian Supreme Court Justice Ivan Rand. Rand was a member of UNSCOP, then meeting in Kadimah House, in virtual seclusion.

However, UNSCOP held some meetings in the Jerusalem YMCA which were open to the public. They were sort of an open forum. Pastor Hull managed to get to Rand during an intermission, at which time he invited Rand to dinner. Rand accepted immediately and later they dined at the Eden Hotel. Hull wrote in his book *The Fall and Rise of Israel*, "Canada had played a large part in the UNSCOP decision (which brought the new state of Israel into existence). Judge Rand inspired, supervised, and shaped the drafting of the plan, and then his determination and fair play saw it through. The inscrutable Justice Rand was compelled to reveal how deeply he had been stirred by what he had seen and heard in Palestine and what a tremendous impression Jewish enterprise and courage and faith had made upon him."[10]

As they sat at dinner in the Eden Hotel, Rand fired a salvo of questions at Pastor Hull, expressing to him how deeply he appreciated being able to talk to a Canadian clergyman who could give him a biblical perspective as well as a contemporary view of Israel and the Palestine situation. He confessed that his knowledge of the situation in Palestine was somewhat lacking. UNSCOP signed its final report at 11:00 P.M. on August 31, 1947.

Opposition to the partition plan was great and debate had been fierce. Nevertheless, three months later on November 29, 1947, after long debate the General Assembly of the United Nations mustered a two thirds vote in favor of the partition plan and the establishing of Israel's sovereign nationhood. Rand was the strongest pro-Israel voice in UNSCOP, as numerous historians have recorded. We think that the strongest influence on Rand was the biblical witness of Rev. William Hull, a Pentecostal believer.

In the book *State in the Making* by David Horowitz the author writes, "It may be said that Canada, more than any other country, played a decisive part in all stages of the U.N.O. discussions of Palestine. The activities of Lester Pearson and his fellow delegates were a fitting climax to Justice Rand's beneficent work on UNSCOP."[11]

Pastor Hull told me the story of how God used him, a Pentecostal pastor, to sow the seed of God's Word about Israel into the heart and mind of Canadian Supreme Court Justice Ivan C. Rand, humbly thanking God for being assigned to this sublime task. Hull would often start his story with "It all began. . . ." Not a vain or boastful man, he was always giving glory to God for putting him into strategic contact with Rand at just the most opportune moment of history.

Skeptics abound. Some ridiculed Hull, imagining that his claims were the wishful thinking of an old man who embellished his role at the crossroads of history. Sorry, skeptic, for Justice Rand himself wrote glowingly of the influence that Pastor Hull had upon his thinking.

Rand wrote in a forward to one of Hull's books: "When in June 1947, as a member of UNSCOP, I first set foot in Palestine, I was indeed a stranger in a strange land. . . . What, in such circumstances, one seeks is a vantage point from which to view the issues freed so far as possible from the vapors of partisanship."

Rand continued, "It was a relief, then, when shortly after my arrival I had the good fortune to meet Rev. William Hull. Here he was, a Canadian, clergyman who for years had been carrying on a mission in Jerusalem, who was, I saw at once a man of good will. . . . Here, I thought was one whom I could trust to express himself with honesty and frankness.

"Somewhat to my surprise, I listened to words of high admiration for the Jewish people, their standards of life and the tremendous work they had done since returning to their ancient homeland. . . . The controversy at once appeared unclouded by irrelevancies and shadowy prejudices and became one for decisions in the light of subtle appreciations and comprehensive understandings. Mr. Hull knew nothing of the effect of that luncheon talk until this forward had been perused by him, but I feel confident that he will count that day as not having been without its fitting deed."[12] And so, "It all began. . . ." How easily God has an obedient, Spirit filled messenger at the crossroads of time and destiny. Israel became a nation.

Pastor Hull lived into his 90s and only recently passed on to his eternal reward. I should think that when we renew our acquaintance upon that golden shore we will feel humble in the presence of this man of God who allowed the Spirit of the Lord to guide him to the right place and action at the precise moment of destiny. Israel — thus it all began. We pay tribute to brother William Hull, a man of God, a Pentecostal pastor.

In a previous chapter I shared a bit of my own story with you, how as a boy of 10 years I accepted Christ, then at the age of 11 I heard a

German evangelist teach about the Jewish people. Reverend Bretschneider told us that the Jews would return to Palestine. It seemed so unlikely in 1943 that people in our little village mocked him for his belief. But God reached my heart and there was born in me a love for the Jewish people.

When I began my evangelistic, Bible teaching ministry in June 1954, speaking about Israel became the major theme. It was not until 1968 that I first traveled to Israel. At that time God opened the windows of heaven. I was caught up into the mainstream of prophetic fulfillment, met some leaders of Israel, fell in love with the land and the people.

How my heart is blessed now that my oldest daughter, Rebecca, and son-in-law, Thomas, live and work in Jerusalem. We take our grandchildren there and God is sowing precious seed in their lives.

In 1969 the late Rev. Zeev Kaufsman, a Jewish Christian, pastor of Messianic Assembly on Gershon Agron Street in West (new) Jerusalem laid hands on me and prophesied that I was called to be an ambassador to his beloved country of Israel. I was also called to be an ambassador for Israel to the churches. This was simply a confirmation of what God had already put into my heart. Kaufsman prophesied that I would meet with the leaders of the land and that new doors would be opened. Since then we have met with many leaders of Israel, spoken in yeshivas and synagogues, conferred on 15 occasions with Prime Minister Menachem Begin, seven times with Prime Minister Yitzhak Shamir, on various occasions with the presidents of Israel, and with many ambassadors.

CHRISTIANS UNITED FOR ISRAEL

In 1975 we launched Christians United for Israel. With about 100 colleagues we stood in front of President Gerald Ford's White House under a banner that read, "Christians United For the Biblical Right of Israel to Its Land." A few of us were asked to come into the Old Executive Office Building at the White House to confer with Robert Oakley for an hour. He was one of Ford's Mid-East experts. We gave him a letter that was hand delivered to Gerald Ford. That meeting in Lafayette Park created shock waves that are still being felt.

As mentioned before, in 1978 we participated in sponsoring an historic meeting at the Hyatt Regency Hotel in Washington, DC where we launched The National Christian Leadership Conference for Israel. As an interdenominational umbrella for Christian pro-Israel leaders NCLCI has no creed but the one idea that Israel has a divine right to exist in secure and defensible borders. On that basis alone do we find our agreement and basis for action. Outside of the conference room and the arena of public action, we each walk our own path in our respective churches.

UNITED STATES HOLOCAUST MEMORIAL COUNCIL, CHURCH RELATIONS COMMITTEE

I was selected to serve on the Church Relations Committee of the United States Holocaust Memorial Council, a congressional committee in the private sector. It has been my privilege to participate in the planning of the Holocaust Museum on the Capital Mall in Washington, DC, near the Smithsonian and next to the Bureau of Engraving. The museum is now open to the public. To visit it is an incredible experience. We thought most people would spend an hour in the museum, but find that most are spending three hours or more. Of the 12 members of the Church Relations Committee, USHMC, I solely represent the Pentecostal and Evangelical communities. I humbly thank God for the privilege to serve in this capacity. It has been rewarding.

Thus my own life is a further witness of the Pentecostal connection to God's earthly Zion — Israel. Why did God pick out a little ragamuffin boy from the poorest of families and send him on a continuous mission around the world? I can only say that I am grateful that He has chosen to use me in His service. I could not begin to name

The Holocaust Museum, Washington, DC.

the host of pastors and leaders in the churches with whom we have joined hands in this great work. The Assemblies of God abounds with true friends of Israel and the Jewish people. Currently we are working on a worldwide directory of organizations, publications, churches, and leaders who support Israel in the Evangelical, Pentecostal, and Fundamentalist churches. It is a much bigger task than we ever envisioned. If your organization should be listed, please let us know.

AN UNENDING ACCOUNT

Time and energy would fail us to tell the whole story of Pentecostals, Evangelicals, and their bond to Israel. It would take a huge volume to contain the account. How can I not mention former District Superintendent Rev. Earl Young of the Western Ontario District of the Pentecostal Assemblies of Canada? We had a part in inspiring and encouraging him to take his annual district council to Jerusalem. About 800 pastors and spouses went to Jerusalem with him. He set a wonderful example for Christian leaders everywhere.

The late Richard Champion, former editor of the *Pentecostal Evangel*, recognized as a friend of Israel, was selected by the Israeli Government to represent the interests of Pentecostals on a government sponsored VIP journalist's tour of Israel. Champion was known to be a fair minded man in matters relating to Israel and the Mid-East.

G. RAYMOND CARLSON

Former Assemblies of God General Superintendent G. Raymond Carlson, a man truly full of grace, proved to have an open heart toward Israel. His love for the Jewish people is genuine. He allowed me to bring in Rabbi James Rudin of the American Jewish Committee for dialogue with top leaders of the Assemblies. Later it was Amnon Linn-Lipzen from the Israeli Chicago Consulate who came at our invitation and conferred with Superintendent Carlson; Assistant Superintendent Everett Stenhouse; Richard Champion, editor of the *Pentecostal Evangel;* Dr. Zenas Bicket, president of the Berean College; Loren Triplet, head of the Department of Foreign Missions; and National Secretary Joseph Flower. A warm and lively exchange took place for over two hours. Frank questions were asked and frank answers given. Shortly after this meeting Reverend Carlson went on his first trip to the Holy Land, as an honored guest of the Israeli government.

NEW LEADERSHIP, RENEWED VISION

New leadership in the Assemblies of God was elected in recent months. We are encouraged as we report that these men have the same historic vision for Israel that our church has traditionally known. In recent conversation with Rev. Thomas Trask, our new general superintendent, and with James K. Bridges, our new general treasurer, I found a high level of interest and sympathy with our cause.

JAN WILLEM VAN DER HOEVEN, ICEJ, FEAST OF TABERNACLES

Prior to the election of the new officials we had invited Ambassador Jan Willem van der Hoeven to come to Springfield. This Pentecostal Dutchman, representing the International Christian Embassy of Jerusalem, met at a breakfast meeting with the above listed brethren plus Rev. Tom Trask, who was then the national treasurer for the Assemblies (now the general superintendent), and possibly others. How van der Hoeven challenged us! His fervent spirit kindled a flame in our hearts. When he was through, Brother Stenhouse warmly responded, "Jan Willem, if you are about to give the altar call I am ready to respond!" Thus do anointed Pentecostal leaders respond to representatives of the Jewish people and to Israel. This warm benevolence is reflected in our local congregations.

Each year there is a Christian Celebration of the Feast of Tabernacles in Jerusalem. In 1992 6,000 Christians from 86 nations came to Jerusalem for the feast. It is estimated that 85 percent of them were Pentecostals and Charismatics. The atmosphere was most definitely Pentecostal, as is the leadership of the International Christian Embassy, sponsor of the event. You should have been with us in the

Barry Hitchcock and Raymond Bowerman carry the CUFI banner in the Jerusalem parade.

great Jerusalem Day Parade, marching with about 15,000 Israelis and 4,000 Christians. See our Scripture banners! See the posters, the costumes. Listen to our voices singing the glad songs of David and Zion. Come with us to the Feast of Tabernacles. Your life will be enriched.

In 1961 the World Conference of Pentecostal Churches met in Jerusalem. The Israeli government struck a special 59mm bronze medallion to honor the Pentecostal convention. A medallion was presented to each of the delegates. The reverse side of the medallion shows an emblem of the Pentecostal Fellowship — a wreath of leaves and plants, the Star of David in the center. Beneath the emblem is a quotation from Isaiah in English: "For out of Zion shall go — the law and the word of the Lord from Jerusalem" (Isa. 2:3). The words "Zion" and "Jerusalem" are in Hebrew.

It has been said that a majority of the pro-Israel Christian groups are headed up by Pentecostal leadership. With no thought of minimizing the efforts of other Evangelicals, I must say that it is my perception that this could be true. Time and space would fail if I tried to list all the Pentecostal leaders like Dan Betzer, Frank Eiklor, Mark Gentry, Jess Gibson, John Hagee, Bobbi Hromas, Robert Johnson, Elmer Josephson, Timothy King, Johann Luckhoff, Joan McWhirter, George Morrison, Jay Rawlings, Ivan Rogers, Jerry Rose, Gwen Shaw, Cary Summers, Hilton Sutton, Ed Thompson, Clarence Wagoner, Merv and Merla Watson, Bill Wolford, and literally hundreds of other pastors and church leaders who are not only sympathetic toward Israel, but active in her cause.

1961 Israeli Medallion, struck for the World Conference of Pentecostal Churches

Reverse side of the medallion, with emblem and Isaiah quotation.

DANGER OF THEOLOGICAL ANTI-SEMITISM

The danger of wrong interpretation of the Bible in relationship to Israel is two-fold. First of all if we refuse to believe what the Bible says we introduce a doctrinal and theological anarchy into the Word of God. Every person becomes a law unto himself or herself. Nothing means anything for sure under this allegorical method. If it is not literal in Luke 1 then why should I take anything literally? I can twist any passage to make it mean what I want it to mean. The Bible is a big book and if you ignore its entire context you can select a line here and there and prove any preconceived notion you may have.

THE 1945 GENERAL COUNCIL — STAND AGAINST ANTI-SEMITISM

The minutes for the 1945 General Council of the Assemblies of God show the brethren and sisters of the fellowship standing guard on the ramparts, ever vigilant to oppose the forces of evil. The resolution against hatred of the Jews reads:

Anti-Semitism

WHEREAS, We have witnessed in this generation an almost universal increase in anti-Semitism and this has resulted in the greatest series of persecutions perpetrated in modern times, and

WHEREAS, Even in the United States of America there has been an alarming increase in anti-Semitism;

THEREFORE BE IT RESOLVED, That the General Council hereby declare its opposition to anti-Semitism and that it disapprove of the ministers of the Assemblies of God identifying themselves with those who are engaged in this propaganda.

BE IT FURTHER RESOLVED, That the editor of publications be instructed to prepare an article including Section I of this resolution in which our position on anti-Semitism is set forth, and that it be published in the Pentecostal Evangel.[13]

From the minutes of the 1945 General Council of the Assemblies of God, p. 38. The resolution was passed and the *Pentecostal Evangel* carried the designated article.

JESUS, SAVIOUR, JEWISH MESSIAH

Of our Lord it is written "... the Lord God will give unto him the throne of his father David. And he will reign over the house of Jacob forever, and of His kingdom there will be no end" (Luke 1:32-33).

He will rule over the house of Jacob. Theologians say that there are Scripture passages which may infer that the Church is a "spiritual" Israel. That is debatable, but, for sure, *never, never, never* is the Church called Jacob. Jacob always refers to the natural seed of Israel. We former Gentiles are the wild branches grafted into Israel's olive tree, and now we are no longer aliens from the commonwealth of Israel. We share a glorious destiny with restored and redeemed natural (national) Israel. But we do not replace Israel in the economy of God.

Jesus was a Jew. Paul makes that clear in Romans 9:3: "For I could wish that myself were accursed from Christ for my brethren, my kinsmen according to the flesh: Who are Israelites; to whom pertaineth the adoption, and the glory, and the covenants, and the giving of the law, and the service of God, and the promises; Whose are the fathers, and of *whom as concerning the flesh Christ came*, who is over all, God blessed for ever. Amen." (Italics mine.)

Only one person, in the history of the world, had the privilege of choosing the circumstances of His birth, the place of His birth, who His parents would be, and of what nation He would be a member. That person was Jesus and He chose to be born in the Judean town of Bethlehem. He chose to be an Israeli. He chose to be born of a mother from the lineage of David, of the tribe of Judah.

Jesus was and is a Jew. He has now ascended to the third heaven, where He is mediator for all mankind. God, who became man, is still the perfect divine-human person (see 1 Tim. 2:5). Jesus is still a man as well as God, and He is still a Jew for He shall return as the conquering "Lion of the Tribe of Juda!" (Rev. 5:5). That is something for Christian anti-Semites to think about.

Pentecostals have always been noted as a movement of people who were willing to take a stand on vital issues. In these last days, as the world's hatred of Israel, always seething in the pagan Gentile heart, threatens to erupt, it is time to take a stand again.

Am Israel Chai! The people of Israel live. It is a fulfillment of prophecy. Israel has a right to exist in her own land. Those who know our ministry know that we work for liaison between Jewish people and Arab leaders. We want to see equity and justice for all people of the region. But we will never compromise the basic premise that Israel has a right to exist in secure borders in the land that God has given her.

Notes

[1]Wilbur Smith, *Israeli/Arab Conflict* (Glendale, CA: Gospel Light/Regal Publications, 1967/1982 8th ed.), p. 49-52.

[2]David Rausch, *Zionism Within Early American Fundamentalism, 1878-1918* (New York, NY: Edward Mellon Press, 1979).

[3]*The Weekly Evangel,* December 22, 1917.

[4]*Statement of Fundamental Truths,* article 14 (Springfield, MO: The General Council of the Assemblies of God).

[5]Louis H. Hauff, *Israel in Bible Prophecy* (Springfield, MO: Gospel Publishing House, 1961/1974), p.iii.

[6]Ron Banuk, *Om Saleem: Prophecy in 1933* (Huntington Beach, CA: Ron Banuk, 1993), p. 6.

[7]David A. Lewis, *Jerusalem Courier,* Vol. 11, No. 2, July 1993 (Springfield, MO: David A. Lewis Ministries), p. 3.

[8]Ralph M. Riggs, *The Pentecostal Evangel,* July 30, 1967, p. 7; reprinted July 11, 1976, p. 12 (Springfield, MO: Gospel Publishing House).

[9]Riggs, *The Pentecostal Evangel.*

[10]William L. Hull, *The Fall and Rise of Israel* (Grand Rapids, MI: Zondervan Publishing House, 1954/1961), p. 275.

[11]David Horowitz, *State In The Making* (New York, NY: Alfred A. Knopf, 1953).

[12]Hull, *The Fall and Rise of Israel,* p. 7

[13]*Pentecostal Evangel,* October 20, 1945, p. 4.

13

INTERNATIONAL CHRISTIAN EMBASSY — JERUSALEM

A Voice for the Church and Israel

> *Some have been given the responsibility of embarking on the voyage of healing Christian-Jewish relations. In the light of history, the Jewish people should not be expected to meet Christians halfway. Building bridges of understanding, razing walls of bitterness, is not only praiseworthy but actually is to walk with God.* — Dr. David Rausch[1]
>
> *They that sleep in the night... But let us, who are of the day, be sober, putting on the breastplate of faith and love; and for an helmet, the hope of salvation* (1 Thess. 5:7-8).

Battered through long centuries of suffering and wandering, the people of Israel returned home in 1948 to the land promised to them.

Buffeted by enemies and frequently betrayed by friends, the new nation refused to be ground into submission. The wounds of friends, however, cut deep.

Jerusalem is the eternal capital of Israel. No other nation has ever claimed Jerusalem as its capital. The three thousandth anniversary of King David making Yerushalaim the capital of United Israel will occur in 1996.

Each nation of the world has the power to select its capital city. Other nations establish peaceful relations and place their embassies in the designated capital. That is the way it works — everywhere except in Israel.

In 1980 the Israeli Knesset (Parliament) passed the Jerusalem Law which declared Jerusalem as Israel's indivisible capital. As a response of protest all 13 foreign government embassies that were in Jerusalem at the time left Jerusalem. They bowed to petrodollar blackmail and made their cowardly move to Tel Aviv.

One ray of hope, like a flickering little candle beamed light into that dark hour of Israel's despair. A little band of Christians boldly proclaimed that they represented the true attitude of millions of believing Christians throughout the world. They established the International Christian Embassy of Jerusalem on Rehov Rashba in the Holy City.

"They took a stand believing Jerusalem to be the biblical, present and future capital of Israel and the Jewish people. They also believe that Jerusalem is their spiritual capital as it is the city where Jesus ministered, died and rose again, and to which He will return. Although the ICEJ cannot claim to represent all Christians to

ICEJ opened offices in Jerusalem in 1980. They now occupy a large building at #10 Brenner Street. Ambassador Jan Willem van der Hoeven, right.

the regathered nation of Israel, it does represent those who identify with its purposes."[2]

Events since then have testified to the fact that the presumed credentials of these Jerusalem Christians are based in reality. They do represent the voice of millions of us worldwide.

While Christians United for Israel has no organizational ties to the embassy we have stood firm in our support of the concepts proclaimed by the ICEJ. We consider the embassy to be a sister organization, with common goals. Today the embassy occupies the quarters formerly occupied by the Chilean Embassy. It is located at #10 Rehov Brenner in Jerusalem, not far from the prime minister's residence. It is your embassy in the Holy Land. Did your tour leader take you there for a visit on your trip to Israel? Pastors, this is an important visit for your group and is easily arranged.

In a 1980 article in *Israel Scene Magazine* Evans Johnson wrote glowingly of the work of the recently opened Christian Embassy. Johnson quoted Jan William van der Hoeven, chief spokesperson for ICEJ: "Van der Hoeven, who believes that 'Israel is here in fulfillment of biblical prophecy' received inspiration in prayer to found the [Christian] Embassy in response to the withdrawal of 13 national embassies from Jerusalem to Tel Aviv in the face of oil blackmail.

"The opening of the embassy was timed to coincide with a conference of 'Bible-believing Christians,' which took its inspiration from Psalm 122, verses 6-9: 'Pray for the peace of Jerusalem! May they prosper who love you.' "[3]

A VISION SHARED

In 1979 while visiting with Prime Minister Begin I made a suggestion to him which could indicate that God was speaking to

Right to left: Meyer Levenon, David Lewis, Professor Rivlin, Ralph Harris. 1970.

several people about the same thing.

Before getting into this I must go back a few years and give you some background information. Then we will discuss one of our 1980 meetings with Begin.

In 1969 I told Meyer Levanon and others in Jerusalem that I believed that one day Begin would be the prime minister of Israel. Levanon laughed and told me several reasons why that was impossible. Begin was the head of Israel's smallest party, with only two seats in the Knesset. He was ruined politically because of his feud with the late David Ben Gurion. And so forth. . . .

In 1972 I met and became friends with Ben Jaffe, head of external relations for the World Zionist Organization. After that I visited the Jaffe home every time I was in Jerusalem. I mentioned my "prediction" about Begin to Benjamin on several occasions. He always smiled tolerantly, and told me how mistaken I was.

In February, 1977 Ramona and I were in the Jaffe home for dinner. I said, "Ben, you have an election coming up. This is it. Begin will be elected as your new prime minister." He knew I wasn't joking, but he could not take me seriously.

Ben chuckled and said, "David, how many times have you been in Israel, and you still don't have us figured out. No, Begin will never be elected as our prime minister."

He laughed, but Begin was elected in the spring, just a few weeks later. In September 1977, when I was back in Jerusalem, Benjamin took me to see the prime minister. He had told Begin about my "prediction" after Begin had won the election, and Begin had asked to meet me.

When we arrived at Begin's home Jaffe was visibly nervous. He and Begin were political opponents, al-

The late Benjamin Jaffe (photo taken in 1982).

though they respected each other. Ben anxiously introduced me, "Mr. Prime Minister, this is David Lewis, the man I told you prophesied your election. And I am the man who told him it was impossible!"

Begin, always the proper Swiss gentleman, stiffened visibly, then seeing the humor of the moment relaxed, put his hand on Bennie's shoulder and said, "You are both prophets. It was impossible — but here I am." Ezer Weizman, now president of Israel was there, being at that time the defense minister. Malcolm Benjamin, head of the Likud-Herut party affairs in England was there, along with a few other dignitaries. Begin chose me to sit at his right hand as the evening's guest of honor.

His first question to me was, "Are you one of the Evangelical born-again Christians?" I told him that I was. He said, "Well, you are the first one I have talked to." The Holy Spirit prompted me and I launched into a discussion about Evangelical perceptions of Jewish apocalyptic literature and why we believe that modern Israel fulfills many prophecies of the Bible. Begin was fascinated and responsive. A local TV crew was brought in to tape our conversation for later release. This was arranged by the party secretary after our conversation had begun, I believe at Begin's request.

That evening I was bold to make some suggestions to the prime minister.

I suggested that closer ties should be established between the

Meeting with Prime Minister Memechem Begin.

Evangelical community and Israel. In the following years I was able to take many Christian leaders to Menachem Begin. In fact, several outstanding Christian leaders first got to Begin because I recommended them to Harry Hurvitz, one of Begin's senior advisors. We have never told these men how they got to Prime Minister Begin.

I remember talking to Harry one day outside the prime minister's office. He mentioned the name of an internationally famous Fundamentalist television preacher who is a good friend of Israel. This person had asked for an appointment with Mr. Begin. Harry asked me, "Who is this man? We have never heard of him. Should the prime minister see him?"

My response was so quick and affirmative it surprised Harry. I told Harry that this man reached millions of Evangelical viewers on American television. He is already a friend of Israel, and meeting Begin will inspire him and strengthen him in his resolve. The pastor had an appointment that day. Later that evening he hailed me across the hotel lobby where we were both staying (he was not part of my group). The pastor said, "David, guess what, I had a meeting with the prime minister today."

I simply said, "That's wonderful." Someday when I write my memoirs you will get the details of many fascinating behind the scenes stories!

Now, back to the 1980 conversation with Prime Minister Begin. I said to him, "I think at this stage we need a house of communication,

an idea center, where Christians and Jews can come together without feeling threatened and explore the areas of our common interest (like survival in a hostile world)." I said, "What we need is a sort of Christian Embassy. Every tour group of Christians could come to such a house of information to be properly instructed as to the true nature of things in the Mid-East. This might serve to offset the lies

Johann Luckhoff, director of the International Christian Embassy of Jerusalem.

of the secular media." Begin was very enthusiastic about this idea. Later I shared it with Christian residents in Jerusalem. Little did I know that God was already speaking to Johann Luckhoff, Jan William van der Hoeven, Merv and Merla Watson, Jay and Meridel Rawlings, Joan McWhirter, Bill Wolford, and others who were among the original founders of the International Christian Embassy of Jerusalem. Evidently God had witnessed the same thing to many of us.

When I heard of the launching of the embassy I was ecstatic. What a fulfillment of my very heart's desire. God had, however, let me know that my work was primarily in America, among Christians, and I was not to have an official role in the Jerusalem Embassy. Although I have been asked to join the staff there on several occasions, I have not been released from the work in North America.

I could desire nothing more than to take up residence in Jerusalem, but for now that is not to be. Some of us have to do the work here. We had launched Christians United for Israel in 1975 and had been active long before that. Later in 1978 I became one of the original founders of the National Christian Leadership Conference for Israel, and now serve as chairman of the board for NCLCI. Bishop John Burt (Episcopal) is our president. Sister Rose Thering runs the NCLCI office in New York, and our office on Seton Hall University campus in New Jersey.

WHY BE CONCERNED?

It could be that some may be thinking, "Why should I get involved? I am not to blame for the Inquisition, the Holocaust, or current anti-Semitism." Dr. Michael Brown says that there is a principle we must not violate. We must make restitution for the past if we want our present and future to be blessed.

Brown points out that when there was a three-year famine in Israel during the reign of King David, ". . . the Lord answered, It is for Saul, and for his bloody house, because he slew the Gibeonites (2 Sam. 21:1).

> David took it upon himself to make restitution for sins he had not personally committed. David not only was not involved, he was ignorant of what had been done by Saul. Yet, the Gibeonites had to be avenged. Saul was dead. David was the only one who could do it. He had to take the responsibility upon his own shoulders. After David made amends, "God answered prayer in behalf of the land" (2 Sam. 21:14).

In the very same way, the Church will never completely see the way out of spiritual famine until it repents for shedding Jewish blood.

"But I'm not guilty!" You say. Neither was David! Yet who else could right the wrongs done to the Gibeonites by the former king of Israel if not by the present king himself? And who else can right the wrongs done to the Jewish people by the Church in former years if not the present Church itself?

"But I'm not related!" you say. "The Church that persecuted Israel wasn't the true Church." David wasn't directly related to Saul either! Yet as God's present representative, only he could repair what his carnal predecessor had done. It is the same with the Church and the Jewish people: We who are the spiritual representatives of the Lord Jesus must repair what our carnal predecessors have done in His name."[4]

EMBASSY ACTIVITIES

ICEJ has been at the forefront participating in bringing home the Russian and Ethiopian Jewish immigrants. While promoting the security of Israel, the embassy has also worked to promote understanding among Arabs as well. We love the Arab peoples and are concerned for them. And, one should not think that all Arabs are anti-

Our tour group marches in the Jerusalem parade. Over 4,000 Christians and 12,000 Israelis marched together.

Israel. The embassy has done a lot of social relief work among the Lebanese and the Palestinians.

THE FEAST OF TABERNACLES — CELEBRATION OF FAITH

One of the great activities of the embassy has been promotion of the annual Christian Celebration of the Feast of Tabernacles (Succoth). We go to the Feast to do the works of the Almighty and sing His high praises (see Ps. 150).

What pageantry! What color! What praise and worship! Truly you should see and participate at least once before the Millennium when it will be mandatory upon all the nations, as foretold by the prophet Zechariah: "And it shall come to pass, that every one that is left of all the nations which came against Jerusalem shall even go up from year to year to worship the King, the Lord of hosts, and to keep the feast of tabernacles" (Zech. 14:16).

The Feast of Tabernacles (Succoth) has a deep and, as yet, unfulfilled significance in Scripture. It was on the occasion of this Feast that King Solomon dedicated the first temple of Israel, Zerubbabel led the Jews back from Babylonian captivity and Ezra refreshed the people's memory of the Scriptures. Several biblical scholars maintain that Jesus was actually born during the Feast of Tabernacles. Looking forward in prophecy, Zechariah tells that when Messiah reigns, all

Christians from the Philadelphia Church of Iceland marching in the Jerusalem parade.

nations will come to Jerusalem to keep and rejoice in the Feast of Tabernacles. Others believe the rapture of the Church will be during the Feast. That, of course, is open to question, and is speculative.

We have participated in several of the feasts and have taken groups of Christians for the celebration. Such an anointing of God came upon the night services in the Binyanei Ha'ooma auditorium (Jerusalem's largest) that one would think he was back in the Upper Room days of early Christianity. Add to this the excitement of the praise walk down the Mount of Olives to the Western Wall, the participation of over 5,000 Christians in the annual Jerusalem March. We marched with colorful costumes, bands, banners, flags, and songs of joy.

The Feast of Tabernacles is celebrated by Jewish people annually, for a full week. The Feast, also called Succoth, falls sometime during the months of September and October. In Israel, a highlight of the Feast is the annual Jerusalem March, when tens of thousands of Israelis converge on the Holy City from all over the country. Now they are joined by thousands of Christians each year. These Christians come from over 80 nations.

Last year when the Israelis saw the Christians marching they cheered and applauded. The *Jerusalem Post* wrote: "The Christian contingents struck a surprisingly deep chord with their proclamation that Israel is not alone." We endeavor to fulfill God's command to

All over the world bands of Christians marched in behalf of the Russian Jews.

"Comfort ye my people, speak ye comfortably to Jerusalem" (Isa. 40:1-2).

One of the marchers last year told how the crowds threw flowers to the Christians, blew kisses, and shouted, "We love you!" She was overwhelmed to see tears in the eyes of several young Israeli soldiers as they read the banners proclaiming solidarity with Israel in her isolation.

Another highlight is the evening time feast in the desert at Qumran. Yet another night features the meeting under the stars in the Sultan's Pool, an outdoor natural amphitheater.

We have given you only a small idea of what goes on in Jerusalem when the Christians from many nations move in to celebrate with Israel in the great feast of rejoicing.

Sobering moments must also be remembered. When we gathered for the Mordecai Outcry, a prayer demonstration for the enslaved Soviet Jews, a heavy spirit of intercession came upon us all. Now, with the in-gathering of over a half million Russian Jews, we can rejoice and hope. ICEJ has paid for the transport of several 747 plane loads of Russian Jews to make their aliyah to the Holy Land.

MIXED EMOTIONS

I know a tough old Israeli. He is one of the founding warrior-pioneers of the State of Israel. His place in history is established. He fought in the underground before there was a state of Israel. His mild and gentle demeanor today would never lead one to think of him as a freedom fighter.

Having fought in Israel's wars for survival, and having been a member of the Irgun in the pre-state days, he has his own way of looking at things. When he looks at the Embassy's activities, he is moderately pleased, strangely drawn, and not a little puzzled. He mildly complains, "All this prayer, praising, and dancing around — what good does it do? You Christians need to get politically active if you want to help Israel."

What some may not yet perceive is that the greatest power of the universe is the power of God and it is brought into action by prayer, not politics. In an age when Christians are (rightly) becoming more politically aware and active, this may sound strange. Indeed, I have urged Christians to get involved in the political arena, to permeate our positive influence there. But we must not leave our foundation. While we constantly emphasize that "faith without works is dead," it is also true that "works without faith is dead."

BEGIN UNDERSTOOD

Most Israelis have a positive attitude toward the embassy and all the goodwill Israel can get. The late Prime Minister Menachem Begin understood the embassy and responded very positively to it. This was also true of former Prime Minister Yitzhak Shamir, with whom Mrs. Lewis and I met on seven occasions. Moshe Auman, foreign ministry; David Bar Ilon, editor of the *Jerusalem Post;* former Mayor of Jerusalem Teddy Kollek; Yehuda Levy, publisher of the *Jerusalem Post;* Yaakov Kirshen, political cartoonist *(Dry Bones)* and author of the book *Trees;* all look with favor on the embassy.

Each prime minister of Israel has spoken to the opening night crowd at the Christian Celebration of the Feast of Tabernacles, and has received standing ovations from the thousands of delegates. I remember that Begin was almost overwhelmed at the enthusiastic response he received from the Christian community.

While visiting in the home of Amnon and Tamar Gil-Ad in Jerusalem, Amnon told us that he had just been to a meeting for European travel agents in Eliat. Amnon was then working for the Ministry of Tourism in Jerusalem, and later came to America to run the North American Israel Government Tourist Office in New York.

Prime Minister Begin had spoken to the over 400 travel agents on a theme designed to promote European tourism in Israel. In the midst of his speech he paused, looked at the crowd, and said, "You may think that Israel has no friends, but I want to tell you that we have some friends that will never let us down. I am speaking of the Christian Embassy in Jerusalem and people like David Lewis with Christians United for Israel in America." It seemed out of context, birthed out of his very spirit. He paused, then went back to his prepared remarks.

MISUNDERSTANDING AND OPPOSITION

Some orthodox Jews and some Christians have misunderstood the embassy and have opposed the work of the embassy.

The orthodox Jews who oppose the embassy remember only bitter experiences with Christianity. They recall the persecutions fostered by Christians. You may argue that these persecutors of Israel were not truly born-again Christians, but to the orthodox a Christian is a Christian is a Christian. . . . They make no such fine distinctions. They read the reeking pages of history which testify that Hitler could never have succeeded had there not been a climate of theological anti-Semitism preached by both the Roman and Protestant churches of Germany. That is the fact, there is no denying it.

The Evangelicals in Germany were largely apathetic and did nothing to protest Hitler's evil persecution of the Jews. Thank God, there were always notable exceptions, like the Evangelical Ten Boom family in Holland who hid Jews from the Nazis, and like the raffish entrepreneur, Catholic Oskar Schindler who spent millions of dollars and risked his very life to rescue around 1,200 Jews.

CHRISTIANS WHO OPPOSE THE CHRISTIAN EMBASSY

A few Christian voices are raised in opposition to the embassy on two grounds. First there are those who hate the Jews and see the embassy and those of us who have a similar point of view as traitors to the cause of Christ. They do not hesitate to label us as antichrist. The scurrilous attack which some of us have endured is almost unbelievable. The embassy has born the brunt of this in Israel. We and other colleagues have endured much of it in America.

Other Christians, while not anti-Semitic, feel that we are undermining the cause of Christian missions to the Jews. Friends, there are hundreds of Christian missionaries in Israel. They are not appreciated by the Orthodox, but they are there. They are tolerated by most of the secular 80 percent of the Israeli population. ICEJ does not fight with these people. The embassy wages no war with them. Why do some of the Christian, Messianic Jews oppose us and try to manipulate us? This is not true of all the Messianic Jews, only a misguided few.

If our colleagues in the ICEJ are following what they perceive to be their calling from the Lord why should anyone object? Why resist a little handful of believers who are obedient to their heavenly vision?

If God has a plan for Israel then that calls for the survival of Israel, why shouldn't some of us cooperate actively with the purposes of God, for the preservation of Israel? God usually uses human instrumentality to bring His purposes to pass. One day you want to stand before Him and hear the words, "Well done, thou good and faithful servant," not just "well thought out. . . ." We are called to implement the plan and purposes of God. Belief without action is deception. "Be ye doers of the word and not hearers only . . ." (James 1:22).

Those who are called to witness to the Jewish people ought to be happy for the fact that God has called a few of us to simply protect and preserve them. Why shouldn't we educate the churches in their responsibility for the survival of the Jews and their little nation?

OTHER CHRISTIAN OPPONENTS

"New Age cult" exposers point out that the "New Age" movement is strongly anti-Semitic, and linked to Nazism in the past. That some of these people would hate the Jews is no surprise. But when leaders in the Evangelical "Kingdom Now" movement attack those of us who support Israel, it comes as a shock and serves us a serious warning. These are people in the Evangelical, Charismatic, and Pentecostal realms. We had better wake up and alert the Church before it is too late. Remember the Nazis could never have succeeded if the Church had not remained silent. Why not find out what your church believes about Israel, and then decide what to do.

One television preacher accused the American branches of the ICEJ of collecting and sending billions of dollars to Israel. He said, "the people [Jews], who for the most part control the money markets of the world." If it were not serious it would sound like a bad joke. The ICEJ struggles to exist. All the American branches barely maintain an office. No money is being used to "support national Israel" or to buy them weapons as this preacher claims in his book. The only financial aid is in the form of social relief, food, blankets, vitamins, mostly for elderly immigrants in need. Our principal aid is moral support which arises from our belief in the Word of God.

It is horrendous that Satan is trying to begin a new Holocaust through the Church which finds its very roots in Israel. This is not to indicate that the "Kingdom Now" movement is manipulated by the "New Age" groups. Some have indicated that this is the case, but we have no evidence.

STANDING IN THE GAP

ICEJ intends to stand in the gap and intercede for the peace of Jerusalem. They will work for implementation of the plan and purpose of God for Israel. Along with ICEJ, we do not compromise our Christian principles nor theology. We believe Jesus is our Saviour and Messiah.

We are fully aware of the controversy this brings us into with our Jewish friends, but there is a whole new non-threatening communication that is taking place. We see a merging destiny for the Church and Israel and that destiny finds its fulfillment in the Messiah and His Messianic kingdom. ICEJ and CUFI are working to build bridges of communication where none existed previously. There are areas of biblical truth yet to be explored by our theologians, but our Jewish friends may be assured, we have no hidden agenda. We are very thankful that, in general, Israeli response has been very encouraging.

Israel Scene Magazine reported:

"Christian Zionism has always been a force within Christianity," says van der Hoeven. Christians did not need to be told of the significance of Israel, but there was a great gap between belief in the Bible and active support of the Jewish state.

For Israelis, bruised by a barrage of international condemnation, the sight of Christians marching in the streets under banners that announced "Jerusalem, you are not alone" and "Pray for the peace of Jerusalem," brought an amazed and emotional response.

Jerusalem Mayor Teddy Kollek said that the opening of the embassy was 'one of the most moving ceremonies I have ever attended' after flag-bearers from 23 nations had filed past him and planted their standards in the embassy garden.

He spoke of the embassy, "Your pure, your idealistic idea that came from the bottom of your hearts," and he asserted that "Jerusalem has been strong only because of its spiritual values.

"Those embassies which left us represented only the governments," he added. "You represented the people."

Israel's Chief Rabbi Shlomo Goren blessed the Christians, saying, "After such a terrible wave of hatred against us all over the world, seeing you make this tremendous effort to come, showing your sympathy, solidarity and belief in the future of Israel, this to us is tremendous. We bless you and consider you a part of the prophetic vision spoken of by Zechariah in chapter 14. Your presence here will always remain a golden page in the book of eternity in heaven. May the Lord bless you out of Zion."

Perhaps, though, the sentiment was most aptly conveyed by Israel's former President Yitzhak Navon: "Your presence," he told the pilgrims, "has not only caused us to remember. It has caused us to be comforted."[5]

HELPFUL THOUGHTS

Our valued colleague, Dr. David A. Rausch, professor at Ashland College offers encouragement and well-suited advice to us all. In his noteworthy book *Building Bridges* David says, "The challenge is laid at our door, because Christian-Jewish relations today desperately need quality interaction, an interaction that encompasses compassion, unconditional love, respect, honesty, vulnerability, and knowledge.

"The Bible teaches that each human being is created in the image of God and as such is not to be treated as a project or an object. Human life is sacred and not to be toyed with — human beings are of infinite worth in God's sight. God's 4,000 year love affair with the Jewish people is undeniable; the contribution of Judaism and the Jewish people to Christianity is unparalleled."[6]

WE ENCOURAGE OUR FRIENDS AT ICEJ

In a most exemplary fashion the dedicated staff of volunteers and executives at ICEJ have fulfilled, to a great degree, the aspirations expressed by Dr. Rausch.

To our dear friends at ICEJ we exhort: Keep on working, praying, marching, praising, worshipping God, and celebrating the goodness of our Lord. Your witness of good deeds has done more to bring healing and has done more to atone for the sins of our blinded Christian forefathers than all the do-nothing theologians put together.

A WORD OF HOPE TO ISRAEL

I speak a loving word to Klal Yisrael: we believe, with you, that the *atchalta de geula* is near at hand. We long to participate in the Torah development of Yerushalayim Ir Hakodesh and the Bet Hamikdash on the Har Habayit. Our prayers are with you. May the Malchut Bet David be restored as described in Gemara. May each Ben Yisrael of Klal Yisrael individually and collectively receive Kadusha benefit from the Almighty, blessed be He forever. Amen.

Israel will survive. The Jewish people will survive.

Notes

[1]David A. Rausch, *Building Bridges* (Chicago, IL: Moody Press, 1988), p. 232.

[2]*Washington for Israel Summit, Program Book,* (Jerusalem: ICEJ, 1992), p. 21.

[3]Evans Johnson, *Israel Scene Magazine,* August 1981 (Jerusalem: WZO), p. 20-21.

[4]Michael L. Brown, *Our Hands Are Stained With Blood* (Shippensburg, PA: Destiny Image Publishers, 1992), p. 168.

[5]Johnson, *Israel Scene Magazine,* August 1981, p. 21.

[6]Rausch, *Building Bridges,* p. 232.

14

DR. THEODORE HERZL AND PASTOR WILLIAM HECHLER

Pioneers Who Led the Way to Zion

> How shall we sing the Lord's song in a strange land? If I forget thee, O Jerusalem, let my right hand forget her cunning. If I do not remember thee, let my tongue cleave to the roof of my mouth; if I prefer not Jerusalem above my chief joy (Ps. 137:4-6).
>
> He who enters the mystery of adhesion to God, debekut, attains equanimity, and he who has equanimity attains solitude, and from there he comes to the Holy Spirit and to prophecy. — Isaac b. Samuel of Acre, *Meriat Enayim*, 14C.

Theodore Herzl, the honored founder of modern political Zionism looked upon Christian Zionists in his time as natural allies in a common cause.

Strange and mysterious are the ways of God. Yes, He uses human instrumentality to bring His purposes to pass, but sometimes the instruments He chooses would not be those that our intelligentsia might select.

An English Evangelical clergyman, William Hechler, was a man chosen by God to fulfill a task so unusual that Hechler was thought of as a peculiar sort. He was a man of superb intellect, with great career opportunities offered him, yet he chose to follow a path not understood by his peers. Hechler is noted as one of the early Christian Zionists.

Hechler loved to study, preach, and teach Bible prophecy. His dream was for the prophecies concerning the scattered house of Israel to be fulfilled. When he heard of Theodore Herzl's Zionist dream he fastened himself to him and followed him like a shadow. A man of true humility, Hechler did nothing for self aggrandizement. He sought only the glory of God. He knew that Herzl was a vessel chosen by God for his time and for the Jewish nation.

DR. DUVERNOY'S WITNESS

No one has more eloquently told this story than Rev. Claude Duvernoy, a Christian citizen of Israel, in his remarkable book *The Prince and the Prophet*. It is the story of Herzl and Hechler. Duvernoy is a true scholar, writer, and lover of Zion, and deserves great honor for the work he has done.

In times of Herzl's deepest despair, there was Hechler with a Bible verse, a prophecy, a word of encouragement.

When Herzl could not get an audience with some European leader or

Pastor William Hechler, dressed in Middle Eastern garb, while accompanying Dr. Herzl during a visit to the Holy Land (Turkish mandate Palestine).

head of a state, there was Hechler, who curiously had a way of getting through to people, lining up appointments for Herzl.

Dr. Duvernoy notes that at first Herzl hardly knew how to take Hechler. Herzl wrote, "Hechler is at all events a curious and complicated character. He is given to pedantry, undue humility, and much pious rolling of the eyes; but on the other hand, he counsels me superbly, and with unmistakably genuine good will. He is at once shrewd and mystical, cunning and naive. So far, with respect to myself, he has backed me up in quite a wonderful way. . . . I would wish the Jews to show him a full measure of gratitude."[1]

HERZL MEMORIALIZES HECHLER IN HIS DIARIES

In his diaries Herzl makes frequent mention of his association and friendship with the English pastor. I think that it is accurate to say that Herzl mentioned William Hechler more, in his diaries, than any other person. While this is easily demonstrated by reading Herzl's diaries, few historians even make mention of Hechler.

In his diary for March 10, 1896, Herzl wrote: "The Reverend William Hechler, Chaplain of the English Embassy here, came to see me. A sympathetic, gentle fellow, with the long, gray beard of a prophet. He is enthusiastic about my solution of the Jewish question.

"He also considers my movement a 'prophetic turning-point' — which he had foretold two years before. From a prophecy in the time of Omar (637 C.E.) he had reckoned that at the end of forty-two prophetic months (total 1260 years) the Jews would get Palestine back. The figure he arrived at was 1897-98." (Zionism was founded by Herzl in 1897 — Ed.) "When he had read my book he ran at once to Ambassador Monson and said: 'The prophesied movement is here.' "

On March 17 the diaries recorded the fact that Herzl was examined by a doctor and his heart was found to have been affected by all the excitement.

"This Dr. Beck does not know that I am taken up with the Jewish affair; neither do his friends, the Jews among whom he moves."

Herzl made note of the fact that Hechler was often instrumental in getting him appointments to see influential people. Hechler traveled with Herzl on many occasions, or went ahead to make whatever contacts he could. On April 21, 1896, Herzl writes in his diary:

> I wanted to go to Pest tomorrow. Late in the evening I got Hechler's call to Karlsruhe. Strange day, de Hirsch dies and I enter into relation with princes. A new book opens in the Jewish matter. . . .

April 23, 1896. "Arrived here eleven o'clock last night. Hechler met me at the station. He told me the circumstances. The Grand Duke had received him at once, when he arrived, but wanted first to have in hand the report of the councilmen on the Judenstaat.

Hechler showed the Grand Duke the Prophetic Tables — which, it appeared, made an impression. . . .

But he was much more fortunate with the Grand Duke. He was admitted to him several times. The Grand Duke spoke of his dead son, Ludwig, whose tutor Hechler had been, and wept bitterly. Hechler comforted him, and read him a Psalm in which the word Zion occurs.

Then the Grand Duke let him speak further. The Duke's chief fear was that if he went in on the plan it might be falsely interpreted. It might be said of him that

David Allen Lewis. "One of my prized possessions. . . ."

he was driving the Jews out of his country. Also he was pulled up by my position as a journalist. Hechler guaranteed that nothing would appear in the papers.

Then the Grand Duke asked what it was that he could do.

Hechler answered: "Your majesty was the first among the German princes at the gathering in Versailles to call King Wilhelm Kaiser. If now you would only participate also in the second great state-founding of the century. For the Jews will become a grand nation."

Dined with Hechler. He had brought his orders with him and was more excited than I. . . .

Hechler, in excellent mood, said: "Mark this beautiful day, this gentle spring sky over Karlsruhe! Perhaps one year from to-day we shall be in Jerusalem." Hechler said he would ask the Grand Duke to accompany the Kaiser next year to the dedication of the Church of Jerusalem. I was to be there too, and Hechler would go along as the scientific companion of the Grand Duke.

Thus did Reverend William Hechler, Evangelical clergyman and early Christian Zionist make his way to the Holy Land with Theodore Herzl, founder of political Zionism. Is it therefore to be thought strange if Christians today once again join hands with Jewish friends in common cause?

A TREASURE

One of my prized possessions is a rare memorial book about Theodore Herzl printed in 1929. On page 189 there is a record of the words Herzl delivered to the Second Zionist Congress, on the subject of Christian Zionism. Some Jewish leaders frowned on Herzl's affinity for Pastor William Hechler. Herzl replied to them.

It is not through paltry consideration of expediency that we clasp the hands so amicably held out to us, for they show above all that there is a conciliatory force inherent in Zionism. Thoughts free from hatred flourish in this soil. We hold inviolably to our Jewishness, and nevertheless gain nobly disinterested friends. Is that so bad? They say that we create new differences, and yet we bring people nearer to one another by a negligible effort, without the use of artifices. We show ourselves as we are — we simply tell the truth.[2]

DR. DUVERNOY'S TRIBUTE

Moving words penned by Dr. Duvernoy provide better words than I can find to conclude this treatise on the *Prince and the Prophet:*

> William Hechler, you left this world when I was a little boy. But the same Lord calls us all, beyond times and moments, nations and languages, dogmas and traditions.
>
> You have preceded us — have shown us the way, having become an old master, a friend. We understand you well, beyond words. We are enlisted in the same fight, charmed by the same Jerusalem, loving the same Zion; it is the same Spirit that guides us.
>
>  Flames devoured your touching studies and humble writings more than thirty years ago. But they did not destroy the hope of your prince and yourself — they have not destroyed Israel. They did not and cannot efface the Messianic frontiers of the motherland of the Israel of God.
>
> Old master, you died in the solitude and poverty of the true servants of God 26

Dr. Claude Duvernoy speaking at the First International Christian Zionist Congress in Basel, Switzerland.

years after your prince, who reposes on a high hill in Jerusalem which bears his name. We know the text of your last message to your Jewish brethren by heart . . . and to your Christian brethren.[3]

Dr. Claude Duvernoy sums up what he envisions would be Pastor William Hechler's words to the Church today:

> My name is not important. At the hour of my death who among you remembers me? It is not customary in the Church to remember and love those who love Zion and its people. . . .
> Try not to abandon Israel when she will stand alone, surrounded by enemies, toiling in the desert, overwhelmed by the crushing task of receiving her

Theodore Herzl, founder of modern Zionist movement, 1897.

children from the four corners of the world.[4]

"For God will save Zion, and will build the cities of Judah: that they may dwell there, and have it in possession" (Ps. 69:35).

"The Lord also shall roar out of Zion, and utter his voice from Jerusalem; and the heavens and the earth shall shake: but the Lord will be the hope of his people, and the strength of the children of Israel" (Joel 3:16).

"To appoint unto them that mourn in Zion, to give unto them beauty for ashes, the oil of joy for mourning, the garment of praise for the spirit of heaviness; that they might be called trees of righteousness, the planting of the Lord, that he might be glorified" (Isa. 61:3).

Notes

[1]Claude Duvernoy, *The Prince and the Prophet* (Jerusalem: Francis Naber; c: Duvernoy, 1979), p.43.
[2]M.W. Weisgal, Ed., *Theodore Herzl — A Memorial* (New York, NY: The New Palestine Press, 1929), p. 189.
[3]Duvernoy, *The Prince and the Prophet,* p. 122.
[4]Duvernoy, *The Prince and the Prophet,* p. 123.

15

THE UNBREAKABLE CONTRACT

Father Abraham and His Sons and Daughters

> *My covenant will I not break, nor alter the thing that is gone out of my lips* (Ps. 89:34).
> *The distinctive difference between the Noahic Covenant and the Abrahamic Covenant is that the bilateral, conditional quality of the Mosaic Covenant is lacking.* — R. Russell Bixler[1]

Abraham was commanded by God to leave Ur of the Chaldees and make his way to a land that would be shown to him. That new land was to be the possession of Abraham's promised descendants by the decree of the Almighty. "And I will give unto thee, and to thy seed after thee, the land wherein thou art a stranger, all the land of Canaan, for an everlasting possession; and I will be their God" (Gen. 17:8).

Abraham, out of step with the purposes of God, had a son by Hagar, a mistress. The son's name was Ishmael, but he was not the promised seed.

When he was 100 years old, and the promise of a son still had not materialized, God reconfirmed the promise, telling Abraham that

Sarah would yet have a son. His response was almost predictable: "Then Abraham fell upon his face, and laughed, and said in his heart, Shall a child be born unto him that is an hundred years old? and shall Sarah, that is ninety years old, bear?" (Gen. 17:17).

Nevertheless Isaac was born. Born to be the promised seed to whose descendants the land would be bequeathed.

Isaac had twin sons, Esau and Jacob. Although Jacob was the younger, he was chosen, by divine revelation to be the next in the line of promised seed and inheritor of the land. Jacob's name was changed to Israel and he in turn had 12 sons. That was the beginning of the Israel nation.

"Then will I remember my covenant with Jacob, and also my covenant with Isaac, and also my covenant with Abraham will I remember; and *I will remember the land*" (Lev. 26:42; emphasis mine).

THE COVENANT OF THE LAND

The idea of a land promised to the seed of Abraham through the line of Isaac and Jacob (Israel) was proposed by God himself and confirmed in an unconditional, unilateral covenant with His servant Abraham.

Enemies of Zion, replacement theologians, Kingdom Now advocates, and Dominionists scoffingly ask, "Since when is God in the Real Estate business?" Since Genesis 1:1, which describes the greatest land transaction in history. God created the physical universe and He has an ongoing interest in His real estate holdings. His final intentions for a restored new heaven and new earth are stated in the last book of the Bible. God has a vested interest in Eretz Israel, and He is not going to lose His property!

"In the same day the Lord made a covenant with Abram, saying, Unto thy seed have I given this land" (Gen. 15:18).

If God should break His solemn promise to Abraham, how can Christians be sure that God will not break the New Covenant, which assures the basis of our salvation?

THE COVENANT IS LITERAL, NOT FIGURATIVE

The biblical declarations relating to the Abrahamic and other covenants are meant to be understood literally, not to be spiritualized or allegorized. One of the greatest works on premillennialism is *The Theocratic Kingdom* (three volumes) by a nineteenth century Lutheran pastor and scholar, George N. H. Peters.

No one can be considered a serious eschatologist or prophecy teacher without being familiar with Peters' work.

Peters wrote, "In all earthly transactions, when a promise, agreement, or contract is entered into by which one party gives a promise of value to another, it is *universally* the custom to explain such a relationship and its promises *by the well-known laws of language* contained in our grammars or in common usage. It would be regarded absurd and trifling to view them in any other light . . . the very nature of a covenant demands, that it should be so worded, so plainly expressed, that it conveys *a decisive meaning,* and not a hidden or mystical one that requires many centuries to revolve in order to develop."[2]

God has intentions toward Israel, and He means to keep His promise regardless of what Israel or the Gentiles do. "Thus saith the Lord; If my covenant be not with day and night, and if I have not appointed the ordinances of heaven and earth; Then will I cast away the seed of Jacob, and David my servant, so that I will not take any of his seed to be rulers over the seed of Abraham, Isaac, and Jacob: for I will cause their captivity to return, and have mercy on them" (Jer. 33:25-26).

COVENANTS — CONDITIONAL AND UNCONDITIONAL

A covenant is a contract or agreement. A unilateral covenant is one that proceeds from one party only in the contract. It is unconditional because no response is required from the second party of the contract to assure fulfillment of the agreement.

A unilateral, unconditional covenant always depicts the sovereign determination of God, which He simply announces to mankind, letting man know what He plans to do — regardless of what we do or do not do.

Eschatologist J. Dwight Pentecost correctly assesses the importance of understanding God's covenant relationships to humanity as relates to biblical interpretation and eschatology (prophecy). He writes, "The covenants contained in the Scriptures are of primary importance to the interpreter of the Word and to the student of Eschatology. . . . These covenants must be studied diligently. . . ."[3]

God has made several covenants with mankind, more than one of which are in force today. For example, the Noahic Covenant, after the great flood, is God's agreement that He would never again destroy the whole earth in another universal flood. He set His rainbow in the clouds as a testimony to that contract. It was a unilateral covenant in that it was not initiated by man, nor was man's agreement required to keep it in force. It entirely proceeded from the sovereign will of God. It still endures, inviolable.

As Bixler says, "God did not say to Noah, 'If you and your descendants behave yourselves, I will never again destroy the earth by water.' He simply made an unconditional, unilateral commitment in which the full burden of fulfillment remained upon himself. Only God — the Superior Party — was bound by this pledge. . . . Noah had no more responsibility for fulfilling any aspect of the Covenant than he had the responsibility for placing the rainbow in the sky."[4]

BEING CHOSEN BEARS A PRICE

Being the chosen people has cost the Jewish people a lot. Many today are in bitterness and reject their own spiritual roots. However, the future is good. In *The Greatness of the Kingdom* Alva J. McClain declares, "Through all the bitter prophecies of judgment uttered against Israel, there is never the slightest intimation that God's covenant with Israel can be broken or ultimately fail. Men may fail, but Jehovah never fails in His purposes: 'For I am the Lord, He says, 'I change not; therefore ye sons of Jacob are not consumed' (Mal. 3:6)."[5]

Some replacement theologians confuse the covenants which are conditional and those which are unconditional. But they are right when they point out the obvious fact that covenants may have conditional clauses regarding blessing from the Lord for individuals.

A further comment by Pentecost is appropriate: ". . . it should be observed that an unconditional covenant, which binds the one making the covenant to a certain course of action, may have blessings attached to that covenant that are conditioned upon the response of the recipient of the covenant, which blessings grow out of the original covenant, *but these conditioned blessings do not change the unconditional character of that covenant.* The failure to observe that an unconditional covenant may have certain conditional blessings attached to it had led many to the position that conditioned blessings necessitate a conditional covenant, *thus perverting the essential nature of Israel's determinative covenants.* "[6] (Emphasis mine.)

Some covenants are conditional. The Sinai Covenant with Moses and the children of Israel was a salvation covenant and was conditional. God says over and over, "If you will do certain things, then I will do certain things." Most conservative Christian scholars agree that the Mosaic Covenant and the New Covenant are also conditional.

These are redemption covenants. Salvation is afforded to those who will to receive it: "And it shall come to pass, that whosoever shall call on the name of the Lord shall be saved" (Acts 2:21; also see Rev. 22:17).

God is still in covenant with national Israel (the physical seed of Abraham through Jacob). This does not mean that a Jew is saved because they are Jewish. Salvation has always been a personal matter between the individual and God. But God is in covenant with Israel through the Abrahamic Covenant. He has purposes to fulfill in Israel, therefore He will not allow the destruction of His chosen people. They will possess the promised land. No other nation in the world is given such an unconditional promise. Only Israel.

The covenant with Abraham is unilateral (comes from one side only) because Abraham did not propose it nor was any act of obedience on his part required to enforce it. Abraham obeyed God in leaving Ur of the Chaldees before the covenant was announced to him by God (see Gen. 12,15). When God confirmed the covenant, with the promise of the land (see Gen. 15), He put Abraham into a deep sleep. God wanted it understood that the agreement proceeded entirely from His side. Its fulfillment will be because of God's determination, regardless of what man does or does not do.

"For my name's sake will I defer mine anger, and for my praise will I refrain for thee, that I cut thee not off. Behold, I have refined thee, but not with silver; I have chosen thee in the furnace of affliction. For mine own sake, even for mine own sake, will I do it: for how should my name be polluted? and I will not give my glory unto another. Hearken unto me, O Jacob and Israel, my called; I am he; I am the first, I also am the last" (Isa. 48:9-12; also read Ezek. 36:21-24; Amos 9:14-15).

BIBLE BELIEVERS RECOGNIZE THE COVENANT WITH ISRAEL

The evangelical world had been preaching this since the 1600s when Increase Mather, first president of Harvard College, wrote *The Mystery of Israel's Salvation* in 1669, the first of many books and tracts on prophecy. He wrote that there was no doubt the Jews would return to the land of their fathers.

Dr. Elhanan Winchester wrote in 1800 that "The return of the Jews to their own land is certain." In 1852 a Reverend Bickersteth wrote *The Restoration of the Jews to Their Own Land*.

Inspired by the Evangelical climate in the land, England's

Balfour Declaration in 1917 had given hope to the Jews that they would be restored to the land.

In 1918 Dr. David Baron wrote in great detail about the coming return of the Jews to the land.

During the early 1900s Christian Fundamentalists were conducting prophecy conferences in New York, Chicago, London, and other cities. There was always major emphasis on the Jewish nation. Dr. David Rausch has extensively documented this phenomenon.

ISAAC IS THE PROMISED SEED

Once in a while persons who are not well informed about what the Bible really says will exclaim, "But Ishmael, the father of the Arabs is also the seed of Abraham. Surely they have a right to the land of Israel too." God did promise to make a great nation of Ishmael: "And also of the son of the bondwoman will I make a nation, because he is thy seed" (Gen. 21:13).

To settle the dispute between Sarah, Abraham's wife, and Hagar, his Egyptian concubine, over the rights of their sons Isaac and Ishmael, the Lord instructed Abraham: "And God said unto Abraham, Let it not be grievous in thy sight because of the lad [Ishmael], and because of thy bondwoman; in all that Sarah hath said unto thee, hearken unto her voice; for *in Isaac shall thy seed be called*" (Gen. 21:12; emphasis mine). One more passage should be noted to firmly establish that Isaac is the promised seed and possessor of the land.

"And Abraham said unto God, O that Ishmael might live before thee! And God said, Sarah thy wife shall bear thee a son indeed; and thou shalt call his name Isaac: and I will establish my covenant with him for an everlasting covenant, and with his seed after him. And as for Ishmael, I have heard thee: Behold, I have blessed him, and will make him fruitful, and will multiply him exceedingly; twelve princes shall he beget, and I will make him a great nation. *But my covenant will I establish with Isaac,* which Sarah shall bear unto thee at this set time in the next year" (Gen. 17:18-21; emphasis mine).

A PROPHECY OF ZION'S GLORIOUS FUTURE

"Arise, shine; for thy light is come, and the glory of the Lord is risen upon thee. . . . And the Gentiles shall come to thy light, and kings to the brightness of thy rising. . . . And the sons of strangers shall build up thy walls, and their kings shall minister unto thee: for in my wrath I smote thee, but in my favour have I had mercy on thee. . . . For the nation and kingdom that will not serve thee shall perish; yea, those nations shall be utterly wasted. . . . The sons also of them that afflicted thee shall come bending unto thee; and all they that despised thee shall bow themselves down at the soles of thy feet; and they shall call thee, The city of the Lord, The Zion of the Holy One of Israel. . . . Violence shall no more be heard in thy land, wasting nor destruction within thy borders; but thou shalt call thy walls Salvation, and thy gates Praise" (Isa. 60:1-18).

Never has this prophecy of Isaiah been fulfilled. It will be. Israel will survive!

Notes

[1]Russell R. Bixler, *Unbreakable Promises* (Pittsburgh, PA: Baldwin Manor Press, 1987), p. 79.

[2]George N.H. Peters, *The Theocratic Kingdom* (Grand Rapids, MI: Kregel Publications, 1884/1972), Vol I, p. 290-91.

[3]J. Dwight Pentecost, *Things to Come* (Grand Rapids, MI: Zondervan, 1958/1964), p. 65.

[4]Bixler, *Unbreakable Promises*, p. 79.

[5]Alva J. McClain, *The Greatness of the Kingdom* (Winona Lake, IN: BMH Books, 1959/1987), p.119.

[6]Pentecost, *Things to Come*, p. 69.

16

THE HOLINESS OF GOD AND THE RETURN OF THE JEWS

What Is at Stake from God's Point of View?

> Ho, ho, come forth, and flee from the land of the north, saith the Lord: for I have spread you abroad as the four winds of the heaven, saith the Lord (Zech. 2:6).
>
> The meaning of Israel is clear. The Jew had experienced too much death, and a portion of the Jewish people decided that they would die quietly no more. The Jews returned to Israel because it was their ancient land. — Howard Fast[1]

Far more than eschatological considerations are at stake in the return of the Jewish people to the land of Israel. God's integrity is at stake. His sovereignty has been challenged. How will He respond?

The return of the Jews to the land of Israel is holy in the eyes of the Lord, a thing not to be taken lightly. It is holy because without its accomplishment the name of God is slandered. His ability to perform His Word is brought into question. "Can a woman forget her sucking child, that she should not have compassion on the son of her womb? yea, they may forget, yet will I not forget thee. Behold, I have graven thee upon the palms of my hands . . ." (Isa. 49:15-16).

The Christian might even ask, "If God cannot keep His promise to Abraham, how can we be sure He will keep His New Covenant promise to the believer?"

The re-establishment of the nation of Israel has a very high priority on God's agenda of dealings with the nations. Strong nations rise and fall because of their reaction to this premise. It is best for nations not to attempt blocking the progress of the revealed plan of God regarding Israel.

God made a covenant with Abraham (see Gen. 12,15) in which He promised Abraham that his chosen seed would inhabit the land forever. It is a unilateral, unconditional covenant. Its fulfillment depends only upon the integrity of Jehovah God.

HOW IS GOD'S NAME PROFANED?

When Israel is not in the land the name of God is profaned in the eyes of the Gentiles. God seems unable to keep His Word. His sovereignty is threatened. His reputation is impugned. His holiness is brought into question. We must consider the holiness of the Almighty in relation to His promise. It has nothing to do with the holiness of Israel or the lack thereof. This concept is based on God's own evaluation of His situation, not upon our philosophical ponderings.

The promise is stated in many ways, always without equivocation or wavering. The heathen may rage. Israel may fail, but God will never fail to keep His promise. He will honor the promise. The descendants of Jacob-Israel will inhabit the land.

"Thus saith the Lord, which giveth the sun for a light by day, and the ordinances of the moon and of the stars for a light by night, which divideth the sea when the waves thereof roar; The Lord of hosts is his name: If those ordinances depart from before me, saith the Lord, then the seed of Israel also shall cease from being a nation before me for ever. Thus saith the Lord; If heaven above can be measured, and the foundations of the earth searched out beneath, I will also cast off all the seed of Israel for all that they have done, saith the Lord" (Jer. 31:35-37).

THE MACROCOSM — THE BROAD VIEW

Let us take a look at the promise in the macrocosm. We peer through the wide angle lens to get the broad picture. God spoke through the prophets. Their testimony is uniform, that wherever the Jews are driven in dispersion among the nations, God will bring them back to the land. This is to preserve His own integrity and personal testimony to the world. The Word of the Almighty is not to be viewed casually. This is serious.

"Behold, the days come, saith the Lord, that the plowman shall overtake the reaper, and the treader of grapes him that soweth seed; and the mountains shall drop sweet wine, and all the hills shall melt. And I will bring again the captivity of my people of Israel, and they shall build the waste cities, and inhabit them; and they shall plant vineyards, and drink the wine thereof; they shall also make gardens, and eat the fruit of them. And I will plant them upon their land, and they shall no more be pulled up out of their land which I have given them, saith the LORD thy God" (Amos 9:13-15).

Dr. Arnold Olson, president emeritus of the Evangelical Free Church of America quoted Kuyper, Lightfoot, and Tolstoy commenting on the fate of the Jews: "Dr. Abraham Kuyper, while prime minister of the Netherlands, visited Palestine in 1905. Noting that Baron de Rothschild had assisted a few Jewish settlers from Russia who were going to redeem the land, he commented, 'The Jews have come on a vain mission. Here, in this land where the voice of God has been once heard, man's voice will never be heard again. Only God can check the blight of the inrushing desert. Only a miracle can save the Holy Land!'

"Bishop Lightfoot wrote decades ago, 'You may deny if you will every successful miracle in the Bible, but this miracle — the preservation of Israel — is more convincing than all.'

"It was [historian] Leo Tolstoy, who wrote long before there was any thought that the dream of a homeland for the Jew would come true, 'The Jew is the emblem of eternity. He whom neither slaughter nor torture could destroy; he whom neither fire nor sword, nor inquisition was able to wipe off the face of the earth; he who was the first to produce the oracles of God; he who has been for so long a time the guardian of prophecy, and who has transmitted it to the rest of the world — his nation cannot be destroyed. The Jew is as everlasting as eternity itself.' "[2]

"Fear not: for I am with thee: I will bring thy seed from the east, and gather thee from the west; I will say to the north, Give up; and to the south, Keep not back: bring my sons from far, and my daughters from the ends of the earth . . . I, even I, am the Lord; and beside me there is no saviour. Remember ye not the former things, neither consider the things of old. Behold, I will do a new thing; now it shall spring forth; shall ye not know it? I will even make a way in the wilderness, and rivers in the desert" (Isa. 43:5-6,11,18-19).

THE MICROCOSM — FOCUSING ON THE DETAILS

Let us now look at some of the details of God's promise to Israel. We will see the promise in microcosm. In addition to general promises to preserve the Jews as a people and to bring them back to the land, the Bible is filled with hundreds of details relating to the grand plan. Now we look through the lens of the microscope to examine the minutiae of the Prophetic Word.

RESURRECTION OF A LANGUAGE

The Hebrew language has many unique aspects, but foremost in our attention is its restoration. Never in the history of mankind has a dead language been restored to common usage. Hebrew language was "dead," used only by scholars and rabbis, much like dead Latin is used by the Roman Church. Isaiah predicted a loss of the Hebrew language and Zephaniah saw it restored.

"Woe to Ariel [Jerusalem] . . . Yet I will distress Ariel, and there shall be heaviness and sorrow. . . . And thou shalt be brought down, and shalt speak out of the ground, and thy speech shall be low out of the dust, and thy voice shall be, as of one that hath a familiar spirit, out

Eliezer Ben Yehuda, the man who revived the Hebrew language, working in his study.

of the ground, and thy speech shall whisper out of the dust" (Isa. 29:1-4). Indeed the Hebrew language was reduced to a mere whisper.

"For then will I turn to the people a pure language, that they may all call upon the name of the Lord, to serve him with one consent" (Zeph. 3:9).

In the latter part of the nineteenth century Eliezar Ben Yehuda undertook a revival of the Hebrew language. This amazing story is told and carefully documented by Robert Saint John in his book *Tongue of the Prophets.* [3]

"Thus saith the Lord of hosts, the God of Israel; As yet they shall use this speech in the land of Judah and in the cities thereof, when I shall bring again their captivity; The Lord bless thee, O habitation of justice, and mountain of holiness" (Jer. 31:23).

RETURN OF THE ETHIOPIANS

Thousands of Ethiopian Jews have been rescued by airlifts Operation Moses and Operation Solomon. "From beyond the rivers of Ethiopia my suppliants, even the daughter of my dispersed, shall bring mine offering" (Zeph. 3:10).

To see the Jewish people coming from all nations and diverse cultures, yet preserving and treasuring their Jewish identity brings to mind the words of Isaiah: ". . . and I will preserve thee, and give thee for a covenant of the people, to establish the earth, to cause to inherit

Operation Moses. Record-setting planeload of Ethiopian Jews coming home to Israel.

the desolate heritages" (Isa. 49:8).

Like the Russian Jews, the Ethiopians were persecuted and in virtual bondage and ostracism. They were called "falashas" a derogatory term meaning "stranger." They lived in primitive poverty, most of their rights stripped from them. Isaiah continues: "That thou mayest say to the prisoners, Go forth; to them that are in darkness, Shew yourselves. They shall feed in the ways, and their pastures shall be in all high places" (Isa. 49:9.)

Tom Sawicki says, "The dramatic rescue of Ethiopian Jewry in 1991's Operation Solomon is to be immortalized in *The Guinness Book Of Records.*

"The 1995 edition, now being prepared, will include an entry headed '1,088 people in one aircraft. The record,' notes a detailed, four paragraph item, 'was set on May 24, 1991, when 1,086 Ethiopian Jews were evacuated to Israel in one plane. . . . Two babies were born en route, bringing the total who landed in Israel to 1,088.'

"In all, over 14,000 Jews were flown to Israel in 36 hours. *Guinness* notes: 'On the record breaking flight, some of the rows of 10 seats had as many as 18 people jammed into them.'

"The entry was suggested to Guinness by Arnon Mantver, director general of the Jewish Agency's immigration and absorption department."[4]

WHERE DID I GET THESE CHILDREN?

With Jews with all different appearances, even black Ethiopians, coming to Israel, the need for land and housing is apparent, one can

Ethiopian immigrants in Israel. The Ethiopians have a deep regard for the Word of God.

hear the questions birthed by Isaiah being asked today: "For thy waste and thy desolate places, and the land of thy destruction, shall even now be too narrow by reason of the inhabitants, and they that swallowed thee up shall be far away.

"The children which thou shalt have, after thou hast lost the other, shall say again in thine ears, *The place is too strait for me: give place to me that I may dwell.*

"Then shalt thou say in thine heart, *Who hath begotten me these, seeing I have lost my children, and am desolate, a captive, and removing to and fro? and who hath brought up these? Behold, I was left alone; these, where had they been?*" (Isa. 49:19-21).

OUT OF THE NORTH — THE RUSSIAN JEWS

In the 1970s and throughout the 1980s many of us in the Church began to agitate for the release of the Soviet Jews. Of course Jewish people were at the forefront of this struggle. Were we trying to fulfill prophecy? Of course we were. God frequently uses human instrumentality to bring His purposes to pass. How shortsighted are those who merely examine the purposes of God and never find the blessing of being in partnership with God. "For we are laborers together with God: ye are God's husbandry, ye are God's building. . . . Every man's work shall be made manifest: for the day shall declare it . . . " (1 Cor. 3:9,13).

My own awareness of the plight of the Russian Jews was aroused when, in 1970, I read the book *Three Million More?* by Gunther Lawrence.[5] After detailing the climate of growing anti-Semitism in the Soviet Union, Gunther challenged us with the words, "Yet, protest appears to be the only present effective course of action. Leonid Vladimirov, the Russian-Jewish author of *The Russians* . . . wrote: 'I am absolutely positive that the effectiveness of the world protest movement about the plight of Soviet Jewry

The elderly Russian Jewish grandmother is representative of the over 500,000 who have immigrated to Israel.

is great. It is actually now the only restricting force affecting the Kremlin's wild anti-Semites. So far as the future of the Soviet Jews is concerned, I know only one thing that will never occur, and this is assimilation.' "[6]

Protest we did, but, along with other awakened Christians, added intercessory prayer, the Mordecai Outcry, the Esther Fast, the Jehoshaphat Victory March, letter writing to refusniks, and pleading the cause of the Russian Jews to our own political and church leaders.

Refusniks were Jewish people in the former USSR who applied for an exit visa and were refused. They became targets of persecution because of this. Many were imprisoned in psycho prisons and slave labor camps. By writing carefully crafted letters to these people, Christians participated in building a wall of protection about many of them. The KGB monitored all foreign mail. We wrote letters as if we knew the recipient well. This caused the KGB to think that this Jewish person had friends in the West. Being conscious of world opinion they were less likely to persecute the letter receiver. Some of those who used our letter writing kits have actually been to Israel and have met some of those they aided in this fashion. Some have sought us out. I remember a family bringing a lovely cake to a lady in our tour group whom they credited with their deliverance from Russia. It was a night of celebration!

The vision was clear. Jeremiah even declared a day when the return of the northern Jews would be so great that it would overshadow the Exodus out of Egypt under the leadership of Moses. That was hard to imagine!

"Therefore, behold, the days come, saith the Lord, that they shall no more say, The Lord liveth, which brought up the children of Israel out of the land of Egypt; But, The Lord liveth, which brought up and which led the seed of the house of Israel out of the north country, and from

Tree planting location at the Golani Junction, high above the Sea of Galilee. This is where the Christians United for Israel forest is located.

all countries whither I had driven them; and they shall dwell in their own land" (Jer. 23:7-8). An interesting chapter on the prophetic aspect of the return of the Russian Jews to Israel can be read in my book *Prophecy 2000.* [7]

ROSES — FRUIT — TREES

As we continue our journey in the microcosm, we note that one of Israel's major exports is roses. And guess what country imports tulips from Israel in certain seasons of the year? Right, The Netherlands. "The wilderness and the solitary place shall be glad for them; and the desert shall rejoice, and blossom as the rose" (Isa. 35:1). It has come to pass. Today you can travel through Israel and view vast fields that were formerly wilderness and desert areas, now growing the finest of roses.

Formerly barren hillsides and swampy lowlands now flourish with fruit bearing trees. "He shall cause them that come of Jacob to take root: Israel shall blossom and bud, and fill the face of the world with fruit" (Isa. 27:6).

A large percentage of Israel's vegetable and fruit harvest is now exported to foreign markets. One can stand at the Allenby bridge, spanning the Jordan river, and see truckloads of unmarked fruit going into the Hashemite Kingdom of Jordan for distribution throughout Arab nations.

Behold the trees on the hills of Eretz Israel! During the last century scores of books written by travelers in Turkish-ruled Palestine described the desolation of the land, the erosion of topsoil, and the scarcity of trees. A British author, George Sandys counted the trees and numbered them at less than 1,000 in the whole land. Surely this reflects the fulfillment of Isaiah's warning to ancient Israel; "And the rest of the trees of his forest shall be few, that a child may write them" (Isa. 10:19). For a description of the harsh wilderness Israel had become, read the chapters on Palestine in Mark Twain's *Innocents Abroad.* [8]

But the prophet also foresaw a day when the land would be green once again, and the hills would be covered with forests as in happier times. "I will plant in the wilderness the cedar, the shittah tree, and the myrtle, and the oil tree; I will set in the desert the fir tree, and the pine, and the box tree together: That they may see, and know, and consider, and understand together, that the hand of the Lord hath done this, and the Holy One of Israel hath created it" (Isa. 41:19-20).

Through the efforts of the Jewish National Fund millions of trees have been planted in Israel. Today there are over 350 million fully grown, mature trees on the hills of the Holy Land. About half of them are forest and half fruit trees. We have planted over 5,000 trees in our Christian's United for Israel Forest at the Golani Junction, high above the Sea of Galilee.

My good friend Ya'akov Kirschen, cartoonist of *Dry Bones* fame has produced a cartoon style book *Trees . . . The Green Testament.* Kirschen has tried to impress me with the notion that he is a totally secular man. I told Amy Marcus, the *Wall Street Journal* reporter who interviewed me about the book, "Kirschen has a deep wellspring of faith deep inside him, waiting to gush forth and find expression. He has written a very biblical book."

Trees starts with the Bible account of Adam, Eve, and the Garden of Eden, carries one through centuries of prophecy and fulfillment, and ends with a quotation of Amos 9:9-15. Kirschen is also deeply distressed with the advances of neo-paganism, the New Age movement, and considers his book to be a partial answer to them. I highly recommend that every Christian and Jewish person obtain and read this delightful, entertaining, and informative 192-page book![9]

THE WALLS OF JERUSALEM

Greater Jerusalem contains an ancient walled city, but is not a walled city. After the times of Jesus, for century after long century, Jerusalem was a small town. Sometimes its population waned and reports show a population inside the walls of as low as 4,000 wretched inhabitants. The number of its dwellers never swelled to over 20,000. Living conditions were miserable in the old walled city. There was nothing outside the walls. Robber bands roamed the area and no one

wanted to be outside the walls at night.

When a British Jew, Sir Moses Montefiore, began building houses in the mid-1800s outside the walls, no one would live in them until Sir Moses hired a private security

Elizabeth Howell plants a tree in the C.U.F.I. forest.

police force to protect the people. How unlikely seemed the words of Zechariah spoken 2,500 years earlier.

"And said unto him, Run, speak to this young man, saying, Jerusalem shall be inhabited as towns without walls for the multitude of men and cattle therein" (Zech. 2:4).

Today, Jerusalem is a sprawling metropolis with a population of 500,000.

GOD'S NAME SLANDERED

How was the holy name of God profaned? By Israel not being in the land. See how the heathen scorn God; "And when they entered unto the heathen, whither they went, they profaned my holy name, when they said to them, These are the people of the Lord, and are gone forth out of his land" (Ezek. 36:20).

The heathen could mock God for His seeming inability to keep His Word. "But I had pity for mine holy name, which the house of Israel had profaned among the heathen, whither they went. Therefore say unto the house of Israel, Thus saith the Lord God; I do not this for your sakes, O house of Israel, but for mine holy name's sake, which ye have profaned among the heathen, whither ye went. And I will sanctify my great name, which was profaned among the heathen, which ye have profaned in the midst of them; and the heathen shall know that I am the Lord, saith the Lord God, when I shall be sanctified in you before their eyes" (Ezek. 36:21-23.)

There is no implication that the Jews were any more profane than any other people. The name of God was profaned by Israel being scattered. How will God rectify this unacceptable situation? By regathering and restoring the Jews to their land. "For I will take you from among the heathen, and gather you out of all countries, and will bring you into your own land" (Ezek. 36:24). This land covenant relationship has nothing to do with individual redemption, but rather with national destiny.

THE DAY OF ISRAEL'S SANCTIFICATION

As you read further in this chapter of Ezekiel you will find that following the national, physical restoration of Israel, in a future Messianic Age God will cleanse Israel from all sin (see Ezek. 36:25-27). They will continue to "dwell in the land that I gave to your fathers; and ye shall be my people, and I will be your God" (Ezek. 36:28, also see Ezek. 36:33-35).

"Then the heathen that are left round about you shall know that

I the Lord build the ruined places, and plant that was desolate: I the Lord have spoken it, and I will do it" (Ezek. 36:36).

FOR THE SAKE OF GOD

The concept of the holiness of God's action in re-gathering Israel is expressed in the often repeated phrase, "For mine own sake." "I, even I, am he that blotteth out thy transgressions for mine own sake, and will not remember thy sins" (Isa. 43:25). "For my name's sake will I defer mine anger, and for my praise will I refrain for thee, that I cut thee not off" (Isa. 48:9). "For mine own sake, even for mine own sake, will I do it: for how should my name be polluted? and I will not give my glory unto another" (Isa. 48:11).

For His own sake God loves Israel. He loves all mankind, but it is for His own sake that He must preserve the Jewish people and establish them in their own land. Listen to the voice of Jeremiah as he prays, "Do not abhor us, for thy name's sake, do not disgrace the throne of thy glory: remember, break not thy covenant with us" (Jer. 14:21). God assures, "I wrought for my name's sake, that it should not be polluted before the heathen, in whose sight I brought them out" (Ezek. 20:14). Daniel understood the importance of the return; "O Lord, hear; O Lord, forgive; O Lord, hearken and do; defer not, for thine own sake, O my God: for thy city and thy people are called by thy name" (Dan. 9:19).

"For Zion's sake will I not hold my peace, and for Jerusalem's sake I will not rest, until the righteousness thereof go forth as brightness, and the salvation thereof as a lamp that burneth. . . . And they shall call them, The holy people, The redeemed of the Lord: and thou shalt be called, Sought out, A city not forsaken" (Isa. 62:1,12). These are prophecies yet to be fulfilled! What a glorious future for Israel.

BIBLE! BIBLE! BIBLE!

A professor in an Evangelical seminary said, "Last night my dog got hold of our Bible and ate the Book of Revelation. I wish that dogs would eat the Book of Revelation right out of every Bible!" Another "intellectual" said to me, "Bible, Bible, Bible! Is that all you can talk about?" Yes, that is about right. Nothing gives more reliable information than the Bible. The Bible is never adjusted to fit circumstances of the moment. All phenomena must line up with the Word of God.

Please do not grow weary with reading Scripture. The solid foundation of all our research and teaching is the Bible itself. Surveys show that when an author includes chapter and verse references in an article, without printing out the text, readers seldom find the time to look up the passages. It's a busy world. That is why I am having the following references printed out in full for your convenience. Here are more glorious promises for you to examine. Please read them all. The emphasis is on God's determination to preserve His own reputation and holiness in the eyes of all mankind. Note how many passages include the words, "for mine own sake." This is not an isolated concept.

MULTIPLE WITNESS

"For I will defend this city, to save it, for mine own sake, and for my servant David's sake" (2 Kings 19:34; Isa. 37:35).

"I, even I, am he that blotteth out thy transgressions for mine own sake, and will not remember thy sins" (Isa. 43:25).

"And I will add unto thy days fifteen years; and I will deliver thee and this city out of the hand of the king of Assyria; and I will defend this city for mine own sake, and for my servant David's sake" (2 Kings 20:6).

"For Jacob my servant's sake, and Israel mine elect, I have even called thee by thy name: I have surnamed thee, though thou hast not known me" (Isa. 45:4).

"But I wrought for my name's sake, that it should not be polluted before the heathen, among whom they were, in whose sight I made myself known unto them, in bringing them forth out of the land of Egypt" (Ezek. 20:9).

"But I wrought for my name's sake, that it should not be polluted before the heathen, in whose sight I brought them out" (Ezek. 20:14).

"Nevertheless I withdrew mine hand, and wrought for my name's sake, that it should not be polluted in the sight of the heathen, in whose sight I brought them forth" (Ezek. 20:22).

"And ye shall know that I am the Lord, when I have wrought with you for my name's sake, not according to your wicked ways, nor according to your corrupt doings, O ye house of Israel, saith the Lord God" (Ezek. 20:44).

"In those days the house of Judah shall walk with the house of Israel, and they shall come together out of the land of the north to the land that I have given for an inheritance unto your fathers" (Jer. 3:18).

"And I will gather the remnant of my flock out of all countries whither I have driven them, and will bring them again to their folds; and they shall be fruitful and increase. Behold, the days come, saith the Lord, that I will raise unto David a righteous Branch, and a King shall reign and prosper, and shall execute judgment and justice in the earth. In his days Judah shall be saved, and Israel shall dwell safely: and this is his name whereby he shall be called, the Lord our righteousness. . . . . But, The Lord liveth, which brought up and which led the seed of the house of Israel out of the north country, and from all countries whither I had driven them; and they shall dwell in their own land. The anger of the Lord shall not return, until he have executed, and till he have performed the thoughts of his heart: in the latter days ye shall consider it perfectly. . . . Am I a God at hand, saith the Lord, and not a God afar off?" (Jer. 23:3-23).

"Thus saith the Lord, The people which were left of the sword found grace in the wilderness; even Israel, when I went to cause him to rest. The Lord hath appeared of old unto me, saying, Yea, I have loved thee with an everlasting love: therefore with loving kindness have I drawn thee. Again I will build thee, and thou shalt be built, O virgin of Israel: thou shalt again be adorned with thy tabrets, and shalt go forth in the dances of them that make merry. Thou shalt yet plant vines upon the mountains of Samaria: the planters shall plant, and shall eat them as common things. For there shall be a day, that the watchmen upon the mount Ephraim shall cry, Arise ye, and let us go up to Zion unto the Lord our God. For thus saith the Lord; Sing with gladness for Jacob, and shout among the chief of the nations: publish ye, praise ye, and say, O Lord, save thy people, the remnant of Israel. Behold, I will bring them from the north country, and gather them from the coasts of the earth, and with them the blind and the lame, the woman with child and her that travaileth with child together: a great company shall return thither. They shall come with weeping, and with supplications will I lead them: I will cause them to walk by the rivers of waters in a straight way, wherein they shall not stumble: for I am a father to Israel, and Ephraim is my firstborn. Hear the word of the Lord, O ye nations, and declare it in the isles afar off, and say, He that scattered Israel will gather him, and keep him, as a shepherd doth his flock. For the Lord hath redeemed Jacob, and ransomed him from the hand of him that was stronger than he. Therefore they shall come and sing in the height of Zion, and shall flow together to the goodness of the Lord, for wheat, and for wine, and for oil, and for the young of the flock and of the herd: and their soul shall be as a watered garden; and they shall not sorrow any more at all. Then shall the virgin rejoice in the dance, both young men and old together: for I will turn their mourning into joy, and will comfort them, and make them rejoice from their sorrow" (Jer. 31:2-13).

"O Lord, according to all thy righteousness, I beseech thee, let thine anger and thy fury be turned away from thy city Jerusalem, thy holy mountain: because for our sins, and for the iniquities of our fathers, Jerusalem and thy people are become a reproach to all that are about us" (Dan.9:16).

"Seventy weeks are determined upon thy people and upon thy holy city, to finish the transgression, and to make an end of sins, and to make reconciliation for iniquity, and to bring in everlasting righteousness, and to seal up the vision and prophecy, and to anoint the most Holy" (Dan. 9:24).

"For behold the stone that I have laid before Joshua; upon one stone shall be seven eyes: behold, I will engrave the graving thereof, saith the LORD of hosts, and *I will remove the iniquity of that land in one day"* (Zech. 3:9.)

"Thus saith the Lord; I am returned unto Zion, and will dwell in the midst of Jerusalem: and Jerusalem shall be called a city of truth; and the mountain of the Lord of hosts the holy mountain" (Zech. 8:3).

CONTEMPORARY JEWISH COMMENTARY

Allow me to share some Jewish commentary with you. Here are some wonderful insights. Rabbi Shlomo Riskin, dean of Ohr Tora Institutions and chief Rabbi of Efrat, Israel has some distinct thoughts on the sanctity of the return of the land itself. He begins an essay titled, *The Land and Its Sanctity* with a quotation from Genesis 15:18-21. This is the passage that describes the ideal and greater boundaries of Israel, perhaps to be realized in the Messianic Age.

Riskin writes, "With all the pandemonium and ferment created by the Palestinian 'peace' agreement which cedes all of Judea, Samaria and Gaza to the Palestinians, it is important to define what is included under the rubric of the 'sanctity of the land' (Kedusha ha'Aretz), and what are the ramifications of such an inclusion are."

After citing various opinions he notes that "Hatam Sofer (in Response to Yoreh Deah) . . . [Maimonides] believes that there is an eternal, spiritual sanctity to every inch of the Land within biblical borders, based upon the blessing, responsibility and inherent owning implied in the passage, 'It is the land which the Lord God seeks eternally, the eyes of the Lord your God being directed towards it from the beginning of the year until the end of the year' " (Duet. 11:12).

Referring to the teachings of Maimonides Rabbi Riskin writes, "The difference is because the lands of ten nations constitute Greater

Israel, encompassing boundaries which will be realized only during the Messianic period. ..."

Still referring to Maimonides for authority Riskin says, "Towering above the entire world is Jerusalem, which Maimonides sees as embodying eternal sanctity. He insists that in addition to the ethereal and spiritual aspects of God there is also a spiritual dimension to His being in Jerusalem, the divine presence, the Shekhina, is most manifest. The city of Jerusalem may be conquered, the Holy Temple destroyed, and the people of Israel exiled and dispersed, but in the words of Maimonides; 'Hashekhina lo betela,' the indwelling of God will never be nullified. (Laws of Beit Habehira. Chap. 6, Law 16)."

After the Jews returned from Babylon in 536 BC by the decree of Cyrus the Persian who conquered Babylon and made it part of his vast Persian Empire, the Jewish leader Ezra "unveils a new kind of Jew, one who cried out, 'If I forget thee Jerusalem, may my right hand forget its cunning!' Such continual and historic connection creates a dimension of sanctity beyond the level granted to Joshua's military conquests.

"In the language of Maimonides Joshua's conquest was 'kibush,' and Ezra's was 'hazuka.' Hazuka presumes ownership, not simply because one conquers land, but because one lives on it and works it. . . . Fascinatingly enough returning confers upon the Land a higher degree of sanctity than did the original conquest. From the Maimonides concept a magnificent idea emerges: holiness does not exist in a vacuum. The sanctity of the Land of Israel (except for Jerusalem whose holiness is spiritually Shekhina-oriented) depends not only on geography but upon demography. The common denominator is that Israel must be sanctified by Jews living on and working the land.

"Thus the Jewish settlements of Judea, Samaria, Gaza and the Golan represent a most profound sanctity. According to most authorities, they are areas to which Jews returned during the Second Commonwealth. Moreover, they were liberated in our own times by the Israeli Defense Force as the result of a war fought in self defense (Kibush Rubim, Maimonides, Laws of Heave Offerings, chapter 1) and further sanctified by Jewish settlement. They are an integral part of our Jewish homeland, from which it is inconceivable that any Jew — in this post-Holocaust age — can ever be 'transferred.' " The underlying reason for this position is that the Land of Israel has awaited the People of Israel to sanctify it from the time of Abraham's Covenant until today.

ISRAEL'S FUTURE TEMPLE

Riskin ventures to comment on the future temple of Israel: "The image of the return is twofold, the Shekhina — the loving, faithful mother — constantly awaits the return of her children to the ancestral home, the place wherein the Holy Temple will eventually be restored as a house of prayer for all nations.

"At the same time, the Land awaits the return of its nation in order for it to be sanctified. God is waiting for us, and the Land is waiting for us. Hopefully neither will be disappointed."[10]

Isaiah 49:3 "And said unto me, Thou art my servant, O Israel, in whom I will be glorified."

There is much to be noted in Rabbi Riskin's essay concerning the Holiness of the Land in the eyes of God. No other land than Israel and no other city than Jerusalem has been chosen and designated as the *Holy Land* and the *Holy City*. Examine the following proof texts carefully.

HOLY LAND, HOLY CITY

Canadian church leader, A. C. Forrest, severe critic of Zionism, calls Israel *The Unholy Land.* Forrest, for 15 years was the editor of an influential paper, The *United Church Observer* and wrote a syndicated column for the *Toronto Star* and many other newspapers. He spares no effort to damn Israel and defend the Palestinians. His criticism of Jan Willem van der Hoeven is sharp; "It is one of the strangest mixtures of premillenialist anti-communist nonsense I have ever heard. . . . His comments are a travesty of the Gospel."[11]

I have known Jan Willem for years. He is outspoken. Many disagree with some of his interpretation of end-time prophecy. He has many accusers. But I will tell you this — van der Hoeven loves Jesus with all his heart. He loves the Jewish and the Arab peoples. He is a defender of Zion. He has not compromised the major tenets of orthodox, Evangelical Christian theology. The difference between A.C. Forrest and Van Der Hoeven is that Forrest denies that Israel is the Holy Land. Jan Willem Van Der Hoeven believes that it is. Who is right? Let's allow the Bible to be the referee in this dispute: Israel is the Holy Land: "And the Lord shall inherit Judah his portion in the holy land, and shall choose Jerusalem again" (Zech. 2:12).

The New Testament refers to Jerusalem as the Holy City: "Then the devil taketh him up into the holy city, and setteth him on a pinnacle of the temple" (Matt. 4:5). "And came out of the graves after his resurrection, and went into the holy city, and appeared unto many"

(Matt. 27:53). "But the court which is without the temple leave out, and measure it not; for it is given unto the Gentiles: and the holy city shall they tread under foot forty and two months" (Rev. 11:2).

Isaiah speaks of the holy mount in Jerusalem: "And it shall come to pass in that day, that the great trumpet shall be blown, and they shall come which were ready to perish in the land of Assyria, and the outcasts in the land of Egypt, and shall worship the Lord in the holy mount at Jerusalem" (Isa. 27:13).

Not Paris, London, Rome, Brussels, New York, nor any city but Jerusalem, is called *Holy* by the Almighty. "To dwell in Jerusalem the holy city, and nine parts to dwell in other cities" (Neh. 11:1). "All the Levites in the holy city were two hundred fourscore and four" (Neh. 11:18). "There is a river, the streams whereof shall make glad the city of God, the holy place of the tabernacles of the most High" (Ps. 46:4).

Zion, Jerusalem, the Holy City! "Awake, awake; put on thy strength, O Zion; put on thy beautiful garments, O Jerusalem, the holy city: for henceforth there shall no more come into thee the uncircumcised and the unclean" (Isa. 52:1). "And they shall call thee, The city of the Lord, The Zion of the Holy One of Israel" (Isa. 60:14). "For I will defend this city to save it for mine own sake, and for my servant David's sake" (Isa. 37:35).

CHOSEN PEOPLE

The chosen people: "For thou art an holy people unto the Lord thy God: the Lord thy God hath chosen thee to be a special people unto himself, above all people that are upon the face of the earth" (Deut. 7:6).

Chosen — peculiar. "For thou art an holy people unto the Lord thy God, and the Lord hath chosen thee to be a peculiar people unto himself, above all the nations that are upon the earth" (Deut. 14:2). "Thou art an holy people unto the Lord thy God. Thou shalt not seethe a kid in his mother's milk" (Deut. 14:21).

"And to make thee high above all nations which he hath made, in praise, and in name, and in honour; and that thou mayest be an holy people unto the Lord thy God, as he hath spoken" (Deut. 26:19). "And they shall call them, The holy people, The redeemed of the Lord: and thou shalt be called, Sought out, A city not forsaken" (Isa. 62:12).

Yes, Israel will survive! God has too much at stake to let His great enterprise fail now.

Notes

[1]Howard Fast, *The Jews — Story of a People* (New York, NY: Dial Press, 1968), p. 366.

[2]Arnold Olson, *Inside Jerusalem — City of Destiny* (Glendale, CA: Gospel Light/Regal Books, 1968), p. 28-29.

[3]Robert St. John, *Tongue of the Prophets* (North Hollywood, CA: Wilshire Book Company, 1952).

[4]Tom Sawicki, *The Jerusalem Report* (Jerusalem, Israel: Jerusalem Report Publications, Ltd., Feb 24, 1994), p. 6.

[5]Gunther Lawrence, *Three Million More?* (Garden City, NY: Doubleday, 1970).

[6]Lawrence, *Three Million More?* p. 202.

[7]David Allen Lewis, *Prophecy 2000* (Green Forest, AR: New Leaf Press, 1987/1993; 6th Ed.), p. 404-420. This chapter gives more biblical prophetic reference to the return of the Russian Jews.

[8]Samuel Langhorm Clemens (Mark Twain), *Innocents Abroad,* Vol. 2 (New York, NY: Harper and Brothers, 1869/1897/1899), p. 212-388.

Note: Many editions of Twain's works have been produced, some in one volume. Simply look for the chapters on Palestine. In my set they are listed as chapters 18-24. Chapter 18 ends the Syrian travels and begins in Northern Israel at Mt. Hermon and Caesarea Philipi (Banias).

[9]Ya'akov Kirschen, *Trees* (New York, NY: Vital Media Enterprises, 1993).

[10]Shlomo Riskin, *The Jewish Press,* October 23, 1993, Brooklyn, NY.

[11]A.C. Forrest, *Unholy Land* (Toronto: McClelland and Stewart, Ltd., 1971), p. 141.

17

TRUST AND VIGILANCE

Should the UN Provide for Israel's Security?

> The treacherous dealers have dealt treacherously; yea, the treacherous dealers have dealt very treacherously (Isa. 24:16).
> Behold . . . the ambassadors of peace shall weep bitterly (Isa. 33:7).

This chapter was originally written for the newsletter of the National Christian Leadership Conference for Israel.[1]

We are as hopeful as the next person that the peace process will work. May God grant it! On the other hand I see Israel at the hour of greatest risk. And risk taking is a dangerous gamble. Israel's objective friends must be more vigilant than ever. This could be the most important hour of NCLCI's existence. It is a time for hope — and for caution.

Arafat assumes that he will ultimately rule not only Gaza and Jericho, but also Jerusalem, Judea, and Samaria (misnamed "West Bank" by the media). Hafez Assad assumes that he will soon occupy the Golan Heights. How far do their ambitions really reach? The PLO Covenant, calling for the extinction of Israel still has not been changed. It is not a hidden agenda. It may be ignored, but not hidden.

On September 13, 1993, the very day he made his speech on the White House lawn, PLO Chairman Yassir Arafat also made a speech to the Palestinian people over Jordanian TV. We have seen no mention of that speech in the media. Arafat never mentioned peace. He said, "We are coming back to Palestine. Our flags will wave over Jerusalem . . . . Since we cannot defeat Israel in war we do this in stages. We take any and every territory that we can of Palestine, and establish a sovereignty there, and we use it as a springboard to take more when the time comes, we can get the Arab nations to join us for a final blow against Israel."

This speech was made on the very day of the famous handshake on the White House lawn! Surely this is the stuff trust is made of.

I am deeply concerned over the destiny of Jerusalem. The PLO, the media, and, unfortunately, many in the American Jewish community seem to take it for granted that there will be a major compromise on the status of Jerusalem. The Christian world must be alerted to this danger, and motivated to do something about it.

In some cases just getting church leaders not to take an anti-Israel stance would be an accomplishment, but we hope for more than that. We want you to talk to your fellow church members, pastors, and church leaders. We want you to get on the White House opinion line and voice your thoughts. We want you to call your senator and congressperson. Make your voice heard! The White House number is 1-202-456-1111. To call a senator or congressperson the number is 1-202-224-3121.

Israel is being asked to take great risks, putting trust in the USA and the UN.

Israel should trust the USA and the UN? After all it was the USA and the League of Nations that declared that World War I was the "war to end all wars." The USA and the UN promised to solve Somalia's problems. The USA and the UN have come up with such innovative ways to protect the Bosnians. Trust us, we have such a good track record.

We asked you not to respond to Saddam Hussein in the Gulf War. You trusted us and took 39 skud missile hits on your cities.

Israel, trust us, we still have your best interests at heart. If we commit troops to the Golan to protect you from Syria, and a few hundred get blown away by terrorists, we will have to abandon you because of political pressures back home. (Remember Lebanon?) It will be with the deepest of regrets that we will desert you, and leave you with insecure borders. You may even become the new Lebanon of the Middle East. We will view this development with deep sorrow and make appropriate speeches voicing our objections in the UN. However, if you defend yourself too vigorously, you can count on us — to join the UN in condemning you. Why should you be any different from the Bosnians, or the Lebanese? Such chutzpah you have. Imagine, wanting to survive at any cost!

After the Second World War we said we did not know about the Holocaust. If we had only known we could have done something. Then we declared that we would never let it happen again. The Holocaust was a model of what should never be done to any people — never again. But now we watch the Sarajevo horror show each night on our television screens. No excuse, we know what is going on there. Genocide. Never again? Tell the Bosnians about trust.

Trust us Israel.

But keep your eyes open.

LEGITIMATE CONCERNS

The Jewish community has legitimate concerns. In the interest of presenting an American Jewish point of view and issuing a strong call to action we offer the following essay:

DESTROYING THE FOUNDATIONS OF ISRAEL
by Emanuel A. Winston
Middle-East analyst and commentator
The views of an American Jewish Journalist

For 2,580 years the Jews, dispersed across the planet, have been drawn back to Israel by forces not always understood by them. This magnet, with Jerusalem at its center, has been captured and recaptured but always its conquerors left dissatisfied, because they could not own or keep the essence of the one God. Once again Yassir Arafat says his Palestinian State flag will fly over the mosques, churches, and synagogues of Jerusalem.

The Jews have now returned and after six miraculous wars which, based on equipment, numbers of men and scant resources, should have been lost to overwhelming forces. Many Jews and Christians understood the meaning of this return and the winning of impossible battles to be a miraculous sign of things to come.

Once again, however, an evil has arisen with the strength and intent to test and thwart God's will. Israel now seems ready to return major portions of her lands to Islam. The peace treaty should not require a return of lands. Instead of "land for peace" the slogan should be "peace for peace."

Israel has engaged in a program initiated by George Bush and James Baker to appease the PLO (Arafat) giving up land thousands of Jews have died for. Judea and Samaria (called the West Bank in the media) are to be turned over to Arafat. With the West Bank goes 33 percent of Israel's precious water resource. Israel is a land where drought followed by famine of Biblical proportions have been frequent visitors, and once the waters are under control of hostile Arab states, they may find no need to attack as they've promised.

General Earle Wheeler, head of the U.S. Joint Chiefs of Staff, conducted a deep military, intelligence analysis and concluded that Israel could not survive if it returned the West Bank and the Golan Heights. They also recommended keeping a protective enclave around the tip of the Sinai and the Gaza Strip. What demands have been used to force Rabin and Peres to ignore these grave findings? What pressures been brought upon them by the Western world that have forced them into the present untenable position?

It seems that Israel's political leaders have refused to consult with their own generals and excellent intelligence services while secret deals were made to give up large segments of territory from what was already a minuscule and vulnerable state. Neither military advice, potential loss of water, the reality of continued Arab terrorism nor the fact that more that 350 treaties between Arab countries have been broken, seem to be sufficient to override a trend toward self destruction.

Presently negotiations are going on to give away the Golan Heights which will leave Israel's northern border exposed to attack from what will once again be Syria's high ground. Peres and Rabin will have put into the hands of a genocidal dictator control over an additional 43 percent of Israel's water resource. This leaves only the depleted aquifers on the coastal plains which already are infiltrated with sea water. Turkey's building a huge dam on the Euphrates River puts Syria in a position of desperately needing water, and thereby intensifies the danger to Israel.

Many Christians and Jews speculate as to why Rabin is taking Israel down a path of virtual national suicide.... Many believe he is simply being blackmailed and threatened by abandonment by the West.

There are still undisclosed secret discussions going on and one can only imagine all that is being promised to Arafat, Assad, and Hussein through Jim Baker's former team, now operating under Clinton and Christopher.

Today's news that, in addition to giving up Judea and Samaria, and the Golan Heights and Gaza, Mr. Peres is now negotiating with King Hussein to cede to Jordan's sovereignty of the Dead Sea area and parts of the Arava desert . . . only to lease them back! In a word the cave of Qumran where the Dead Sea Scrolls were buried and Masada would be in the hands of the Arabs again as the key holders of the land. In Hebron, the cave of the Machpelah where Abraham, Sarah, Isaac, Rebecca, Jacob, and Leah are buried is again to be denied to the Jews who wish to worship there.

Clearly, a war of such massive dimensions is being prepared that the entire world could be engulfed in its flames. Iran and Syria are currently being armed by the same countries and companies that covertly armed Iraq. Germany, France, Belgium, Switzerland, and even the United States is presently furnishing these radical fundamentalist Islamic nations with the best weapons and technology that money can buy. Missiles capable of carrying nuclear, chemical, and biological warheads that can reach Israel and beyond are being delivered to those radical hostile nations. $58 billion has been spent from January 1991 to July 1993 for weapons in this region.

There is no longer a question that forces have been coalesced whose interests lie in the phased elimination of Israel. Business greed, coupled with an unquenchable hatred of the Jewish people is forcing a massive confrontation between Islam and the Judeo-Christian civilization. World governments and their intelligence services are frantically assessing the problem of the 2,000-3,000 ballistic missiles that will be in the hands of the Arabs by the year 2000. There simply isn't enough of Israel to give away to satisfy the Arab nations who smart from losing six wars to an enemy they are told to hate.

The prophet Isaiah has a word for Israel's enemies. 'For it is the day of the Lord's vengeance, and the year of recompenses for the controversy of Zion. And the streams thereof shall be turned into pitch, and the dust thereof into brimstone, and the land thereof shall become burning pitch. It shall not be quenched night nor day; the smoke thereof shall go up for ever: from generation to generation it shall lie waste; none shall pass through it for ever and ever' (Isa. 34:8-10).

To Israel there is a word of hope from the prophet's pen: "The wilderness and the solitary place shall be glad for them; and the desert shall rejoice, and blossom as the rose. It shall blossom abundantly, and rejoice even with joy and singing: the glory of Lebanon shall be given unto it, the excellency of Carmel and Sharon, they shall see the glory of the Lord, and the excellency of our God" (Isa. 35:1-2).

We must be a source of renewed strength and encouragement to Israel's leadership in confusing, stressful and dangerous times. We can call out to them not to yield to pressures of the West, but put confidence in the Almighty and His unfailing promises.

Isaiah says, "Strengthen ye the weak hands, and confirm the feeble knees. Say to them that are of a fearful heart, Be strong, fear not: behold, your God will come with vengeance, even God with a recompense; he will come and save you. And the ransomed of the Lord shall return, and come to Zion with songs and everlasting joy upon their heads: they shall obtain joy and gladness, and sorrow and sighing shall flee away" (Isa. 35:3-4,10).

The land of Israel is being given away as you read this. We *must take action now!* President Clinton must be told that grass-roots Jews and Christians do not accept the phased dismemberment of Israel, even when self-anointed spokesmen gush euphorically over the empty word of Peace. "Land for Peace" is the formula for war, not peace. A war that would bring Hell up to the surface of the planet earth.

Call the White House Opinion Line, your senators, and members of congress. If you do not know the name of your senators or members of congress, call and ask your local public library. They will tell you who to call, and they will give you phone numbers.

Convey this message: I do not believe that Israel should give up land for peace. Let the peace treaty be negotiated first. Then let the local Israelis and Arabs work on negotiating borders. Israel is being forced to give up too much in advance of an actual treaty. Let there be an exchange of peace for peace.[2]

Notes

[1] David Lewis serves as Chairman of the Board for NCLCI.
[2] Emanuel A. Winston, *Destroying the Foundations of Israel* (Highland Park, IL: Winston-Gray, Inc., 1994).

18

PEACE AT LAST?

> Moloch comes riding with uplifted sword,
> And all men acclaim him, their chosen lord.
> So join in the shouting, likes fools and slaves,
> And let him thrust you into your graves. —
> Sneor[1]
>
> I exhort therefore, that, first of all, supplications, prayers, intercessions, and giving of thanks, be made for all men; For kings, and for all that are in authority; that we may lead a quiet and peaceable life in all godliness and honesty (1 Tim. 2:1-2).

September 13, 1993. For most of the world it was business as usual.

A group of scientists in Hamburg had informed the public that 1992 was the worst war year since 1945. At the end of 1992 there were 52 wars being waged in the world. The situation has gotten worse, today I read in the *Middle East Intelligence Digest* that there are now 70 conflicts in progress.

United Nations forces were (in self defense) killing the people of Somalia, whom they have been sent to aid and defend. Yes, guerrilla soldiers were the target, but civilians were being slaughtered. Sadly, this is the way of the world.

The "former" Soviet Union (long live the new Russian Empire) still has 30,000 nuclear bombs mounted on 12,000 missiles, mostly targeted at the USA, Europe, and Israel. Politicians continue to reassure us that the cold war is over. We wonder why Russia has by far the greatest military machine in the world today. *McAlvany's Intelligence Advisor* clues us in to the fact that the KGB is bigger and stronger than ever before.

But in one tiny area of the world, as I write, the talk is all about peace, and the whole world is taking notice. Israel is the focus of attention. I can only wonder what the situation will be as you read this. The situation is volatile. Things could change overnight. We pray for tranquillity in the Middle East, but watch with caution. Is the USA selling Israel out to Syria? Can Arafat be trusted? Can he control his own factious PLO? What about Hamas, Hezbolah, and other terrorist organizations? What about the threat of civil war in Israel over the dispossession of the settlers? Can Israel survive in this turmoil?

BEHIND CLOSED DOORS

The world media revealed the astounding information that secret negotiations had been conducted in Norway for over a year, led by the late Johann Joergen Holst, the Norwegian foreign minister. Holst presided over 14 secret meetings involving representatives of the Palestine Liberation Organization (PLO) and of Israel.

Israel and the PLO have been bitter enemies since the founding of the PLO in 1964. The PLO Charter calls for the destruction of Israel and Israel has refused to recognize the PLO as the legitimate (unelected) representative of the Arabs, who since 1964 have been called Palestinians. Prior to 1948 about the only people calling themselves Palestinians were the Jews who lived there under the Turkish and later the British mandate.

The Palestinian Arabs are human beings who have rights and needs that must be met. But is the PLO the honest broker for this peace? We hope that Israel has not made a tragic mistake. Jomo Kenyata, head of the 1950s terrorist Mau Mau bands, slaughtered thousands of innocent Christians and others, but reformed and became the moderate, responsible president of Kenya. Could he be a role model for Arafat? Let us hope so.

Israel possesses less than 1 percent of the land mass of the Middle East, yet it is the most hotly contested real estate in the world.

PASTOR KAUFSMAN PROPHESIED

In 1968 when Pastor Zeev Kaufsman of Jerusalem told me that

the nations would gradually turn against Israel and put inexorable pressure upon her to give up land for peace it sounded unreal. Israel was then the darling of the Western World. Zeev prophesied to me that when the West-World Antichrist confirms an agreement with Israel (see Dan. 9:27) that it would be by coercion. He predicted that the world leaders would come to Israel saying, "All right, you Jews, we have had it with you. Trouble, trouble, trouble! Here is a treaty for you to sign, and you will sign or be abandoned."

What transpired in Washington, DC on the White House lawn is not that treaty of Daniel's vision, but it is a foreshadowing. This treaty could serve good purposes, but deception lurks in the shadowy future.

Peace is not evil. It is good. Good treaties, honored by the parties thereto are not bad, they are good. It is better to have peace than war. But these are dangerous times for Israel, and for all of us. We walk a tightrope over chasms of unimaginable depth.

We fully expected the peace accord or something like it. We predicted it. In August, 1993 we printed an article which referred to secret negotiations. We have prayed for the peace of Jerusalem, so if peace is achieved, thank God for it.

THE DAY OF THE HANDSHAKE

On September 13, 1993, at about 11 a.m. Eastern Time, Israeli

Signing of the peace accord between representatives of Israel and the PLO, September 13, 1993.

Prime Minister Yitzhak Rabin, PLO leader Yasser Arafat, and Israeli Foreign Minister Shimon Peres, along with U.S. President Bill Clinton, and Secretary of State Warren Christopher, walked onto the White House lawn for the signing of one of the most incredible documents of our time, a peace accord between the PLO and Israel. It was the day of the incredible handshake.

Oh brave New World Order have you brought us hope for mankind's survival, or do even more sinister agendas lurk in the shadows of international politics and pressure?

What manipulative tactics did you use on Mr. Rabin? What threats fell on his ears? What geo-political blackmail and arm twisting was exercised? Look at the distress in Mr. Rabin's face. What anguish has driven him as he comes to meet and shake hands, reluctantly, with his old enemy?

But we must remember, peace treaties are not made with your friends. Peace treaties are made with your enemies. Without enemies there is no need for peace treaties! Some conservative Israelis have taken offense at this concept, but it is true nevertheless. I know this chapter is giving various points of view, but the Bible is not a deck of Tarot cards. We know what the final outcome will be, but there is a lot of foggy bottom land to be traversed until Messiah comes. We simply do not know what is coming in this process, or what this is the time for, on the prophetic timetable. So while we see the peace process as being terribly flawed, and not very hopeful, yet we hope, yet we pray for the peace of Jerusalem, and all her neighbors roundabout.

We all want peace, but this is a wicked, greedy, and deceitful world that has shown negligible success in keeping peace through the long history of humankind. For all the efforts of sane and hopeful leaders we still live in a world steeped in war and violence. Jesus did not gloat when He said, "There shall be wars and rumors of wars." Rather, He was weeping over the inability of rebellious humanity to solve its deepest problems.

What does the peace effort mean in the light of Bible prophecy? When each of the World Wars ended it was said by some, this treaty being signed is the beginning of the tribulation of seven years, and one of the signers or sponsors of the treaty must be the Antichrist.

The peace accord of September 13 is not the Antichrist covenant. We are not in the Tribulation. What we see evolving may be the framework that will develop into that agreement with hell (see Isa. 28:18), but it is not in focus yet. One thing we have learned in recent years is that prophecy and world events can move at lightning speed.

See the Berlin wall falling down! Observe the upheaval in the USSR and Eastern Europe. Watch how the European Community advances toward the formation of New Rome.

JORDAN'S FUTURE

The Beast will rule over all the earth. A shaky world coalition will be under his dominion. All the nations except one. That nation is Jordan. Of the Antichrist, Daniel predicts: "He shall enter also into the glorious land [Israel], and many countries shall be overthrown: but these shall escape out of his hand, even Edom, and Moab, and the chief of the children of Ammon" (Dan. 11:41). Edom, Moab, and Ammon are regions of the Hashemite Kingdom of Jordan. Whatever judgments may fall on Jordan, there will be a space of time when that nation will be protected by God, for the accomplishing of His own purposes in the region.

HAVE YOU HEARD OF PETRA?

Prophecies given by individuals are never the basis upon which we interpret the Bible. But there is a gift of prophecy operative in the church. Some of these prophecies line up with Scripture and are at least of interest to us.

We mentioned the Jordan prophecies in detail in an earlier chapter. Since writing that chapter Ron Banuk has sent us more translations and explanations which we are studying carefully. To refresh your memory, please recall how in 1933 Om Saleem, an Arab Christian housewife spoke prophecies in a church in Amman, Jordan. It is a matter of documented fact that one of the prophecies was that the Jews would return to Palestine in 1948 and would establish a new nation. She also spoke of friendship between Jordan and Israel, and of the prophecies relating to Petra.

PEACE WITH JORDAN?

For over 20 years we have predicted a Jordan-Israel peace treaty. Since the days of Israeli Prime Minister Golda Meir, secret negotiations between Israeli and Jordanian leaders have taken place, with a hope to bring about a peace treaty. Treaties have value when honored. They are seldom permanent, however.

In an article appearing in our *Jerusalem Courier* for August 1993 we wrote: "I have long taught that there would be a peace treaty between Jordan and Israel. Israel will find a place of shelter in Jordan during the Tribulation, at the lost city of Petra and perhaps elsewhere in the Hashamite Kingdom. . . . Our contacts tell us that ongoing secret negotiations between Jordanian and Israeli leaders may bring a peace treaty in the next five years. May God grant it. Beh Ezrat Hashem!" Since starting the writing of this book things have changed again. The negotiations between Jordan and Israel are out in the open!

Since Jordan's population is 70 percent Palestinian, it stands to reason that King Hussein would not dare to make any accord with Israel without including a solution for the Palestinians' plight. Realizing this, a number of years ago I became involved in efforts to privately bring Israelis and Palestinians together for dialogue.

A MEETING IN RAMALLAH

One such meeting was conducted in Ramallah, involving an Israeli government official, myself, and several leaders of the Palestinian District Leagues (now defunct). There was anger around the conference table. Accusations were hurled. Finally, a sense of calm and reason prevailed. At the end of the meeting all agreed that while there were many problems to work out it is time to stop the killing and violence, and create a framework of communication in which Palestinians and Jews can work out solutions to the problems of the area.

Peace is good. God is the author of peace. William Tecumseh Sherman, a great Civil War general declared, "War is hell." These words were part of his graduation address at Michigan Military Academy, June 19, 1879. "War is at best barbarism. . . . Its glory is all moonshine. It is only those who have neither fired a shot not heard the shrieks and groans of the wounded who cry aloud for blood, more vengeance, more desolation. War is hell."

THE WAY OF THE BEAST

We all prefer to live in a tranquil society rather than a state of chaos. The goal of prophecy and divine history is a state of peace, the Regnum Millennium (Kingdom of a thousand years). In general peace treaties are good. One is evil. The Beast will use humanity's weariness with war and longing for peace to weave a subtle deception that culminates in devastation. Daniel writes of the awful purpose of the Antichrist: "He shall magnify himself in his heart, and *by peace shall destroy many:* he shall also stand up against the Prince of princes; but he shall be broken without hand" (Dan. 8:25). When Satan is the promoter of peace, watch for deception.

Does the September 13 signing mark the onset of the Great Tribulation? No, it does not. That day comes, but not now. It may come swiftly and unexpectedly, but it has not started yet.

In 1978 Anwar Sadat, Menachem Begin, and Jimmy Carter met

at Camp David for the signing of a similar peace accord for Egypt and Israel. Some cried, "This is it." But it was not. In 1979 the actual peace treaty was signed in Cairo and in Jerusalem. More cries, "This must be it" arose. But it was not. Articles and booklets circulate proving that Sadat, or Begin, or Carter was the Antichrist. Watch for a repeat of this genre of error, for some people never learn. Soon you will read that Arafat, or Rabin, or Clinton is the "son of perdition." Pick the Antichrist of your choice. Play your games if you must, but leave me out.

How could Israel consider making peace with her enemy, the PLO, with terrorist Yassar Arafat? Very simply, there is no need to make a peace treaty with friends. Peace treaties are made with your enemies so that they will stop killing you and hopefully you can stop killing them.

FOLLOW PEACE

We are to "Follow peace with all men" (Heb. 12:14). Jesus advised, "Agree with thine adversary quickly, whiles thou art in the way with him . . . " (Matt. 5:25). Moses wisely said, "When thou comest nigh unto a city to fight against it, then proclaim peace unto it" (Deut. 20:10). Making peace is better than going to war. In the Proverbs we read, "When a man's ways please the Lord, he maketh *even his enemies* to be at peace with him" (Prov. 16:7).

What good can come of the peace effort? Out of his deep pit of anguish the sufferer Job asked, "Who can bring a clean thing out of an unclean? not one" (Job 14:4). Wrong, Job. God can bring good out of evil, purity out of impurity. That is the theme of redemption. God can take a broken, ruined life and bring forth a new creation. "Therefore if any man be in Christ, he is a new creature: old things are passed away; behold, all things are become new" (2 Cor. 5:17).

God will take this ruined planet and renew it. The thousand year reign of Messiah is but the inauguration of an eternity of perfection.

God brings good out of evil. Satan brings evil out of good. "By peace shall he destroy. . . ." Therefore it behooves us to "Be sober, be vigilant; because your adversary the devil, as a roaring lion, walketh about, seeking whom he may devour" (1 Pet. 5:8).

Evil is ever alert, unceasingly probing, continually watching, looking for an opening. We are not ignorant of the devil's devices.

We join the search for peace, but remember that "Hate is strong and mocks the song of peace on earth, good will to men." We are wary. We live in hope, but observe with caution.

WHEN MESSIAH REIGNS

Wars and violence will not completely cease until Messiah reigns from Jerusalem. Perhaps we can look forward to advancing peace in the Middle East and a time of relative peace in many parts of the earth. But the tide will turn for, "When they shall say, Peace and safety; then sudden destruction cometh upon them, as travail upon a woman with child; and they shall not escape" (1 Thess. 5:3).

SEDUCTION

"Because they have seduced my people, saying, Peace; and there was no peace; and one built up a wall, and, lo, others daubed it with untempered mortar" (Ezek. 13:10).

The Beast will use peace to destroy: "The words of his mouth were smoother than butter, but war was in his heart: his words were softer than oil, yet were they drawn swords" (Ps. 55:21).

"We looked for peace, but no good came; and for a time of health, and behold trouble!" (Jer. 8:15). "Behold the ambassadors of peace shall weep bitterly" (Isa. 33:7). Antichrist "shall confirm the covenant with many for one week" [week of years = seven years] (Dan. 9:27).

ISRAEL'S GUARANTEED SURVIVAL

Only Israel, of all nations, is guaranteed survival. Only Israel resists the Antichrist. While the entire Gentile world bows to the Beast, Israel stands alone and bravely counterattacks his awesome forces. Judah takes up arms against the armies of hell. "And Judah also shall fight at Jerusalem" (Zech. 14:14). Great leadership arises in Judah! Israel declares of the Beast: he "shall tread in our palaces, then shall we raise against him seven shepherds, and eight principle men" (Mic. 5:5).

Listen devil, look out for the two mighty prophets, the seven shepherds, and the eight principle men. They are on your trail, oh loser of all time and eternity. Your evil intention will not prevail.

TREATY BY FORCE

The ill-advised, seven-year-treaty *forced* on Israel cannot last: "And your covenant with death shall be disannulled, and your agreement with hell shall not stand" (Isa. 28:18).

The Beast makes his last ditch stand. It is a darkening day for Israel. Satan seems to have the upper hand. "Thy life shall hang in doubt before thee" (Deut. 28:66). But God is about to bare His mighty arm. Shortly the skies will open and Messiah will appear on a white horse with saints of all ages in His entourage. In the face of darkest doom a light breaks through the eastern sky. What a day that will be. God fights for Israel and Israel alone.

WHAT ANGERS THE ALMIGHTY?

What is it that so provokes the wrath of God that He launches the Armageddon campaign against the armies of all nations? It is not pornography, crime, human abuse, cultism, wars in general, abortion, violence, crooked politics nor prostitution. These are evil sins that offend the Almighty, sins He will deal with in the final judgment, but they are not what triggers Armageddon.

What brings the Armageddon battle is when the nations attack Jerusalem and threaten Israel. God cannot allow Israel to be destroyed. His Holiness and reputation are at stake (see Ezek. 36:19). God cannot break His promise to Abraham.

"And it shall come to pass in that day, that I will seek to destroy all the nations that come against Jerusalem" (Zech. 12:9).

"If I whet my glittering sword, and mine hand take hold on judgment; I will render vengeance to mine enemies. . . . Rejoice, O ye nations, with his people: for he will avenge the blood of his servants, and will render vengeance to his adversaries, and will be merciful unto his land, and to his people" (Deut. 32:41,43).

"Then shall the Lord go forth, and fight against those nations, as when he fought in the day of battle. And his feet shall stand in that day upon the mount of Olives, which is before Jerusalem on the east. . . . And the Lord my God shall come, and all the saints with thee. And the Lord shall be king over all the earth: in that day shall there be one Lord and his name one. Jerusalem shall be safely inhabited" (Zech. 14:3-11). We have arrived at the Regnum Millennium, the kingdom of a thousand years.

"Pray for the peace of Jerusalem: they shall prosper that love thee" (Ps. 122:6). "And I will give peace in the land" (Lev. 26:6).

MILLENNIAL PEACE TREATY — AT LAST!

Then, think of the promised Millennial peace treaty involving Israel, Iraq, and Egypt! "In that day shall there be a highway out of Egypt to Assyria [Iraq], and the Assyrian shall come into Egypt, and the Egyptian into Assyria, and the Egyptians shall serve with the Assyrians. In that day shall Israel be the third [in partnership] with Egypt and with Assyria, even a blessing in the midst of the land: Whom the Lord of hosts shall bless, saying, Blessed be Egypt my people, and Assyria the work of my hands, and Israel mine inheritance" (Isa. 19:23-25).

Our privilege and mandate for the present season, before the Regnum Millennium is clear:

IN THE NOW SEASON

First of all we are given personal peace. "Therefore being justified by faith, we have peace with God through our Lord Jesus Christ" (Rom. 5:1).

Next we are commanded to pursue peace. "Let us therefore follow after the things which make for peace, and things wherewith one may edify another" (Rom. 14:19).

Finally we are promised a time when the kingdom of God will be visibly manifested. "And the God of peace shall bruise Satan under your feet shortly. The grace of our Lord Jesus Christ be with you. Amen" (Rom. 16:20).

Notes

[1]J. Leftwich, *Golden Peacock* (Science-Art, 1939) p. 114. (Leftwich cites Sneor's "War Comes").

19

A MIDDLE EAST COMMON MARKET?

A Revolutionary Idea to Benefit Both Arabs and Israel

> *To every thing there is a season, and a time to every purpose under the heaven . . . a time of war, and a time of peace* (Eccles. 3:1,8).
> *Beside that he had of the merchantmen, and of the traffic of the spice merchants, and of all the kings of Arabia, and of the governors of the country* (1 Kings 10:15).

The very thought of a successful Arab-Israel alliance strikes cold fear into the heart of American and European Socialist Capitalists. It would be so powerful, so competitive that it could bring about the collapse of Western Socialist Capitalism and the Machiavellian Multi-National Corporations. What relationship might this have with the fall of end-time Economic Babylon? We have long said that if the super power nations would get out of the Middle East and let the local people reach normal accommodations, many of the problems of the area could be considerably cooled down.

The Middle East has always been a place of mystery, intrigue, and secret dealings. Israel has sought peace and cooperation with her neighbors for over 40 years. Several farsighted leaders in Arab countries have joined in private meetings with Israeli leaders seeking solutions to their mutual problems. Both sides can recognize the great beneficence that would befall the area if the joint efforts of the involved parties could pool their resources for peaceful goals.

PIPELINE TO EUROPE

One of those secret deals presently brewing is referred to in an article in *U.S. News:* "Israel and Qatar, one of the oil-rich Arab gulf states, have quietly agreed to formally study whether a natural-gas pipeline between them would be economically viable. The Goal: allowing Qatar to transport its natural gas to Europe via an Israeli port on the Mediterranean. The secret accord was worked out during a private meeting in London late last month between Israeli Foreign Minister Shimon Peres and his Qatari counterpart, Sheik Hamad Jassim bin Jabor al-Thani. The potential stumbling blocks: the reaction of Saudi Arabia, whose territory such a pipeline would cross, and Qatar's insistence that Israel must first conclude a peace agreement with Syria before any construction could begin."[1]

We found further confirmation of this amazing news in the pages of the *Jerusalem Report*. Moshe Shahal, Israel's energy minister was quoted in the *Report* as saying that, "Israel has plans and is ready to start work on a major facility for the trans-shipment of Arab oil to the West. . . . The most likely location for what could become 'the Rotterdam of the Middle East' is Ashkelon, on the Mediterranean coast south of Tel Aviv." Ashkelon already has a deep-water oil port, oil storage facilities, and oil jetty.

Shahal confirmed that the Gulf Arabs and the Japanese have shown strong interest in Israel as an oil transit point, being the pivotal cross roads between the East and the West.

"At the same time, he noted that studies by Japanese groups and the international Armand Hammer Institute agree that potential exists for five oil pipelines across Israel with an annual volume of as much as 70 million tons; Israel's current petroleum consumption amounts to only 10 million tons a year. 'If all this oil goes through Israel,' he said, 'it's only natural that we develop a major oil industry near an oil port, with storage, refinery, and trade facilities, like Rotterdam. Like us, the Dutch have no oil of their own.'

"The fact that Israel is not an oil producer is particularly important to Gulf Arabs. Shahal said that one of the leaders of an Arab Gulf nation said to him, 'If we ship our oil through Israel, we know you can be trusted not to close the taps.'"[2]

In a related article *The Jerusalem Report* notes, "The Qataris see Israel as a serious business partner." The *Report* quotes a Gulf diplomat, "Everyone in the region recognizes the strategic potential of ties with Israel." Other Gulf nations are involved. "The signs are that Oman, a sultanate at the southern tip of the Gulf that once controlled the slave trade of East Africa, and that is fast becoming one of the more advanced political communities of the Gulf is already playing around with a similar logic."[3]

THE DEAD SEA

The Dead Sea is the richest single mineral deposit on earth. Its borders are shared by Israel and the Hashemite Kingdom of Jordan. S. Drori told us that there are enough of 11 vital minerals to meet the needs of all the nations of the world for hundreds of years to come. These minerals include molybdenum, magnesium, and titanium; metals of the future. Perhaps of even greater importance is the presence of an enormous quantity of potash, necessary for fertilizer used in reclaiming wilderness areas and deserts of the world, all of which can be transformed into fertile farm land given a supply of water and these fertilizers.

SOLUTION TO WORLD HUNGER

Solar power experiments at the Dead Sea, and in a related project at the Salton Sea in California promise technology and a source of power that would allow the cheap desalinization of sea water for irrigation purposes. In effect, here at the Dead Sea we have the necessary components for the transformation of desert lands and the solution to world hunger. Must we wait for Messiah and the Millennium, or will the powers of the Middle East lay down their guns and create a haven of tranquillity for the benefit of all mankind? We can hope. We can pray. We can act. We must do all that we can to serve our generation well in our own time.

CANAL OF THE SEAS

For years there has been a dream in the hearts of certain Israeli scientists and planners to build a canal from the Mediterranean Sea to the Dead Sea. Israel has always had an enormous financial burden in supplying military security for the nation. For a lack of funding the Dead-Med Canal project has been on hold for some time. Now another idea has come forth.

A highly informed and well positioned Israeli described secret negotiations to us. The purpose of these meetings between Jordan and Israel, is to build a canal from the Red Sea to the Dead Sea. This canal would run from the northern end of the Red Sea, along the Israel-Jordan border to the Dead Sea. The Dead Sea needs a controlled source of fresh water to make up for the loss of Jordan River water which has been diverted for agricultural irrigation. The Dead Sea has gotten dangerously low. If not corrected this could even destroy the delicate balance of conditions that allow for the utilization of this liquid mineral mine.

Water from the Red Sea, controlled by a series of locks could supply significant hydroelectric power for the two nations. The water from the Red Sea would drop to the thirteen hundred feet below sea level at the Dead Sea. This falling water, passing through a series of locks could be harnessed to turn giant turbines which would power powerful electric generators. The resultant electrical power production would supply 10 to 15 percent of Jordan's and Israel's needs for electricity.

The incredible mineral wealth of the Dead Sea can be harvested by both countries. Solar power development would go forward. Shlomo Drori, head of the Dead Sea Works department of information told me that the World Bank is ready to fund the project, providing Jordan and Israel enter into a peace treaty.

WILL ISRAEL JOIN THE ARAB LEAGUE?

How can this even be considered to be a serious question?

Nevertheless, Mendel Weinbach asks in the "David's Slingshot" column of *The Jewish Press,* "Will Israel Join the Arab League?" As preposterous as it sounds, this question demands careful consideration.

Weinbach writes, "One of the arguments prominently presented by the sponsors and supporters of the accord with the PLO is that it will enable Israel to develop friendly relations with all of the Arab states in the region."[4]

Sheba and Dedan, mentioned in Ezekiel 38 are Arab nations that will befriend or be in league with Israel. They stand with Israel to protest the end-time Magog-Russian invasion of the land.

We offer seven reasons why Russia will still invade Israel in our sixth edition of *Prophecy 2000.* [5]

Prime Minister Yitzhak Rabin and Shimon Peres, foreign minister of Israel, have had secret meetings in Morocco, Jordan, Syria, and possibly Saudi Arabia. We have reported on such secret meetings going on by peace seeking Israeli leaders since the leadership of Prime Minister Golda Meir who had meetings with King Hussein of Jordan.

A month before the Intifada started in 1987 we reported to you of secret talks going on between the Likud government of Israel and King Hussein of Jordan, the end in mind being a peace treaty between Jordan and Israel.

Mendel Weinbach continued, "Who would have imagined that this honeymoon spirit would extend so far as to consider making Israel a member of the Arab League?

"Strange as it may seem, this is exactly the idea which was brought up during a recent convention of the Swedish Socialist Party.

"The heads of the Young Guard of the Israel Labor Party and of the PLO Youth were guests of honor at this convention and it was they who came up with the strange initiative. They discussed a proposal to change the name of the Arab League and to hold a meeting in Tunis in the very near future which would issue a call for admitting Israel to that organization.

". . . Some observers pointed out that the same idea was kicked around back in the '50s by Prime Minister David Ben-Gurion and Jordan's King Abdulla, who hoped to use Israeli membership in the Arab League as a springboard for recognition of Israel by the Arab world. (It was such ideas which won the Jordanian ruler the hatred of Arab radicals and led to his assassination)."[6]

Even before the state of Israel was born a far-sighted Christian in the Roosevelt administration envisioned the benefits of cooperation between the people in the region. In his magnificent book *Palestine, Land of Promise* Walter Clay Lowdermilk, a noted American soil conservationist visited British Palestine and came to some remarkable conclusions. He spoke of a huge reclamation project capable of supporting not only the two million Jews and Arabs living there in 1938 but also at least four million Jewish refugees.

Dr. Lowdermilk proposed a Jordan Valley Authority, based on the experience of America's Tennessee Valley Authority. He noted the "amazing changes the Jewish settlers in Palestine have wrought in the eroded, sterile land by irrigation, drainage, fertilization, reforestation, and other modern methods."[7]

Lowdermilk was sent to Palestine by the U.S. Department of Agriculture. He spent 15 months there, studying the land and its potential. His book grew out of his observations and experiences there. He was a soil conservationist, forestry engineer, and hydrologist of wide experience. He also had an intense interest in history. He wrote, "It is interesting to note that British scholars of the Palestine Exploration Fund who explored Palestine during the second half of the nineteenth century had a very high estimate of the country's capacity. . . . Sir Charles Warren expressed their common opinion in a book on Palestine issued as early as 1875, before even the earliest modern Jewish settlements were founded."[8]

Lowdermilk was impressed that Warren wrote, "Give Palestine a good government and increase the commercial life of the people and they may increase tenfold and yet there is room. The soil is so rich, the climate so varied, that within ordinary limits it may be said that the more people it contains, the more it may accept. Its productiveness will increase in proportion to labor bestowed on the soil until a population of fifteen million may be accommodated there."[9] Lowdermilk moderated the figure, looking at a smaller mandated area, to twelve million.

He wrote, "After the centuries of darkness which crushed the hopes of Palestine's miserable inhabitants, a new force has come into the land and made it live again. The possibility of a new day for the entire Near East is hidden in the fertile lands, the flourishing villages and cities, the co-operatives and factories of Jewish Palestine.[10]

WHAT IS PROPHECY FOR?

Bible prophecy is not a fortune telling system or Ouija board. It is not designed to give us all the details of future events. It does give us the broad picture of the final outcome of all things. It inspires and motivates us to good works, to cooperate with the ongoing plan of God. And finally, it helps us to interpret events as they happen.

It is natural to speculate and wonder about the future. It is even legitimate, as long as we are not dogmatic about our speculations. Now, with that in mind let me ask, "What if there is a Mideast Common Market formed between Israel and her neighbors?"

It seems like a good idea to me. Get it out of your head that there is something wrong with peace. None of us want to send our young men and women to more far-flung battle fields. If you want more war you are sick. Jesus lamented as He said that there shall be wars and rumors of wars. War is not a manifestation of God's will, but rather of the rebellion of mankind against the will of God. Even the wars that God commanded to be waged against the idolatrous, child sacrificing pagans were reaction to the evil that humanity had generated. For all good reasons wars should be prevented as much as possible.

The deception comes and the false peace of short duration will arrive, but in the meantime, this is all we have got, and we have to make the best of it until Messiah sets up His peaceable kingdom. So, what might happen if there is peace in the Middle East? Here is a scenario: Israel, Jordan, Egypt, Saudi Arabia, and probably other nations could join in a Common Market. The deserts would bloom. A great canal from the Red Sea or the Mediterranean to the Dead Sea could bring renewed prosperity to the whole area. Industry would flourish, hunger and poverty would cease, oil would flow, and gold would be mined. The Mideast Common Market (MECM) would be the richest block of nations on earth. The Israeli military might would be refined for common defense of the area.

See Russia and her allies fester with envy, sinking deeper and deeper into the cesspool of poverty. Observe the Western nations resentment rise as the MECM raises the price of oil and gold. Western leaders would growl their malice, again accusing Israel plotting to rule the world. They move against Jerusalem to settle it once and for all. Eureka! It is Armageddon. But from the open skies Jesus and the glorified saints of all ages in His entourage appear to fight the battle for Israel. Then the kingdom of God is manifested on earth and the great prophesied peace treaty between Israel and the Arabs is signed under the auspices of Jesus Christ as foretold by the prophet Isaiah.

THE REAL MID EAST PEACE COMES AT LAST

Any success in bringing peace to the Mideast is but a foreshadowing of a Messianic time of tranquillity and blessing idealized by the prophets of Israel, the sayings of Jesus, and the Book of Revelation.

"In that day shall there be a highway out of Egypt to Assyria [Iraq], and the Assyrian shall come into Egypt, and the Egyptian into Assyria, and the Egyptians shall serve with the Assyrians. In that day shall Israel be the third [in partnership] with Egypt and with Assyria, even a blessing in the midst of the land: Whom the Lord of hosts shall bless, saying, Blessed be Egypt my people, and Assyria the work of my hands, and Israel mine inheritance" (Isa. 19:23-25).

May God hasten the day. I lust not for Armageddon, but I long for the peaceable kingdom of our Lord, Moshiach ben David.

Israel will survive. I see her, not only in the visions of the earliest Testament but in the final pages of the Christian Scriptures.

Notes

[1]Charles Fenyvesi, Ed., "Washington Whispers," *U.S. News & World Report*, February 14, 1994, p. 18 (Washington, DC: USNWP, Inc.,).

[2]Leslie Susser, *The Jerusalem Report*, February 24, 1994, p. 5-6 (Jerusalem: Jerusalem Report Publications, Ltd.).

[3]Ehud Ya'Ari, *The Jerusalem Report*, February 24, 1994, p. 26-27 (Jerusalem: Jerusalem Report Publications, Ltd.).

[4]Mendel Weinbach, *The Jewish Press*, October 23, 1994, p. 9 (Brooklyn, NY).

[5]David Allen Lewis, *Prophecy 2000*, 6th ed. (Green Forest, AR: New Leaf Press, Inc., 1990/1993), p. 387-399. Also see my booklet *Is Russia Off the Hook?*

[6]Weinbach, *The Jewish Press*, p. 9.

[7]Walter Clay Lowdermilk, *Palestine, Land of Promise* (New York, NY: Harper and Brothers, 1944), from the book cover.

[8]Lowdermilk, *Palestine, Land of Promise*, p. 227.

[9]Lowdermilk, *Palestine, Land of Promise*, p. 228. Lowdermilk cites from Sir Charles Warren's book *Land of Promise* (London, 1875).

[10]Lowdermilk, *Palestine, Land of Promise*, p. 228.

20

ISRAEL BRINGS HOPE

New Technology and Energy Source — Solution for World Problems

And I will give her her vineyards from thence, and the valley of Achor for a door of hope: and she shall sing there, as in the days of her youth, and as in the day when she came up out of the land of Egypt (Hos. 2:15).

Out of Palestine is again emerging a better way of life for tillers of the soil and a new realization of man's moral obligation to the good earth which nourishes those who give it loving care. — Walter Clay Lowdermilk, 1944

One month before the Intifada, the Palestinian uprising, started we were conferring with Shlomo Drori, head of the Department of Information for the Israel Dead Sea Chemical Works. No one I have ever met has given me so much knowledge about the Dead Sea as Mr. Drori. His is a love affair with the body of water known in the Bible as the Salt Sea. The Bible never calls it the "Dead Sea," in fact it was not called the Dead Sea until after the destruction of Sodom and Gomorra.

Mr. Drori speaks like a prophet when he talks about the Dead Sea. He sees here the developing technology for the solution to world hunger. As we alluded to in the last chapter, operational solar ponds producing energy point the way to the day when solar energy will be used to cheaply desalinate sea water. This will be used to irrigate the vast deserts of the earth, turning it into fertile farm land. Add to this the bromines and potash from the Dead Sea which are needed for fertilizers, and you have a great start toward defeating famine.

Drori told us in November 1987 that secret negotiations were going on between Jordan and Israel. A new plan has been developed to bring a canal from the Red Sea to the Dead Sea.

The outbreak of the PLO-inspired Intifada put the whole project on hold, if indeed it is even still alive. I think it is alive, and that King Hussein really would prefer to make a peace treaty with Israel.

FORGING AHEAD

In the meantime Israel's scientific community forges ahead with technology to solve energy problems, water problems, and the problem of world hunger. Plans which could bring prosperity to the entire region.

Israel has freely shared its technology in this realm. The Dead Sea solar ponds project has a joint American venture at the Salton Sea in California which works in league with the Israeli project. These are the only two places on earth where this particular technology is being used. We published an article on this in a previous *Jerusalem Courier.*[1]

A very encouraging report was published in the *Wall Street Journal* June 9, 1993. The Journal tells of an Israeli concept called SNAP — "Sneh aero-electric power." Sneh is the Hebrew word for the biblical bush that burned without being consumed.

WIND TOWER MAY YIELD CHEAP POWER

Here is the *Wall Street Journal* report:

A wind dissipated the flood in Noah's day. Another wind parted the Red Sea for the fleeing Israelites. And now a wind may once again play a role in the history of Israel — only this time it would be a man-made wind blowing inside a tower more than half a mile high.

The wind tower is the serious proposal of a team of Israeli scientists, engineers and architects who believe they have found a cheap method of generating electricity. Situated in the desert near the sea, the generating station would consist of a hollow cylinder of 3,300 feet high — twice the height of New York's World Trade Center — and 1,500 feet in diameter.

The idea works like this: Sea water is pumped to the top of the tower and sprayed into the center where it rapidly evaporates in the dry desert heat. As the air is cooled by the evaporation, it grows denser and heavier and begins falling, plunging ever faster down the tower interior. By the time the cold air hits the tower bottom, it's traveling at 50 miles an hour.

If the water is sprayed continuously, the result is a powerful downdraft that can be piped into tunnels to drive wind turbine electric generators. By one calculation, such a wind tower built in the Negev desert and drawing water from the Red Sea, could produce 40 billion to 80 billion kilowatt-hours of electric energy a year.

Line drawing from Wall Street Journal *depicting an aero-electric power plant.*

The energy's cost would be a mere two cents a kilowatt-hour, less than one fifth the cost of generating a kilowatt-hour in, say, California. And in some versions the tower could also desalt sea water, providing cheap water for desert farming.

Even the wind tower's progenitors concede that the idea may at first strike people as so much hot air. "I had good friends who said, 'Dan, why don't you write a book to get it out of your system and then go do something serious,' " says Dan Zaslavsky, the 62-year-old Israeli agricultural engineer who began working on the wind tower concept a dozen years ago.

But most who listen to Dr. Zaslavsky come away impressed with what the inventor has dubbed "sneh aero-electric power," or SNAP (sneh being the Hebrew word for the biblical bush that burned without consuming itself). Those impressed include scientists and engineers at the Technion — Israel Institute of Technology in Haifa, often described as the Israeli equivalent of the Massachusetts Institute of Technology. Dr. Zaslavsky heads the agricultural engineering faculty there.

"The great thing is that neither the structure nor the concept requires any new technology," says the president of Technion Zehev Tazmor.

"Building the tower would be a piece of cake," agrees Wendel R. Wendel, president of Starnet International Corp., an engineering-construction concern in Longwood, Florida. Since the tower unlike a skyscraper, is a cylindrical shell without any infrastructure, it could be built in two years or less at a cost "in the $300 million range," he says.

In the next few days, a plan leading to a SNAP plant will be submitted to the Israeli Ministry of Commerce and Industry by Technion researchers. The plan calls for a $5 million research and development effort culminating in a $25 million pilot version of the tower.

"Dan's project is high on the burner for us," says Lewis Weston, president of the American Technion Society, the institute's fund-raising arm. "This is the kind of project we like because if it works it's not just an Israeli project; it would help the Saudis, the Kuwaitis and anyone else who needs energy.

The Technion is setting up a profit-oriented subsidiary to develop the SNAP concept commercially. One Israel-oriented venture capital fund in Los Angeles, Second Equity Concepts Ltd., is already assembling a group of U.S. companies to raise $275 million.

A SNAP plant could also be a part of the Mideast peace talks. Dr. Zaslavsky, a former water commissioner, headed Israel's negotiating team dealing with water problems at the Vienna peace talks last year. At the talks, he says, Jordan proposed joining with Israel to dig a canal from the Red Sea to the Dead Sea.

"The Red-Dead Canal, by itself isn't all that attractive economically," Dr. Zaslavsky says. "But," he says, "the canal could be dug in sections, with a SNAP generator at the end of each one. That would allow the canal to meet all the electric needs of both countries."

An American physicist, Philip R. Carlson, is credited with first conceiving the downdraft wind generator. About 1965, when he was at Lockheed Aircraft Corporation, he started working on the idea of getting energy from thunderstorms. "Thunderstorms create updrafts that would be hard to harness," recalls Dr. Carlson, now 81. "So I started thinking about downdrafts in a chimney created by evaporating water at the top of the chimney."

Lockheed patented the concept during the energy crisis in the mid 1970's, and the patent was transferred to Agbabian Associates, a Pasadena, California engineering firm, in 1977. Although the patent expired last year, Dr. Carlson and Agbabian, now owned by the Japanese, retain an interest in any SNAP project, Dr. Zaslavsky says.

The height of the tower, which confounds most people, is the least of the problems facing the SNAP project. Michael Bort, the Technion's dean of architecture, devised a tower made of lattice-like walls crocheted of mass produced aluminum or steel struts 12 to 15 feet long and covered with an aluminum facade.

"On a scale of difficulty of one to ten, building the tower would be about a five," says Mr. Wendel, the U.S. engineer-builder. "The struts and facade panels could be extruded on site," he says, "and builders could use the Asian technique of a scaffolding that rises as the tower rises, avoiding moving giant cranes into the desert."

There is, though, one problem still to be solved. The evaporation of sea water at the top of the tower and a steady rain of salty brine inside the tower would leave a lot of salt to dispose of.[2]

BIBLE EXTOLS THE FUTURE OF ISRAEL

The Bible predicts the end-time re-establishment of the nation of Israel, the reclamation of the land, and that Israel will be a blessing to the whole earth. Water will spring forth. Trees will grow. It is already beginning. The greater fulfillment awaits the Regnum Millennium, the reign of Messiah, but thank God for any portion we can see here and now!

"He shall cause them that come of Jacob to take root: Israel shall blossom and bud, and fill the face of the world with fruit" (Isa. 27:6)

"When the poor and needy seek water, and there is none, and their tongue faileth for thirst, I the Lord will hear them, I the God of Israel will not forsake them. I will open rivers in high places, and fountains in the midst of the valleys: I will make the wilderness a pool of water, and the dry land springs of water. I will plant in the wilderness the cedar, the shittah tree, and the myrtle, and the oil tree; I will set in the desert the fir tree, and the pine, and the box tree together: That they may see, and know,

Walter Clay Lowdermilk, a great visionary for the land of Israel.

and consider, and understand together, that the hand of the Lord hath done this, and the Holy One of Israel hath created it" (Isa. 41:17-20).

Again the prophet Isaiah extolls the greatness of God's plans for Israel. "The wilderness and the solitary place shall be glad for them; and the desert shall rejoice, and blossom as the rose. It shall blossom abundantly, and rejoice even with joy and singing: the glory of Lebanon shall be given unto it, the excellency of Carmel and Sharon, they shall see the glory of the Lord, and the excellency of our God . . . for in the wilderness shall waters break out, and streams in the desert. And the parched ground shall become a pool, and the thirsty land springs of water: in the habitation of dragons, where each lay, shall be grass with reeds and rushes. . . . And the ransomed of the Lord shall return, and come to Zion with songs and everlasting joy upon their heads: they shall obtain joy and gladness, and sorrow and sighing shall flee away" (Isa. 35:1-10).

WHEN SHALL IT BE?

We are asked, "But will these problems be solved in the Millennium?"

Indeed, will peace with Jordan come before Messiah appears or only in the Millennium? Why not both now and then? Why not pray in a positive vein? We are not lusting for Armageddon. That will also come in its time. But since I do not know how long that will be, I must be responsible for the quality of life in the now season. I pray for the peace of Jerusalem (see Ps. 122), and for all her neighbors as well. Some people read prophecy and get bloodthirsty. That is not God's intention. That is just sick.

VIDEO AVAILABLE

Leonard Horwin, a Los Angeles attorney, informed us that a special video portraying the role of Israel in solving world problems of famine, soil depletion, and related subjects is available at a subsidized price. It is valuable for home showings, airing on local television, for churches, synagogues, and service groups. The title is *Saving Soil and Water, The Lowdermilks, China, and the Israel Connection.*

A second video, *Building Africa and Saving a People,* is also available.

These videos are suitable for all audiences. Factual data is included, especially from now deceased Inez Lowdermilk (a Methodist missionary, and one of the world's most contributive women on lifting the status of women). Through her and especially the work of her husband, Walter Clay Lowdermilk, great strides were made in saving and restoring the soil in China, Israel, and Africa. Also, information is included from Nigerian Professor Boniface Ossechere, Professor of African Studies, UCLA, and other leading scholars dealing with the African connection with Israel.

If you want the video for a television release, order the 3/4" size. If you want it for a regular VCR/VHS (home player) order the 1/2" version.

To order either video, or for more information write to The California Christian Committee for Israel; P. O. Box 2433; La Habra, CA 90632-2433. The cost of either video is $10.00 postpaid.

Notes

1David A. Lewis, *Jerusalem Courier,* Vol. 2, No. 3 (Springfield MO: David A. Lewis Ministries, Inc. 1983).

2Jerry E. Bishop, *The Wall Street Journal,* June 9, 1993 (New York, NY).

21

A CHANGE IS COMING!

Pagan Gentiles — Get Ready for a Shock

> *I am the Lord, your Holy One, the creator of Israel, your King. Behold, I will do a new thing; now it shall spring forth; shall ye not know it?* (Isa. 43:15,19).
>
> *I appointed the ancient people, and the things that are coming, and shall come, let them shew unto them* (Isa. 44:7).
>
> *And he that sat upon the throne said, Behold, I make all things new* (Rev. 21:5).

This is an age of change. Anyone who says it's the same old world needs to wake up and see reality. The biggest change of all approaches. Are you ready for it?

Politicians campaign under the banner of "change." And it works! It is the road to winning an election. "Change." Before the next election ask a voter, "What change is the candidate talking about?" How vague may be the answer, "But he will change things and we need change, so I will vote for him." Indeed, these are strange and changing times.

We have learned that change is a mine field. We have discovered that change can bring distress. Not all mutation is desirable. Someone forgot to ask the candidate what was going to be changed. Some who got the message chose to ignore it, for the sake of change. Yes, this is the period of change. Never have things changed so rapidly. Social evolution is accelerating exponentially. For morality you are offered a veritable smorgasbord of choices. Nothing is absolute any more. Promiscuity is admired. A virgin is the object of jokes. The UN gives the nod to a pedophile organization, NAMBLA (North American Man Boy Love Association).

How succinct the words of Isaiah, "Woe unto them that call evil good, and good evil; that put darkness for light, and light for darkness; that put bitter for sweet, and sweet for bitter! Woe unto them that are wise in their own eyes, and prudent in their own sight! Woe unto them that are mighty to drink wine, and men of strength to mingle strong drink: Which justify the wicked for reward, and take away the righteousness of the righteous from him!" (Isa. 5:20-23).

Politicians are not the only ones on the bandwagon of revolutionary change. The East-West gurus of the new world religion prophesy that around the year 2000 there will be a major transition. Time will flux. Reality will warp. Pseudo "virtual reality" will replace normal truth perception. The world will leave the old order, the age of Pisces, the era of Christianity, and move bravely into the New World Order, the age of Aquarius. New Age gurus herald a paradigm shift touted to transpire around the turn of the century.

A SURPRISE FOR THIS ARROGANT WORLD

There is a change coming all right, but it is not the change most people think about. The age of the Gentiles is about over, and soon will dawn the millennial age of glory for the Church and for Israel.

We are living in the close of the Church Age and the "times of the Gentiles," as outlined in Luke, Romans, and the Book of Revelation. Jesus predicted: "And they shall fall by the edge of the sword, and shall be led away captive into all nations: and Jerusalem shall be trodden down of the Gentiles, until the times of the Gentiles be fulfilled" (Luke 21:24).

Listen Gentiles, it's about over for you. Born-again Christians are not Gentiles (heathen) and will have a place in the glorious Kingdom that is coming to earth. Paul wrote to three first century churches indicating that believers in Jesus are "former" Gentiles. (See Gal. 2:15; Eph. 2:11.) The word Gentile in Hebrew has shades of meaning. It is translated "heathen" in 138 passages (KJV). Christians may think of themselves as "former" Gentiles: "Ye know that ye were Gentiles, carried away unto these dumb idols" (1 Cor. 12:2). Although my ancestry is British and French (no Jewish ancestors), I am no longer a Gentile. I am no longer an alien to the commonwealth of Israel. It is important for us to know our identity in God. That, however, should not cause us to overlook His continuing plan for national Israel. The existence of the Church, a new people of God, does not negate the continued existence of the original Zion — Israel. My identity with God does not depend on a denial of the original Israel. My identity is established in Christ as noted by the apostle Paul: "Wherefore remember, that ye being in time past Gentiles in the flesh, who are called uncircumcision by that which is called the circumcision in the flesh made by hands; That at the time ye were without Christ, being aliens from the commonwealth of Israel, and strangers from the covenants of promise, having no hope, and without God in the world: But now in Christ Jesus ye who sometimes were far off are made nigh by the blood of Christ" (Eph. 2:11-13).

Paul's brilliant exposition to the Roman church includes a definite statement about natural Israel's future. Note the use of the name Jacob referring to Israel in verse 26. Never in the entire Bible is the name Jacob used to refer in fact or type to the Church. It always, without exception, refers to natural Israel.

"For I would not, brethren, that ye should be ignorant of this mystery, lest ye should be wise in your own conceits; that blindness in part is happened to Israel, until the fullness of the Gentiles be come in. And so all Israel shall be saved: as it is written, There shall come out of Sion the Deliverer, and shall turn away ungodliness from Jacob: for this is my covenant unto them, when I shall take away their sins" (Rom. 11:25-27).

How frequently we hear the weary, worn-out statement, "I don't know about all this prophecy business. There are so many points of view. It's all a matter of interpretation." Exactly! It is a matter of interpretation. Either you believe the Word of God literally or you explain it away; it is as simple as that and there is need for no further complication. Even symbols have a literal meaning, and we find their meanings in the pages of the Bible itself.

There are coming days of change! "Behold, the days come, saith the Lord, that the plowman shall overtake the reaper, and the treader of grapes him that soweth seed; and the mountains shall drop sweet wine, and all the hills shall melt. And I will bring again the captivity of my people of Israel, and they shall build the waste cities, and inhabit them; and they shall plant vineyards, and drink the wine thereof; they shall also make gardens, and eat the fruit of them. And I will plant them upon their land, and they shall no more be pulled up out of their land which I have given them, saith the Lord thy God" (Amos 9:13-15). Am Israel Chai! The People of Israel Live!

God means what He says and it is beginning to come to pass, starting with the revival of the modern nation of Israel. Here we see Ezekiel 36-39 in the process of being fulfilled. There is coming a golden Messianic Age when all of the visions of the prophets will be fulfilled. The Church of redeemed persons, adopted into the commonwealth of Israel, will share in the glory of that age and the complete fulfillment of the hopes and dreams of the ages which are now only realized in a fragmentary way in Israel and in the Church. In the meantime we have God's mandate for the present age in which we live. We know our duty, there is no dilemma.

In 1961 Rev. Louis Hauff wrote,

> The Scriptures show that the eyes of the nations will be upon the nation of Israel in the last days. We are aware that Israel is today the center of attention of the world. All nations are aware of the existence of the nation of Israel and are concerned about what happens there. Each one is taking sides either for or against Israel. This could lead to a world conflict. In July, 1958, a time of crisis occurred when Russian Communists infiltrated Syria and supplied arms to the Syrians. Suddenly, the United States fleet landed Marines in Lebanon and Great Britain flew paratroopers into Jordan. The stage seemed set for a great battle. The battle of Armageddon seemed very close. Look at a map of Israel and you will see that Armageddon (the plain of Megiddo or Esdraelon) was surrounded by the United States to the northwest, Russia to the northeast, Great Britain to the east, Israel to the south, and Egypt to the southwest. Happily, the alert soon ended, but we were able to see how quickly the nations of the world could assemble at Armageddon in a great last conflict.
>
> After the Lord fights for and delivers Israel there will come a spiritual awakening to the people. The prophet Zechariah stated: "And it shall come to pass in

that day, that I will seek to destroy all the nations that come against Jerusalem. And I will pour upon the house of David, and upon the inhabitants of Jerusalem, the spirit of grace and of supplications: and they shall look upon me whom they have pierced, and they shall mourn for him, as one mourneth for his only son, and shall be in bitterness for him, as one that is in bitterness for his first born. .... In that day there shall be a fountain opened to the house of David and to the inhabitants of Jerusalem for sin and for uncleanness" (Zech. 12:9-10; 13:1).[1]

Although written over 30 years ago, this book is still up to date simply because Pastor Hauff relied on the Word of God for his insight into Israel's place in prophecy and world affairs.

MEETING OF CHRISTIAN ZIONISTS

In 1985 hundreds of Christian leaders met in Basel, Switzerland for the First International Christian Zionist Leadership Congress. We met in the Staadt Casino Music Hall, the very place where Theodore Herzl launched the modern Jewish Zionist movement in 1897.

In recognition of the mandate of God's Word relating to Israel, the Second International Christian Zionist Leadership Congress convened in Jerusalem in 1988. In 1987 the conveners of the congress proclaimed:

The State of Israel came into existence 40 years ago because of God's commitment to His covenant made with Abraham some 4,000 years before. Since then, this fledgling state has survived despite overwhelming problems and five wars.

Israel's continuing existence is a modern-day miracle. It is a miracle which has an especially challenging impact because it is the fulfillment of God's prophetic Word. Scripture enjoins us to give heed to the prophetic Word that shines as a bright light in our dark world (2 Pet. 1:19).

It is important, therefore, that Christians recognize and respond to God's eternal love for Israel.

Toward this end, the International Christian Embassy Jerusalem wishes to announce the 'Second International Christian Zionist Congress,' to be convened in Jerusalem from the 10 to the 14 of April, 1988.

At the time of the State of Israel's 40 anniversary, this will be an unequaled opportunity for Christians to come together to honor the Jewish State and pledge their on-going support for her. In recent years, Christian interest in and support for Israel has spread to many nations around the globe. We must, therefore, continue our efforts to focus that support, born out of our love for and commitment to the Lord Jesus Christ. Biblical Christian Zionism includes the following basic tenets:

1. Belief that the restoration of the modern State of Israel is no political accident, but rather a visible fulfillment of God's Word and promise (see Isa. 11:10-12; Jer.31:10-12).

2. Recognition of Christianity's debt to the Jewish people and acknowledgment of the long, dark history of Christian anti-Semitism.

3. The conviction and unswerving belief that the Land of Israel is the rightful homeland of the Jewish people, being promised and bequeathed by God to Abraham and his descendants as an everlasting possession and inheritance (see Gen. 17:7-8).

4. The declaration that in choosing Israel and bringing her back to her promised land, God did not make an exclusive choice, rather an all-inclusive one — promising one day to bring, through Israel, a blessing in which all generations and all nations of the earth would participate.

The Second International Christian Zionist Congress will seek ways by which Christians can turn their beliefs into concrete action. This means that the congress will explore theology, the Israel economy, information and Christian journalism, pilgrimage touring, and ways and means of furthering our struggle against anti-Semitism. Special emphasis will be placed on the on-going plight of Soviet Jewry.

It must be recognized, however, that many Christians from different backgrounds have a deep and sincere commitment to Israel. Their position is not necessarily motivated by prophetic belief but by other concerns relative to the history of Israel and her people. This congress provides a platform for such love and commitment to be expressed and deepened.

While primarily Christian leaders from all over the world will be attending, the congress is open to all Christians who have a love for Israel. The leadership of the International Christian Embassy believe that God is calling us to meet in Jerusalem at this time. Clearly the timing of this gathering is very significant. With this in mind, we cordially invite you to be a part of the Second International Christian Zionist Congress.

The First International Christian Zionist Congress met in Basel, Switzerland, in August of 1985. That congress, convened in the same hall that Theodore Herzl used for his historic Zionist Congress in August of 1897, brought together Christian leaders from different parts of the world. For three days the delegates listened to well-known Jewish and Christian speakers addressing the many implications of the restoration of the State of Israel. The strong consensus of the approximately 600 delegates was that the time spent together at Basel was challenging, enriching and a significant step forward in Jewish-Christian relationships.

The Basel Congress laid a vital foundation upon which we must build. Only as we do this can we hope to consolidate what has gone before and at the same time open up new areas of understanding, love, encouragement and comfort between Christians and Jews.

It is hoped that the Second International Christian Zionist Congress will enable Christians to further harmonize their stand on behalf of Israel and her destiny and by so doing add to the work begun at Basel in 1985."[2]

I have attended and spoken for each of the Christian Zionist Leadership congresses. These reports, therefore, are those of an on-the-spot observer.

A VISION FOR THE FUTURE

Change is coming, change so complete, so overwhelming, that it can be comprehended only by the aid of the Holy Spirit (see 1 Cor. 2:9-10; John 16:13). Premillennialists have caught a glimpse of what is coming, but as long as they sit in their cloistered study halls only pondering what the future holds their vision will be dim at best. Only those who put works with their faith and go out to do battle on the front lines will see with a clear eye.

The nation of Israel exists as a testimony to the miracle-working power of God. Anyone who works to insure the continued existence of Israel cooperates with the Divine plan.

THY WILL BE DONE

One could take a fatalistic attitude and say, "Well, if it's God's will for Israel to exist then it will exist." This is true. God's will shall ultimately be done. However, there are many ways the human race can follow in arriving at that ultimate fulfillment. We must recognize that in this present age God's will normally is not done. What we see in the world today — wars, violence, calamities, immorality, and drug abuse, is a result of humanity's rebellion against the will of God. People question why God, being all powerful and loving, does not stop the wars and suffering of the world.

Actually, the sufferings of humanity are a manifestation of man's rejection of the will of God. God's will toward man is good. Satan is the prince of death (see John 10:10). That is why the prayers and good works of God's people are so important. God ever seeks a person who will intercede for the nations so that destruction may be averted. Listen to the lament of God, "I sought for a man among them that should make up the hedge and stand in the gap before me for the land, but I found none" (Ezek. 22:30). In that dark and bitter hour of Israel's history there was no one to stand in the gap. Calamity fell upon the land. What will it be in our day? Will the believers cry out to God? Will Christians bless Israel and thus receive blessing from the Almighty? The choice is yours.

CAN THERE BE PEACE?

In 1978 I talked to a man who professed to be very interested in Bible prophecy. He inquired as to my opinion of the potential peace treaty between Israel and Egypt. I told him that we should pray for peace in the Middle East. His response was, "What do you want that for? I hope they have a war tomorrow, and kill each other off. It will bring the coming of Jesus that much closer." This is nothing more or less than a spiritually sick attitude that, unfortunately, infests the Church and especially those who are interested in certain aspects of prophecy. I call it Armageddon lust.

I know Armageddon is coming. But God did not call us to be

promoters of Armageddon. We are followers of the Prince of Peace. As a man of the Millennium, I long to see peace here and now to whatever degree it is possible. Why should we long for war and destruction? When Jesus stood on the Mount of Olives and said, "There shall be wars and rumors of wars," He was not gloating over the misfortunes of mankind. He was weeping over man's refusal to accept God's peace.

God commands us to pray for the peace of Jerusalem (see Ps. 122). This demands that we pray for the peace of nations around Jerusalem and for a normalization of relations between Israel and her neighbors. The end of the age will come in due season, but as long as the believers are here, our mandate is to pray for and believe for the peace of Jerusalem.[3] This statement was published 12 years before the peace accord was signed, September 13, 1993, on the White House lawn. We pray that our farsighted hopes are not in vain.

Perhaps the present peace process between Rabin and Arafat is a test of our faith. However flawed the political leaders may be, we must pray that God will change them, and use them for good.

True believers should be supportive of Israel. The Jews have returned to the land a second time (see Isa. 11:11) and they will not be driven out of the land again (see Amos 9:13-15). This is the divine plan. We are not merely spectators, but we are called to end-time involvement in that plan of the Almighty. How shall we be involved?

THE POWER OF PRAYER TO EFFECT CHANGE

First of all we are called to intercession. God intervenes in human affairs when we invite Him to do so. His will is not always done on earth. We are instructed to pray for God's will in the Lord's prayer. "Pray for the peace of Jerusalem, they shall prosper that love thee" (Ps. 122). God would not command us to pray a prayer that was designed to frustrate us. If it were not possible for this to be fulfilled, then why pray? Final prophetic events are predetermined but many details along the way can be determined by our cooperation (or lack thereof) with the known will of God. We do not know how far we are from the end of the age. It may be close at hand, but we should not abandon our responsibilities and use prophecy as an escapist mentality. We must strive to serve our generation well in our own time. We urge you to pray for all the people of the Middle East and their leaders. We highly recommend the reading of *Smashing the Gates of Hell in the Last Days.*[4]

This book has been described as a manual for spiritual warfare and end-time victory. It will help you understand how to pray effectively for the Church, your nation, for Israel, and international events.

THE NEW CIA — CHRISTIANS IN ACTION!

To our prayers we add works. "Faith without works is dead" (James 2:20). There are ways in which you can be a Christian agent for change in the most positive and beneficial ways. Two things we need to work on are the false image of Israel portrayed to the Church and the bad image of the Church in the eyes of the Jewish people.

For centuries Christianity has misrepresented its own teaching to the Jewish world by bad actions and anti-Semitism. We are so hardened to this reality that we can hardly admit that it is true. The Jewish historian is not wrong when he writes that it was "Christian" anti-Semitism that made acceptance of Hitler possible. Hence the persecution of the Jews becomes a "Christian" phenomenon in Jewish eyes.

That is, of course, a short-sighted view. For one thing, anti-Semitism is a Satanic, not Christian philosophy. From Haman to Antiochus there have been pre-Christian attempts to eradicate the Jews. But "Christians" have opted to cooperate with hell on all too many occasions. We deny the validity of such a manifestation of "Christianity" and disassociate ourselves from it. We must now accept the responsibility of presenting to Israel the true spirit of Christianity, a spirit of love and concern. This is one of the purposes of Christians United for Israel, The National Christian Leadership Conference for Israel, and a number of other similar organizations. (A partial listing of some of these organizations may be found in the back of this book.)

Perhaps you would like to become a member of Christians United for Israel. Members receive a membership card. You will also receive the next four issues of our newspaper, *The Jerusalem Courier*. It is published irregularly. Readers of this book may receive a complimentary membership in C.U.F.I. by writing to C.U.F.I.; P.O. Box 11115; Springfield, MO 65808.

Notes

[1]Louis Hauff, *Israel in Bible Prophecy* (Springfield, MO: Gospel Publishing House, 1961/1974), p. 22-23.

[2]*Jerusalem Courier,* Vol. 6, No. 2, p. 11 (Springfield, MO: David A. Lewis

Ministries, 1987).

[3]*Jeruaslem Courier,* Vol. 1, No. 1, p. 1.

[4]David Allen Lewis, *Smashing the Gates of Hell in the Last Days* (Green Forest, AR: New Leaf Press, 5th Ed., 1987).

22

IF AMERICA ABANDONS ISRAEL

Twilight of the USA?

> *And there went out another horse that was red: and power was given to him that sat thereon to take peace from the earth, and that they should kill one another: and there was given unto him a great sword* (Rev. 6:4).
>
> *If my people, which are called by my name, shall humble themselves, and pray, and seek my face, and turn from their wicked ways; then will I hear from heaven, and will forgive their sin, and will heal their land* (2 Chron. 7:14).

Authors of recent books on American destiny feel free to appropriate Old Testament promises made to Israel, transferring them to America and/or the Church. It is acceptable to draw from the well of Old Testament inspiration and apply principles found there to our nation, as long as there is a recognition that the primary application was and still is to the nation of Israel.

The problem with this approach is that many authors overlook a truly foundational premise that we should be taking very seriously.

God firmly states that He will bless those who bless Israel (the great nation promised to Abraham through his promised seed Isaac and Jacob/Israel) and curse those who curse her. This is found in Genesis 12:1-3 where God states this concept to Abraham.

Why is Israel so critical to America's survival? Why even mention Israel in connection with America's chaotic problems? And, when we say America here, these principles apply to any nation.

TROUBLE IN AMERICA — BETRAYAL OF ZION

America is now experiencing troubles that are in part due to the fact that our nation is slowly turning away from being supportive of Israel. There are other things that call for the wrath of God on America but this is an important matter that must be shouted from the house-tops. Recently I reread a prophecy made by Jan William van der Hoeven in the mid 1980s stating that the president elected in 1988 would turn against Israel. And I predicted later that he could not be re-elected if he did not change his policies toward Israel.

I would like to warn the present administration that if they do not stop trying to strangle Israel, demanding unreasonable "land for peace" deals they will bring further distress on our nation and calamity upon their own heads. How can Evangelicals be unconcerned? Should we not pray and work for a reversal of this negative attitude toward the Jewish state?

When I gave testimony on the Middle East before the Senate Foreign Relations Committee in Washington, DC, I was questioned by Senator Percy on my book *Magog, 1982 Canceled* which is about the Lebanon war. At one point I told the senators that Israel's 1982 invasion into Lebanon, where a bloody civil war had been raging for seven years, gave Lebanon a chance to become a viable nation once again.

At the Senate Foreign Relations Committee hearings I further indicted the U.S. State Department for stopping General Ariel Sharon from finally pushing the PLO terrorists out of Beirut. The sorry result of that policy was the debacle of the PLO fighting its own factions and in the same time frame we saw our Marine bases blown up with the loss of over 200 American lives. I spoke about this to the senators with authority. Some of them wrote me letters of appreciation. Now things are on the decline again. Will we wake up in time?

LISTEN, MR. PRESIDENT!

I warned former President Gerald Ford in a letter, which was hand-delivered, that if he did not alter his policy toward Israel, he could not be re-elected. History renders the verdict.

Christians United for Israel placed a full-page ad in the Atlanta Constitution when President Carter was in Atlanta to address the Southern Baptist Convention. In this letter, signed by over 100 Christian clergymen and leaders, we appealed to President Carter to bless Israel. A group of our partners gave out thousands of reprints at the Baptist convention.

A copy of this advertisement was placed in Carter's hands at the convention. His Mideast policies failed because they were not based on biblical concepts, even though Carter is a born-again Christian. His recent book, *The Blood of Abraham*, reveals that while he has a political grasp of certain aspects of the Middle East, he has still not come to grips with his Christian, biblical heritage, regarding the Jewish people. He seems to have little grasp of Israel's right to the land, according to the Scriptures.

I warned George Bush in a statement given at a press conference at the National Press Club in Washington, DC. (Statements were also made by other Christian and Jewish leaders and a U.S. Senator). Here is the text of my statement:

FRIENDS OF JERUSALEM PRESS CONFERENCE
WASHINGTON, DC. — OCTOBER 28, 1991

Statement by David Allen Lewis
Chairman of the Board, National Christian Leadership
Conference for Israel.
President, Christians United for Israel.

I have recently returned from Israel where on this and other occasions, I have had the opportunity to observe first hand the wrenching need which the State of Israel has in providing for her persecuted exiles from Russia, Eastern Europe, and Ethiopia.

In spite of the tortured mathematical Rubic twists of the opponents of Loan Guarantees to Israel, and the quoting of dubious sources of information about Israel's inability to repay the loans, as an Evangelical leader, and as the Chairman of the Board of the National Christian Leadership Conference for Israel, I urge our president and other leaders to move forward with these loans to enable Israel to borrow money from private lending institutions at favorable rates for the following reasons:

1. Israel's record of repaying loans in a timely manner is impeccable and unique among nations who have received such guarantees from us. Let the record be clear — this is not foreign aid. This is a business deal with one of our best customers.

2. A strong argument can be put forth for Israel's ability to repay these loans enhanced by the fact that much of the money will go into self amortizing ventures in Israel's private sector into which repayment is factored.

3. Much of the money will be spent to purchase products in the U.S., and interest will be paid to American lending institutions to the benefit of our own economy.

4. As U.S. Senator Robert W. Kasten, Jr. indicated on September 10, the loan guarantees will cost the American taxpayers nothing. Even the substantial "origination fee" will be pre-paid by Israel.

5. Furthermore the $1.6 billion dollar deposit which the U.S. will put in trust as a guarantee will be the source of considerable earnings for our economy in the form of interest.

6. Not only will these funds be used to meet enormous humanitarian needs, they will contribute immensely to Israel's economy and increase her already significant role as a U.S. client. Israel is one of our best trading partners, spending over $1.5 billion dollars in 42 states in 1989-1990 alone.

7. Finally I have serious concerns about the moral ground on which the needs of refugees, whose flight from persecution we have encouraged, are held hostage to preserving some "delicate balance" with Arab countries in whose streets we hear the cry "Death to America, Death to Israel." On the other hand Arab countries such as Syria, the world's biggest drug dealer and money launderer, sell drugs on our streets (See *Narco Terrorism* Rachel Ehrenfeld), use their "bonuses" for participating in the Gulf War, to purchase Scud C Missiles and other sophisticated weaponry and build plants to manufacture such weapons to be aimed solely at Israel as in

the case of Egypt and Syria.

Mr. President, Mr. Baker, Israel was asked to wait six months before applying. When they did apply in September, they were asked to wait an additional four months while the need mounts and the hurting continues. Is this any way to treat a friend?

Additional ad lib comments were made following the reading of this statement.

In similar fashion. I now warn Bill Clinton that disaster will befall his administration and our nation if he does not stop pressuring Israel into making land compromises that will endanger the nation of Israel. No matter what mistakes he can push the leaders of Israel into committing, he will be held responsible.

USA CIVIL WAR II

America is now on the verge of revolution, a violent civil war is potential. Our own 28-year Intifada started in 1965 with the Watts riots in Los Angeles. Rioters rampaged, buildings were blown up or burned, looting was widespread, and many were killed. The police could not control the situation so the National Guard was called in. More deaths resulted.

For the last 28 years, since 1965, south central Los Angeles has been a war zone. Drive-by automatic weapon shootings and gang wars are so commonplace that it almost ceases to be newsworthy. Only when the violence is stepped up, as it was in response to the verdict in the Rodney King case, do the TV vultures descend on the scene again. Once again the National Guard and the Marines are called to restore order. The gangs regroup, the drug pushers continue, violence is perpetuated. The poor and the downtrodden suffer.

Moloch gloats.

The moral and spiritual shaking is worse than the two earthquakes that hit Southern California on June 28, 1992, and the great quake of 1994. A preview of things to come. Missouri will suffer one of the worst earthquakes in history when the New Madrid fault experiences a major shift.

WHEN THE CIVIL WAR GOES NATIONWIDE

Los Angeles is not the only urban center to suffer riots. One day when riots break out in 30 or 40 major population centers, you may be the first to call for "law and order." Widespread violence, looting in the suburbs, bombing the homes of baby boomers and yuppies will create a demand for extraordinary measures. Now the whole Militia must be mobilized to control internal strife and civil disobedience. Martial law can be declared and welcomed. In effect normal governmental processes are put on hold and martial law rules the land. Then America could have an irreversible dictatorship.

A president could become a military dictator over such a junta.

Our last several presidents have signed into law a series of Executive Orders making legal provision for such harsh rulership in the event of internal and seemingly uncontrollable trouble. The president and the military will have legal right to take over all assets, manpower, and energy sources to preserve law and order. Citizens can be forced to move to any area for work assignments.

Is America on the verge of a revolution? The Los Angeles riots are a small picture of what will yet develop on a nationwide scale. Commotion, havoc, chaos, and upheaval will prepare the way for the governmental structure that will bow to and cooperate with the Antichrist.

All of this could happen before the Rapture, or it may be after, during the Tribulation, but it will happen! Don't count on the Rapture as an escape from all troubles. We just don't know the timetable. (See Mark 13:32-33.)

"And I looked, and behold a pale horse: and his name that sat on him was Death, and Hell followed with him. And power was given unto them over the fourth part of the earth, to kill with sword, and with hunger, and with death, and with the beasts of the earth" (Rev. 6:8).

THE BAREFOOTED MASSES

The late Dr. J. Wallace Hamilton wrote a book, *The Thunder of Bare Feet,* in which he pictured the disadvantaged and downtrodden of the world rising up against the overlords of earth, then they become the new corrupted overlords.

Our racial problems in America are easily understood in the proper frame of historical reference. People have been enslaved from time immemorial. There is not a person reading this whose ancestors at some point of time were not slaves. In fairly recent times traders created a market for black African slaves. Black African tribesman and Arabs captured other black Africans and sold them to the white slave traders who brought them to America for ultimate degradation and exploitation. All are guilty! Overworked, beaten, raped, and bullied the black Africans groaned under the oppression and longed for deliverance.

Black Americans, in the midst of your anger, you need to pause and carefully reflect on the fact that while white slave traders and plantation owners sinned against God and man by slave trafficking, on the other hand it was other white men and women who fought against slavery through the abolitionist movement and were willing to lay down their lives in a horrible civil war to bring freedom to the black people. While you criticize the white race, remember to thank God for those white persons who came to your rescue and set you free, and thank Him for those Christians of all races who love you and wish God's best and prosperity for you.

Since there are violent extremists on both sides of this question I tell you that it is inevitable that there will be a mighty upheaval in this country. The question may be, will it be a PLO style Intifada or a Lebanese style civil war? How much of it will hit before the Rapture and Tribulation?

Even now the spirit of Hitler stalks the land. The eternally damned Nazis are rising again and some of you cannot even see it.

The coming upheaval will forward the cause of the perpetrators of world socialism and the New World Order. Out of chaos will arise a New Order that, promising law and order, and peace, will bring about the ultimate enslavement of all mankind, all races of people. Read it in the Book of Revelation. It is plain to see if you do not refuse to see. But of course some people have bought the deceptive bill of goods that it is hard to understand the Book of Revelation. Actually it is one of the easiest books in the Bible to understand. Read it. Believe it.

SURVIVAL

Because of the uncertainty of the times I advocate what I call 60-day survival as a minimum of preparedness. Not everyone can do what I will suggest, but you can do some things to protect your family and home.

What I suggest is quite simple. Stock up a supply of non-perishable food. Dry beans, brown rice, whole-wheat flour, and corn meal should be stored in airtight containers. Good quality multi-vitamins from all natural sources should be stocked. Packaged meals that can be stored at room temperature have a good shelf life.

Have a supply of pure water on hand. Have energy free water purifying devices and water purification tablets. A catalytic heater and a supply of fuel would be a good thing. An electrical generator would be good for some to have. Have battery operated radios and a good supply of alkaline batteries. High quality, solid metal flashlights, and candles are a must.

Some believe that if you are on a farm or live in a village your chances are better. Just remember that while violence will begin in the cities, it will eventually sweep the countryside.

The currency may become valueless, so have some silver bullion on hand for making emergency purchases. If you have old silver coins hang on to them. Buy silver ingots or bars (one to 20 ounces) with a well known mint mark, such as Englehard or Silvertown. When the big economic collapse described in Revelation hits, FDIC will not help you. Your insured accounts will be gone forever.

Have things with which to barter. Tools are a good thing to stockpile for barter. Keep them in the blisterpak or as purchased, with the price tag in place. In hard times everyone needs to fix things up and will need tools. Extra clothing items could be good for barter.

When the last great depression hit and the banks were closed most people lost everything they had in safe deposit boxes as well as their accounts. This poses a real problem. Where shall you store things? In a short-term crisis situation the banks may survive or recover, but don't count on it.

Treat your accumulation as a hobby. This is not an investment. It will never make money for you. It is for a time of emergency. It is like the first aid kit on the shelf. Pray to God that you never need any of your carefully stored things.

Do not put your dependence on things, but upon the Lord. If it makes you stressful and nervous to follow this advice, then maybe you should ignore this chapter. You should be able to do what you do in a sense of calm faith. If you choose to follow none of this advice and rely solely on the Lord's provision, no one can fault you for that. I realize this is not for everyone.

Look at this matter like you would view an auto or health insurance policy. You hope to never need the provisions of the policy, but you buy it just in case.

As a traveling evangelist, I have a problem. I cannot follow my own good advice! If an emergency arises while I am in Oregon, Poland, Iceland, Barbados, or Maine what good will anything at my home base do me? I am going to have to depend upon the Lord for any hour of crisis that may come before the Rapture. This does not indicate any lack of confidence on my part in my own council. I am trying to give you good advice, for those who can receive it.

Note again that I advocate 60-day survival. If a revolution

continues beyond two months you would need a heavy duty arsenal to protect your well stocked domicile. Hooligans will roam through the suburbs and countryside. Bands of looters will break into the National Guard Armory and take heavy weapons. Their grenade launchers and bazookas will blow you off the face of the earth if you resist their demands.

In every country where trouble has erupted in the past, most of the people sat around saying, "It cannot happen here." Wake up, friend.

NOT THE GOSPEL

Survival is not the gospel. What I write is practical advice and not a command of the Lord. Find the will of God for yourself. Take a little responsibility in this. No one else can determine the will of God for you personally. I have no further advice for you at this time.

This is not the gospel, for the gospel must be universal in its application. The gospel must apply equally to the poor and dispossessed as well as to the banker, the lawyer, the Amway representative, the Texas millionaire, and the Connecticut yuppie. All the rest of it is optional. But these could be important options for you, individually.

We are in the intelligence and information service of the King of kings and His kingdom, and it is in this light that I have written this.

"My people are destroyed for lack of knowledge: because thou hast rejected knowledge, I will also reject thee, that thou shalt be no priest to me: seeing thou hast forgotten the law of thy God, I will also forget thy children. They eat up the sin of my people, and they set their heart on their iniquity. And there shall be, like people, like priest: and I will punish them for their ways, and reward them their doings. For they shall eat, and not have enough: they shall commit whoredom, and shall not increase: because they have left off to take heed to the Lord. Whoredom and wine and new wine take away the heart" (Hos. 4:6-11).

REPENTING FOR THE NATION'S SINS

If we want to save America, we must turn away from sin and seek true holiness. Do not allow the demons of television to brainwash you. The average Christian watches "slime-time" TV for four hours or more daily. The average Christian does not spend even 15 minutes a day in Bible reading and prayer. Are you not also appalled that Christians are not appalled at the sin and immorality that is rampant around us? Are you offended by sin? That is one true manifestation of holiness unto the Lord.

"Beloved, now are we the sons of God, and it doth not yet appear what we shall be: but we know that, when he shall appear, we shall be like him; for we shall see him as he is. And every man that hath this hope in him purifieth himself, even as he is pure. Little children, let no man deceive you: he that doeth righteousness is righteous, even as he is righteous" (1 John 3:2-7).

This is a Bible prophecy ministry, but what good is prophecy if it is merely a mental exercise and does not promote holiness unto the Lord?

Television is the greatest corrupter of morals and sound thinking in our times. It is a sower of disinformation and delusions. Having great potential for good the medium has become the voice of Satan for about 95 percent of the time it speaks. TV glorifies and promotes every form of immorality. It scoffs at the God of heaven. Music videos that are vile and obscene are shown in daytime hours. Nudity and violence are paraded across the screen.

The gospel is mocked. The media exudes moral sickness. Safe sex is the mythology of a plague-ridden world. Are these not the last days of Sodom and Gomorrah? How much longer can the wrath of God be withheld?

We must all repent of the sins of stealing, cheating, immorality, murder and abortion. Though you and I may not personally be guilty of these sins, we must repent, as the prophets did, for their nation (see Dan. 9:1-23). Do not be quiet. Speak out against the evils of society.

ISRAEL — THE LITMUS TEST

Since so many are so quiet about our nation's creeping betrayal of Israel, you must shout your protest from the housetops. Insist that your church pay attention to this major end time issue. Learn to refute the lies of the media and the anti-Semites. Don't let lukewarm leadership sweep this issue under the rug. You and I can turn the tide for God and righteousness.

No one said it would be easy. You are mandated to educate yourself so that you can answer on these matters. This is, after all, the most important of all the great issues that face us today. Israel is God's litmus test of the end times. God cannot put maximum blessing on this nation's legitimate Christian reformers if they ignore the issue of Israel's security and survival.

There is still time to correct our course. God declares that even if a judgment has been pronounced, it can be reversed: "At what instant I shall speak concerning a nation, and concerning a kingdom, to pluck up, and to pull down, and to destroy it; If that nation, against whom I have pronounced, turn from their evil, I will repent of the evil that I thought to do unto them" (Jer. 18:7-8).

TWIN TRADE TOWERS — A SHADOW OF THINGS TO COME

The fatal day was Friday, February 26, 1993. At 12:18 p.m. a massive explosion rocked the Twin Towers of New York's World Trade Center, blasting a 100-foot crater three floors deep. Five lay dead, hundreds wounded. Pandemonium prevailed. Shortly after the bombing, U.S. law enforcement officials arrested a suspect who is a member of a Moslem terrorist organization said to be connected in some way to the Moslem Brotherhood and to HAMAS. The terrorist organization HAMAS, we were told, now has its principle headquarters right here in America.

When Israel bombed Saddam Hussein's nuclear reactor at Osirak, outside of Baghdad in 1981, the Jew-hating world howled with rage at the tiny beleaguered nation of the sons and daughters of Isaac. How the hypocrites in the UN condemned what they could scarce understand — then. Understanding came hard. It dawned during the Gulf War when the Western nations fell all over themselves backing down on previous condemnation of Israel [re: Osirak], realizing that if Israel had not taken out the Osirak reactor the consequences would have been beyond devastating for the Allied Coalition. Imagine a Saddam with atomic bombs mounted on his SCUD missiles.

Is it possible that as the tragedy of the bombing of the Twin Trade Tower buildings in New York hits home the USA will gain some little bit of understanding of why Israel expelled over 400 HAMAS connected leaders from her borders? These men are the very infrastructure of that Moslem Fundamentalist terror organization. Israel has exiled them for only two years. Even now they have allowed most of them to come back into the country. After the tragic Hebron Massacre of 1994, at the hand of a mentally disturbed Israeli Army captain, 1,000 terrorists were released from Israeli prisons as an appeasement.

After the Gulf War, Kuwait drove 300,000 Palestinians out of her borders, not for two years, but permanently. Saudi Arabia kicked out tens of thousands of Palestinians — permanently. Where are the cries of outrage in the United Nations for these actions? Double standard! Lying hypocrisy!

Let us imagine for a moment, that when all the terrorists involved in killing and wounding hundreds of our people in New York are apprehended, the USA decides to exile them to a no man's land between Canada and the USA for only two years. Will CNN, ABC, CBS, and NBC cry out against their removal from our soil as they have cried out against Israel?

We ask, "Why this double standard?" In ancient times, during the days of Gideon, the Israelites were forced to battle the Midianites. Today Israel's biggest enemies are the Media-ites.

All the "ites" would do well to read the record in God's Word, the Bible. "Behold, he that keepeth Israel shall neither slumber nor sleep" (Ps. 121:4).

God said that He would bless those who bless Israel and curse those who curse her. When will our political leaders wake up? Will the terrorist afflicted agony of New York City be enough of a catalyst? Will our eyes finally start to open? Shall our blindness continue?

Here is an intriguing thought: Two nations have introduced more anti-Israel resolutions than any other nations in the United Nations, according to Freida Keets, Israeli radio journalist, who spoke in the First Assembly of God Church of Fort Meyers, Florida where Rev. Dan Betzer is the pastor. And what is the identity of those two ill-fated nations? Yugoslavia and Somalia. I rest my case.

It is only a matter of time until a terrorist organization assembles a nuclear bomb in a major city, whether New York, Washington, Paris, London, or Rome. What administration can resist their demands then? "Thus saith the Lord of hosts, Behold, evil shall go forth from nation to nation, and a great whirlwind shall be raised up from the coasts of the earth" (Jer. 25:32).

Wake up, people, our only hope is in God.

Is there hope for the future? Yes, in the short term we can impact and change our world through prayer, intercession, and positive action. In the long term, our hope is in the predetermined plan of a sovereign God who will bring His purposes to pass.

"Blessed is the man that trusteth in the Lord, and whose hope the Lord is" (Jer. 17:7).

We are "Looking for that blessed hope, and the glorious appearing of the great God and our Saviour Jesus Christ" (Titus 2:13).

23

YEHUDA'S STORY

A True Parable

*For all our days are passed away in thy
wrath: we spend our years as a tale that is told*
(Ps. 90:9).
*There is a wheel of justice that turns full
circle with the passing of the years of time.* —
David Allen Lewis

I feel that God sent him to me for many curious reasons. Yehuda
came to the hotel to listen to one of our lecturers. After the meeting we
spent several hours talking of many things. Though now he talks
plainly on matters of our mutual research, that night he spoke to me
in parables.

Everyone in Jerusalem has a story to tell. The air is full of
mystery. Intrigue permeates the atmosphere. One true story Yehuda
told me is like a parable. Though dark may be the night imposed on
humanity by man's brutality to his fellow man, nevertheless there is
a wheel of justice that turns full circle in the passage of time.

Yehuda came to us during the feast of Purim. That is the time
when the Jewish people celebrate the victory of Mordecai and Esther
over Haman, the Hitler of his day. Haman built a gallows on which to
hang the Jews, but God turned the situation about, and Haman hung
on his own gallows.

Yehuda told of an ex-Nazi Luftwaffe officer who engaged in

conversation with him some time ago. The Nazi was loud, arrogant, and boastful. "You Jews," he argued, "are always stirring up the stink of the past. Why can't you leave the past alone?"

Yehuda inquired of him, "I suppose, sir, that you would admit Hitler started the Second World War?"

"You see," said the Nazi, "that's exactly what I mean, always digging up old history. Why can't you forget it and live for today?"

"Well," said Yehuda, "I guess you could further admit that Hitler was responsible not only for the death of six million of my people, the Jews, but also for 50 million other casualties in World War II?"

"Yes, yes, of course — we all admit that Hitler was a devil. We Germans made a mistake about him, but what good does it do to remember it now?"

Yehuda continued, "I must tell you, sir, that the Nazis did a 'good' job on my family. All my family — mother, father, brothers,

sisters — were killed in your death camps. All, that is, but me and one uncle."

"You have a sick mind," the Nazi shouted. "I know you have experienced personal tragedy, but you need to forget it. Leave the past in the past. Furthermore, I have had enough of this conversation."

"Not quite enough. I have one more thing to tell you. Some-

Yehuda
Oppenheim

thing you do not know. You admit that Hitler started the Second World War, but what you do not know is that one Jew, my uncle, ended it!"

"What insanity is this? Surely you Jews are mad, but you especially! I have never heard such nonsense. And who might this uncle of yours be?"

"My uncle was Robert Oppenheimer," said Yehuda as his eyes pierced into the soul of the unrepentant Nazi.

The Nazi literally shook like a leaf in the summer breeze. Unable to say another word, he turned and walked away. You see, he recognized the name Robert Oppenheimer as the man who was chiefly responsible for the atomic bomb.

There is a wheel of justice that turns full circle with the passing of the years of time.

Haman hangs on his own gallows. Hitler burns the Jews in the gas furnaces and then burns himself in his own bunker in Berlin. They that curse Israel are cursed by the Almighty.

Israel will survive.

Robert Oppenheimer, a physicist, was a professor at the University of California and the California Institute of Technology. He directed atomic energy research and the manufacture of the atom bomb during the Second World War. From 1947 until 1966 he was director of the Institute for Advanced Study at Princeton University.

Oppenheimer served as chairman of the general advisory com-

Robert Oppenheimer.

mittee of the U.S. Atomic Energy Commission until 1954. After seeing the horrible effects of the atomic bomb, he refused to work on the hydrogen bomb. He was accused of being a security risk and was suspended from the A.E.C. in 1954.

Allegations against him were never proven. It is well known that this man was responsible for guiding the research and production of the atom bomb, which so dramatically brought the Second World War to its conclusion, with victory falling into the hands of the free world.

"Daniel answered and said, 'Blessed be the name of God for ever and ever: for wisdom and might are his' " (Dan. 2:20).

"For I will give you a mouth and wisdom, which all your adversaries shall not be able to gainsay nor resist" (Luke 21:15).

PEACE FOR THE MIDDLE EAST

Let's Face the Facts

THE PLO COVENANT

Israel is being pressured by the United Nations, including and especially the USA and United Europe, to give up land for peace, without any assurance that her neighbors will normalize relations with Israel. No, Israel should not give land for peace. Let there be an exchange of "peace for peace," then every other item on each nation's agenda may be discussed and negotiated on a normal basis. Egypt is the only Arab nation that recognizes Israel's right to exist. Don't be fooled by peace conferences. We are hopeful but cautious.

Further, the same nations that convened the original convention that brought the PLO into existence along with the PLO Charter should reconvene, revise the PLO Charter, and remove the passages that call for the destruction of Israel. One of the promises PLO Chairman Yassir Arafat made was to change the PLO Charter. We are still waiting, hopefully. There can be normalization of relations, but not while the threat to destroy Israel is still in the Charter. Let's begin with basics.

No doubt you have heard about the PLO Charter, but few ordinary people in the Western Nations have ever seen it. Here it is, complete. There is no other. Evaluate it for yourself. The words in square brackets have been added to define and clarify the PLO Charter.

THE PALESTINE NATIONAL CHARTER
(THERE IS NO OTHER)

Article 1: Palestine [all of Israel] is the homeland of the Arab Palestinian people; it is an indivisible part of the Arab homeland, and the Palestinian people are an integral part of the Arab nation.

Article 2: Palestine, with the boundaries it had during the British mandate, is an indivisible territorial unit. [Includes all of Israel and the Hashemite Kingdom of Jordan].

Article 3: The Palestinian Arab people possess the legal right to their homeland and have the right to determine their destiny after achieving the liberation of their country in accordance with their wishes and entirely of their own accord and will.

Article 4: The Palestinian identity is a genuine, essential and inherent characteristic; it is transmitted from parents to children. The Zionist occupation and the dispersal of the Palestinian Arab people, through the disasters which befell them, do not make them lose their Palestinian identity and their membership of the Palestinian community, nor do they negate them.

Article 5: The Palestinians are those Arab nationals who, until 1947, normally resided in Palestine regardless of whether they were evicted from it or have stayed there. Anyone born, after that date, of a Palestinian father—whether inside Palestine or outside it—is also a Palestinian.

Article 6: The Jews who had normally resided in Palestine until the beginning of the Zionist invasion will be considered Palestinians. [See note at end of section].

Article 7: That there is a Palestinian community and that it has material, spiritual and historical connection with Palestine are indisputable facts. It is a national duty to bring up individual Palestinians in an Arab revolutionary manner. All means of information and education must be adopted in order to acquaint the Palestinian with his country in the most profound manner, both spiritual and material, that is possible. He must be prepared for the armed struggle and ready to sacrifice his wealth and his life in order to win back his homeland and bring about its liberation.

Article 8: The phase in their history, through which the Palestinian people are now living, is that of national struggle for the liberation of Palestine. Thus the conflicts among the Palestinian national forces are secondary, and should be ended for the sake of the basic conflict that exists between the forces of Zionism and of imperialism on the one hand, and the Palestinian Arab people on the other. On this basis the Palestinian masses, regardless of whether they are residing in the national homeland or in Diaspora, constitute—both their organizations and the individuals—one national front working for the retrieval of Palestine and its liberation through armed struggle.

Article 9: Armed struggle is the only way to liberate Palestine. Thus it is the overall strategy, not merely a tactical phase. The Palestinian Arab people assert their absolute determination and firm resolution to continue their armed struggle and to work for an armed popular revolution for the liberation of their country and their return to it. They also assert their right to normal life in Palestine and to exercise their right to self-determination and sovereignty over it.

Article 10: Commando action constitutes the nucleus of the Palestinian popular liberation war. This requires its escalation, comprehensiveness and the mobilization of all the Palestinian popular and educational efforts and their organization and involvement in the armed Palestinian revolution. It also requires the achieving of unity for the national struggle among the different groupings of the Palestinian people, and between the Palestinian people and the Arab masses so as to secure the continuation of the revolution, its escalation and victory.

Article 11: The Palestinians will have three mottoes; national unity, national mobilization and liberation.

Article 12: The Palestinian people believe in Arab unity. In order to contribute their share towards the attainment of that objective, however, they must, at the present stage of their struggle, safeguard their Palestinian identity and develop their consciousness of that identity, and oppose any plan that may dissolve or impair it.

Article 13: Arab unity and the liberation of Palestine are two complementary objectives, the attainment of either of which facilitates the attainment of the other. Thus, Arab unity leads to the liberation of Palestine; the liberation of Palestine leads to Arab unity; and work towards the realization of one objective proceeds side by side with work towards the realization of the other.

Article 14: The destiny of the Arab nation, and indeed Arab existence itself, depends upon the destiny of the Palestine cause. From this interdependence springs the Arab nation's pursuit of, and striving for, the liberation of Palestine. The people of Palestine play the role of the vanguard in the realization of this sacred national goal.

The liberation of Palestine, from an Arab viewpoint, is a national duty and it attempts to repel the Zionist and imperialist aggression against the Arab homeland, and aims at the elimination of Zionism in

Palestine. Absolute responsibility for this falls upon the Arab nation—peoples and governments—with the Arab people of Palestine in the vanguard. Accordingly the Arab nation must mobilize all its military, human, moral and spiritual capabilities to participate actively with the Palestinian people in the liberation of Palestine. It must, particularly in the phase of the armed Palestinian revolution, offer and furnish the Palestinian people with all possible help, and material and human support, and make available to them the means and opportunities that will enable them to continue to carry out their leading role in the armed revolution, until they liberate their homeland.

Article 16: The liberation of Palestine, from a spiritual point of view, will provide the Holy Land with an atmosphere of safety and tranquillity, which in turn will safeguard the country's religious sanctuaries and guarantee freedom of worship and of visit to all, without discrimination of race, color, language, or religion. Accordingly, the people of Palestine look to all spiritual forces in the world for support.

Article 17: The liberation of Palestine, from a human point of view, will restore to the Palestinian individual his dignity, pride and freedom. Accordingly the Palestinian Arab people look forward to the support of all those who believe in the dignity of man and his freedom in the world.

Article 18: The liberation of Palestine, from an international point of view, is a defensive action necessitated by the demands of self-defense. Accordingly, the Palestinian people, desirous as they are of the friendship of all people, look to freedom-loving justice-loving and peace-loving states for support in order to restore their legitimate rights in Palestine, to reestablish peace and security in the country, and to enable its people to exercise national sovereignty and freedom.

Article 19: The partition of Palestine in 1947 and the establishment of the State of Israel are entirely illegal, regardless of the passage of time, because they were contrary to the will of the Palestinian people and to their natural right in their homeland, and inconsistent with the principles embodied in the Charter of the United Nations, particularly the right to self-determination.

Article 20: The Balfour Declaration, the mandate for Palestine and everything that has been based upon them, are deemed null and void. Claims of historical or religious ties of Jews with Palestine are incompatible with the facts of history and the true conception of what constitutes statehood. Judaism, being a religion, is not an independent nationality. Nor do Jews constitute a single nation with an identity of its own; they are citizens of the states to which they belong.

Article 21: The Arab Palestinian people, expressing themselves by the armed Palestinian revolution, reject all solutions which are substitutes for the total liberation of Palestine and reject all proposals aiming at the liquidation of the Palestinian problem or its internationalization.

Article 22: Zionism is a political movement organically associated with international imperialism and antagonistic to all action for liberation and to progressive movements in the world. It is racist and fanatic in its nature, aggressive, expansionist and colonial in its aims, and fascist in its methods. Israel is the instrument of the Zionist movement, and a geographical base for world imperialism placed strategically in the midst of the Arab homeland to combat the hopes of the Arab nation for liberation, unity and progress. Israel is a constant source of threat vis-a-vis peace in the Middle East and the whole world. Since the liberation of Palestine will destroy the Zionist and imperialist presence and will contribute to the establishment of peace in the Middle East, the Palestinian people look for the support of all the progressive and peaceful forces and urge them all, irrespective of their affiliations and beliefs, to offer the Palestinian people all aid and support in their just struggle for the liberation of their homeland.

Article 23: The demands of security and peace, as well as the demands of right and justice, require all states to consider Zionism and illegitimate movement, to outlaw its existence, and to ban its operations, in order that friendly relations among peoples may be preserved, and the loyalty of citizens to their respective homeland safeguarded.

Article 24: The Palestinian people believe in the principles of justice, freedom, sovereignty, self-determination, human dignity, and in the right of all peoples to exercise them.

Article 25: For the realization of the goals of this Charter and its principles, the Palestine Liberation Organization will perform its role in the liberation of Palestine in accordance with the Constitution of this Organization.

Article 26: The Palestine Liberation Organization, representative of the Palestinian revolutionary forces, is responsible for the Palestinian Arab people's movement in its struggle—to retrieve its homeland, liberate and return to it and exercise the right to self-determination in it—in all military, political and financial fields and also for whatever may be required by the Palestine case on the inter-Arab and international levels.

Article 27: The Palestine Liberation Organization shall cooperate with all Arab states, each according to its potentialities; and will adopt a neutral policy among them in the light of the requirements of the war of liberation; and on this basis it shall not interfere in the internal affairs of any Arab state.

Article 28: The Palestinian Arab people assert the genuineness and independence of their national revolution and reject all forms of intervention, trusteeship and subordination.

Article 29: The Palestinian people possess the fundamental and genuine legal right to liberate and retrieve their homeland. The Palestinian people determine their attitude towards all states and forces on the basis of the stands they adopt vis-a-vis the Palestinian case and the extent of the support they offer to the Palestinian revolution to fulfill the aims of the Palestinian people.

Article 30: Fighters and carriers of arms in the war of liberation are the nucleus of the popular army which will be the protective force for the gains of the Palestinian Arab people.

Article 31: The Organization shall have a flag, an oath of allegiance and an anthem. All this shall be decided upon in accordance with a special regulation.

Article 32: Regulations, which shall be known as the Constitution of the Palestine Liberation Organization, shall be annexed to this Charter. It shall lay down the manner in which the Organization, and its organs and institutions, shall be constituted; the respective competence of each; and the requirements of its obligations under the Charter.

Article 33: This Charter shall not be amended save by (vote of) a majority of two-thirds of the total membership of the National congress of the Palestine Liberation Organization (taken) at a special session convened for that purpose.

If the United Nations somehow pressures Israel into giving up land to the point where her fragile security is intolerably threatened, Israel will be forced to arm to the teeth, prepare field nuclear missiles and long range nuclear missiles. Let another war be triggered off either by a nation or a group of wild eyed fanatics and it will spell devastation for all the people in the Middle East. Mr. Clinton, Mr. Christopher, John Major, you would not want that on your conscience would you? That goes for the successive leaders of the Western nations and the UN.

Appendix # 2

Some of Israel's Friends

Christian Organizations and Leaders
Who Support Israel

Indicates organizations that involve Christian and Jewish leaders.

American Christian Trust
Bobbi Hromas
PO Box 9517
Washington DC 20016-9517

*American-Israel Friendship
    League, Inc
Samuel M. Eisenstat
134 E. 39th St.
New York NY 10016
212-213-8630, FAX 212-683-3475

Baptist International Seminary
Dr. Roy Stewart
PO Box 260
Oxon Hill MD 20750
301-567-1918, FAX 301-567-3805

Baptist Leader
American Baptist Churches USA
PO Box 851
Valley Forge PA 19482

Rev. Dan Betzer
First Assembly of God Church
6901 Harbor Lane
Ft. Myers FL 33919
813-936-4420

Bible Light International
Elmer Josephson
PO Box J
Ottawa. KS 66067
913-242-2290

Blossoming Rose
Dr. DeWayne Coxon
360 West Pine Street
Cedar Springs MI 49319
616-696-3435, FAX 616-696-3790

Pat Boone Entertainment Inc.
9200 Sunset Blvd #1007
Los Angeles CA 90069
310-858-0044, FAX 310-858-3769

Bridges for Peace
Clarence Wagner
PO Box 33145
Tulsa OK 74153
918-749-8811
In Israel: 12 Ibn Ezra St
Rehavia Jerusalem
2-669-865, FAX 2-666-675

Calfornia Christian Committee
    for Israel
Mary Rose Black Ryan
PO Box 5342
Berkeley CA 94705
510-655-2542

Call for Reconciliation
Arie Ben Israel
Am Heiligenstock 2
D-6312 LABACH 6
West Germany
06405/3371

Canadian Friends, International
    Christian Embassy, Jerusalem
Alan C. Lazerte, B.A., LL.B,
    Executive Director
PO Box 636
Oakville, ONT L6J 5C1 Canada
905-338-2272
Rev. Bernice Gerard
National Chairperson
604-266-7740

Prof. Harry James Cargas
Webster University
470 E Lockwood
St. Louis MO 63119

Center for Judaic Christian Studies
Dr. Dwight Pryor
PO Box 293040
Dayton OH 45429
513-434-4550

Christian Action for Israel -U.K.
M. G. Young
Lords Manor Shepreth,
Royston, Herts,
United Kingdom Sg8 6RE
44-799-526838
FAX 44- 799- 526713

Christian Corps for Israel
Marilyn Escue
14506 S.W. 15th Ave
Newberry FL 32669
904-332-5199/904-334-1300

Christian Friends of Israel
PO Box 1813
Jerusalem 91015 Israel
972-2-894172/187
FAX 972-2-894955

Christian Inst. for MidEast
    Studies, Inc.
Mr. Ted Pantalea
605 45th St East
Bradenton FL 34208
813-748-5742

Christian-Israel Friendship League
Elva Lanowick, Secretary
PO Box 400
Paradise CA 95967
916-877-6003

Christian Israel Public Action
    Committee (CIPAC)
Richard Hellman, President
2013 Que Street N.W.
Washington DC 20009
202-234-3600, FAX 202-332-3221

Christians United for Israel
David Allen Lewis, Founder,
    President
304 E. Farm Road 186
Springfield MO 65810
417-882-6470, FAX 417-882-1135

Christians United for Israel
Ambassador at Large
Rev. Sherlock Bally
809 Shadow Lane
Sapulpa, OK 74666
918-227-3907

Christians United for Israel
Arkansas Chapter
Mark Gentry, Chairman
PO Box 111
Natural Dam, AR 72948
501-929-5757

Christians United for Israel
California Chapter
Rev. Richard D. Pruitt, Chairman
1900 Shaffer Road
Atwater, CA 95301
209-358-5701, FAX 209-358-5715

Christians United for Israel
Maryland Chapter
Rev. Donald Nave, Chairman
7323 Prince George's Rd.
Baltimore, MD 21207
410-484-7899

Christians United for Israel
Mississippi Chapter
Rev. Ron Delgado, Chairman
PO Box 9419
Columbus MS 39701
601-329-2279

Christians United for Israel
Missouri Chapter
Rev. Wm. Shackelford, Chairman
(Shofar Ministries)
PO Box 3655
Joplin, MO 64803
417-781-8671

Christians United for Israel
New York Chapter
Rev. James Graziano, Chairman
Faith Tabernacle Church
529 Sunrise Hwy.
West Babylon, NY 11704
516-661-1833

Christians United for Israel
Ohio Chapter
Rev. Ed Smelser, Chairman
8528 Deer Creek Lane NE
Warren, OH 44484
330-856-2333

Christians United for Israel
Oklahoma Chapter
Roberta and Lendell Roberts,
    Chairmen
704 Oakview Dr.
Midwest City, OK 73110
405-737-2412

Christians United for Israel
Washington Chapter
Terry Patton
PO Box 19591
Seattle, WA 98109
206-399-3351

Cornerstone Church
Pastor John Hagee
18755 Stone Oak Parkway
San Antonio TX 78258
210-490-1600 FAX 210- 490-3385

Daughters of Judah
Rev. Sandy O'Connell
PO Box 948
Clinton MA 01510

Exodus Ltd.
Polly Grimes
PO Box 1387
Redondo Beach CA 90278
 310-370-0185

Faith Bible Chapel
Pastor George Morrison
12189 West 64th Ave
Arvada CO 80004
303-424-2121

First Assembly of God
Pastor Edward Thompson
PO Box 360262
Melbourne, FL 32936

For Zion's Sake
Judith M. Classen
947 Alnetta Dr.
Cincinnati OH 45230
513-232-1508 FAX 513-232-1508

Foundation for Israel
Ted Beckett
PO Box 2350
Orange CA 92665
714-997-8452

Friends for Israel
R. J. D. de Jong, Founder
St Nicolaasweg 20
Bunschoten Holland 3752 XP
03499-88015

Friends of Israel
Elwood McQuaid
PO Box 908
Bellmawr NJ 08099
800-257-7843

Harvest Assembly of God
Pastor David Addeja
525 Kempsville Rd
Chesapeake VA 23320
804-547-7710 FAX 804-436-5837

"Hayseed" Stephens
Evangelistic Association
365 Cook Road
Weatherford, TX 76086
817-441-9323

Insight
Fay Hardin
PO Box 540634
Orlando FL 32854-
407-290-0088 FAX 407-290-8339

Inst. of Judaic-Christian Research
Susan Batchelor, Administrator
PO Box 120366
Arlington TX 76012
817-792-3304 FAX 817-275-6317

Interfaith Resources, Inc.
David Blewett
1328 Oakwood Dr.
Anoka MN 55303
612-421-1896

Intl. Christian Embassy Jerusalem
2013 Q Street NW
Washington DC 20009
202-638-5830 FAX 202-638-5833
In Israel: PO Box 1192
91010 Jerusalem
Israel
02669-823 / 619-389
FAX 972-2-669-970

*Intl. Fellowship of Christians
    & Jews
Rabbi Yechiel Eckstein
28 East Jackson Blvd. Suite 1910
Chicago IL 60604
312-554-0450 FAX 312-554-0490

The Issachar Ministry
Pastor Peter McArthur
PO Box 230
Carnarvon Western Australia 6701
61-99-411571 FAX 61-99-412213

Israel the Holy Land
Carol M Dawson
995 56A Street
Delta B.C. V4L 1Y6, Canada

Israel Vistas
Jay Rallings
PO Box 02726
Mevesseret Jerusalem 90805 Israel

Jeremiah Films
Pat Matriesiana
PO Box 1710
Hemet CA 92343
800-828-2290/714-653-1006
FAX 714-652-5848

Mrs. Yvonne Lewerke
1000 Eisenhower Ave
The Willows Apt #110
Mason City IA 50401
515-423-1340

Peter Michas
925 Cherry Lane
Troy, IL 62294

Midnight Call Inc.
Arno Froese
4694 Platt Springs Road
West Columbia SC 29170
800-845-2420

Mission to America
Hilton Sutton
736 Wilson Road
Humble TX 77338
713-446-7181

National Christian Leadership
    Conference for Israel
Bishop John Burt, President
Dr. Rose Thering, Executive
    Director
David Allen Lewis, Chairman of
    the Board
134 East 39th Street
New York, NY 10016
212-761-9393

National Conference of Christian
    and Jews
Don Selvine, Director
2041 Martin Luther King Ave SE,
    Suite 302
Washington DC 20020
202-678-9400

Olive Branch
Bob and Ramona Dicks
8494 State Highway 176
Walnut Shade MO 65771-9100
417-561-4182 FAX 561-5135

Olive Tree Biblical Ministries
4637 Chippewa Way
St. Charles MO 63304
314-926-8273

A Praise in the Earth
Thomas & Rebecca Brimmer
1/12 Ha-Shayish Road
Gilo, Jerusalem, Israel
02-761-274

Progressive Vision International
Tom Hess
117 Second Street N.E. #3
Washington DC 20002

Religious Roundtable
Ed McAteer
5911 Brierdale Ave
Memphis TN 38119

Shalom International
Frank Eichlor
PO Box 310
Corona CA 91718
714-771-1500

Shofar Communications
Jimmy DeYoung
PO Box 2510
Chattanooga TN 37409

Shofar Ministries
William & Sharon Shackelford
PO Box 438
Marionville MO 65705
417-463-2927
FAX 417-463-2211

Ed Steele Agency
Ed Steele
311-C No. Tustin Ave.
Orange CA 92667
714-997-8450/FAX

TV 38
Jerry Rose
One North Wacker Drive
   Suite 1100
Chicago IL 60606
312-977-3838

Voices United for Israel
Esther Levens & Allen Mothersill
5311 Johnson Drive Suite A
Mission KS 66205
913-432-7900 FAX 913-432-7997

World of the Bible Ministries
110 Easy Street
San Marcos TX 78666-7326
512-392-6312 FAX 512-396-1012

Bibliography

Categories

GR - General Reference   PRO - Prophecy
HIT - Hitler   10T - Identity of Israel, Heresies
HZ - Herzl and Zionism   AS - Anti-Semitism
HO - Holocaust   CJ - Christian/Jewish relations
CZ - Christian Zionism   CAS - Christian Anti-Semitism

American Jewish Committee and Jewish Publication Society. *American Jewish Yearbook 1987.* vol. 87. New York, NY and Philadelphia, PA., 1987. (GR)

Amler, Jane Frances. *Christopher Columbus's Jewish Roots.* Northvale, NJ: Jason Aronson Inc., 1970. (GR)

Anderson, Roy Allan and Jay Milton Hoffman. *All Eyes on Israel.* Fort Worth, TX: Harvest Press Incorporated, 1975. (PRO)

Angebert, Jean-Michel. *The Occult and the Third Reich.* New York, NY: McGraw-Hill Book Company, 1971. (HIT)

Archbold, Norma. *The Mountains of Israel: The Bible and the West Bank.* Phoebe's Song Publication, 1983. (PRO)

Armstrong, Herbert W. *The United States and Britian in Prophecy.* Pasadena, CA: The Worldwide Church of God, 1980. (10T)

Ausubel, Nathan. *The Book of Jewish Knowledge.* New York, NY: Crown Publishers, Inc., 1964. (GR)

Ausubel, Nathan. *Pictorial History of the Jewish People: From Bible Times to Our Own Day Throughout the World.* New York, NY: Crown Publishers, Inc., 1966. (GR)

Badsey, Stephen. *Hitler.* London, England: Bison Books Ltd., 1991. (HIT)

Bar-Illan, David, ed. *Eye on the Media.* Jerusalem, Israel: The Jerusalem Post, 1993. (GR)

Baron, David. *Israel in the Plan of God.* Grand Rapids, MI: Kregel Publications, 1983. (PRO)

Begin, Menachem *The Revolt.* New York, NY: Dell Publishing Co., Inc., 1977. (GR)

Beilin, Dr. Yossi. *A Vision of the Middle East.* Tokyo, Japan: State of Israel, 1993. (GR)

Bein, Alex. *Theodore Herzl.* New York, NY: The World Publishing Co., 1962. (HZ)

Ben-Sasson, H. H., ed. *A History of the Jewish People.* Cambridge, MA: Harvard University Press, 1976. (GR)

Berstein, Jack. *The Life of an American Jew in Racist Marxist Israel.* Detroit Lakes, MN: Pro-American Press, 1984. (AS)

Bernstein, Victor H. *The Holocaust: Final Judgement.* Indianapolis, IN and New York, NY: The Bobbs-Merrill Company, Inc., 1980. (HO)

Berry, Harold J. *British Israelism: The Problem of the Lost Tribes.* Lincoln, NE: Back to the Bible Publication, 1974. (10T)

Bishops, Claire Huchet. *How Catholics Look at Jews.* New York, NY: Paulist Press, 1974. (CJ)

Bixler, Russell R. *Unbreakable Promises: How to Know and Receive All that God has Given You.* Pittsburgh, PA: Baldwin Manor Press, 1987. (PRO)

Blum, Howard, *Wanted: The Search for Nazis in America.* New York, NY: The New York Times Book Co., 1977. (HIT)

Bower, Tom. *The Paperclip Conspiracy: The Hunt for the Nazi Scientists.* Boston, MA: Little, Brown and Company, 1987. (HIT)

Boyd, F. M. *Ezekiel.* Springfield, MO: Gospel Publishing House, 1951. (PRO)

Bracher, Karl Dietrich. *The German Dictatorship: The Origins, Structure, and Effects of National Socialism.* London, England: Weidenfield and Nicolson, 1971. (HIT)

Brossard, Chandler. *The Insane World of Adolf Hitler.* Fawcett Gold Medal Book, n.d. (HIT)

Brown, Michael L. *Our Hands are Stained With Blood.* Shippensburg, PA: Destiny Image Publishers, 1992. (CZ)

Browne, Lewis. *How Odd of God: An Introduction to the Jews.* New York, NY: The MacMillan Company, 1934. (GR)

Bullock, Alan. *Hitler: A Study in Tyranny.* New York, NY: Bantam Books, 1961. (HIT)

Burnett, Ken, *Why Pray For Israel?* Hants, UK: Marshall, Morgan and Scott, 1983. (CZ)

Burrows, William E. and Robert Windrem. *Critical Mass.* New York, NY: Simon and Schuster, 1994. (GR)

Butz, A. R.. *The Hoax of the Twentieth Century.* 23 Ellerker Gardens, England: Historical Review Press, 1976. (HO)

Cahn-Lipman, Rabbi David E. *The Book of Jewish Knowledge: 613 Basic Facts About Judaism.* Northvale, NJ: Jason Aronson Inc., 1991. (GR)

Cargas, Harry James. *A Christian Response to the Holocaust.* Denver, Colorado: Stonehenge Books, 1981. (HO)

Carlson, Paul R. *O Christian! O Jew!* Elgin, IL: David C. Cook Publishing Co., 1974. (CJ)

Carpenter, Frank G. *The Holy Land and Syria.* Garden City, NY and New York, NY: Doubleday, Page & Company, 1923. (GR)

Carr, Joseph J. *The Twisted Cross.* Lafayette, LA: Huntington House Publishers, 1985. (HIT)

Carter, Jimmy. *The Blood of Abraham.* Boston, MA: Houghton Mifflin Company, 1985. (GR)

Chitwood, Arlen, L. *Focus on the Middle East.* Norman, OK: The Lamp Broadcast, Inc., 1991. (PRO)

Clarke, Nicholas Goodrick. *The Occult Roots of Nazism: The Ariosophists of Austria and Germany 1890-1935.* Wellingborough, England: The Aquarian Press, 1985. (HIT)

Cohen, Mitchell. *Zion and State: Nation, Class and the Shaping of Modern Israel.* New York, NY: Basil Blackwell Inc., 1987. (GR)

Cohen, Richard. *Let My People Go.* New York, NY: Popular Library Eagle Books, 1971. (GR)

Cooper, Matthew. *The German Army 1933-1945:* Vol 11 Conquest. New York, NY: Kensington Publishing Corp., 1978. (HIT)

Davis, George T.B. *Rebuilding Palestine According to Prophecy.* Philadelphia, PA: The Millon Testaments Campaign, 1935. (PRO)

Davy-Humphrey, A. *The Bible and Palestine's Future.* London, England: Marshall, Morgan and Scott, n.d. (PRO)

Dimont, Max I. *Jews, God and History.* New York, NY: The New American Library, 1962. (GR)

Dolan, David. *Holy War for the Promised Land.* Nashville, TN: Thomas Nelson, Inc., 1991. (CZ)

Dornberg, John. *Munich 1923: The Story of Hitler's First Grab for Power.* Cambridge, MA: Harper and Row Publishers, 1982. (HIT)

Dowty, Alan. *The Rise of Great Power Guarantees in International Peace Agreements. vol. 3* The Hebrew University of Jerusalem, Israel, 1974. (GR)

Dubnow, S. M. *History of the Jews in Russia and Poland: From the Earliest Times Until the Present Day.* Philadelphia, PA: The Jewish Publication Society of America, 1916. (GR)

Duvernoy, Claude. *The Prince and the Prophet.* Jerusalem, Israel: Christian Action for Israel, 1978. (CZ)

Duvernoy, Claude. *Controversy of Zion.* Green Forest, AR: New Leaf Press, 1987. (CZ)

Eban, Abba. *My People: History of the Jews.* Vol.11, New York, NY: Behrman House, Inc., 1979. (GR)

Eckstein, Rabbi Yechiel. *What Christians Should Know About Jews and Judaism.* Waco, TX: Word Books Publisher, 1984. (CJ)

Eiklor, Frank. *A Time for Trumpets: Not Piccolos!* Orange, CA: Promise Publishing Co., 1988. (CZ)

Eisenman, Robert H. ed. *If I Forget You, O Jerusalem: A Handbook of Zionist Prophecy.* Fountain Valley, CA: The Yahwist Press, 1978. (PRO)

Elon, Amos. *Herzl* Rinehart and Winston, 1975. (HZ)

Epstein, Rabbi Dr. I. *The Babylonian Talmud.* 18 volumes. London, England: The Soncino Press, 1952. (GR)

Fast, Howard. *The Jews: The Story of a People.* New York, NY: Dell Publishing Co., Inc., 1968. (GR)

Feder, Don. *A Jewish Conservative Looks at Pagan America.* Lafayette, LA: Huntington House Publishers, 1993. (GR)

Feinberg, Charles Lee. *The Prophecy of Ezekiel: The Glory of the Lord.* Chicago, IL: Moody Press, 1969. (PRO)

Fink, Ruben. *America and Palestine.* New York, NY: Herald Square and Press, Inc., 1944. (GR)

Fisher, Eugene J. *Seminary Education and Christian-Jewish Relations: A Curriculum and Resource Handbook.* Washington, D.C: The National Catholic Educational Association, 1988. (CJ)

Fishman, Precilla. ed. *The Jews of the United States.* New York, NY: Quadrangle/The New York Times Book Co., 1973. (GR)

Fishwick, Marshall W. *Faust Revisited: Some Thoughts on Satan.* New York, NY: Seabury Press, 1963. (GR)

Flannery, Edward H. *The Anguish of the Jews: Twenty-Three Centuries of Antisemitism.* New York, NY: Paulist Press, 1985. (AS)

Flynn, Kevin and Gerhardt, Gary. *The Silent Brotherhood: Inside America's Racist Underground.* New York, NY: The Free Press, 1989. (AS)

Ford, Henry Sr. *The International Jew: The Worlds Foremost Problem.* Dearborn, MI: Henry Ford Sr., 1948. (AS)

Forrest, A.C. *The Unholy Land.* Mc Clelland and Stewart Limited: Toronto, Canada, 1971. (CAS)

Foster, J. Whitfield. *Israel Have I Loved.* Jerusalem, Israel: J. Whitfield Foster, 1958. (GR)

Frank, Waldo. *Bridge Head: The Drama of Israel.* New York, NY: George Braziller, Inc., 1957. (GR)

Frister, Roman. *Israel: Years of Crisis and Years of Hope.* New York, NY: McGraw-Hill Book Company, 1973. (GR)

Fruchtenbaum, Arnold G. *Israelology: The Missing Link in Systematic Theology.* Tustin, CA: Ariel Ministries Press, 1989. (CZ)

Gade, Richard E. *A Historical Survey of Anti-Semitism.* Grand Rapids, MI: Baker Book House, 1981. (AS)

Gaebelein, Arno C. *The Prophet Ezekiel: An Analytical Exposition.* Nepture, NJ: Loizeaux Brothers, 1972. (PRO)

Gerber, David A., ed. *Anti-Semitism in American History.* Chicago, IL: Univeristy of Illinois Press, 1987. (AS)

Gilber, Felix. ed. *Hitler Directs His War.* New York, NY Oxford University Press, 1950. (HIT)

Gilbert, Martin. *The Arab-Israeli Conflict: Its History in Maps.* London, England: Weidenfield and Nicolson, 1974. (GR)

Gilbert, Martin. *Auschwitz and the Allies.* New York, NY: Henry Holt and Company, 1982. (HO)

Gilman, Sander L. *Jewish Self-Hatred: Anti-Semitism and the Hidden Language of the Jews.* Baltimore, Maryland: The John Hopkins University Press, 1986. (AS)

Ginsberg, H. L. ed. *The Book of Isaiah.* Philadelphia, PA: The Jewish Publication Society of America, 1972. (PRO)

Goodman, Paul. *A History of the Jews.* Cleveland, OH: The World Publishing Company, 1943. (GR)

Gould, Allan. ed. *What Did They Think of the Jews?* Northvale, NJ: Jason Aronson, Inc., 1991. (GR)

Graber, G. S. *History of the SS.* New York, NY: Granada Publishing Co., 1978. (HIT)

Greenfield, Richard Pierce and Greenfield Irving A. *The Life of Menachem Begin.* New York, NY: Manor Books, Inc., 1977. (GR)

Greenstein, Howard R. *Judaism: An Eternal Covenant.* Philadelphia, PA: Fortress Press, 1983. (GR)

Grose, Peter. *Israel in the Mind of America* New York, NY: Alfred A. Knopf, Inc., 1983. (GR)

Gur, Lt. Gen. *Mordechai. The Battle for Jerusalem.* New York, NY: Popular Library, 1974. (GR)

Haber, Eitan *Menachem Begin: The Man and the Legend.* New York, NY: Dell Publishing Co., Inc., 1978. (GR)

Haffner, Sebastian. *The Meaning of Hitler.* New York, NY: MacMillan Publishing Co., Inc., 1979. (HIT)

Hagee, John. *Should Christians Support Israel?* San Antonio, TX: Dominion Publishers, 1987. (CZ)

Halperin, A. William. *Mussolini and Italian Fascism.* Princeton, NJ: D. Van Nostrand Company, Inc., 1964. (GR)

Hanson, Calvin B. *A Gentile with the Heart of a Jew.* Nyack, NY: Parson Publishing, 1979. (CZ)

Harkabi, Y. *Arab Attitudes to Israel.* Jerusalem, Israel: Keter Publishing House Jerusalem LTD., 1972. (GR)

Harkabi, Y. *The Palestinian Covenant and its Meaning.* Totowa, NJ: Vallentine, Mitchell and Co., L.T.D., 1979. (GR)

Harris, Rev. Maurice H., Ph. D. *A Thousand Years of Jewish History.* New York, NY: Bloch Publishing Co., 1927. (GR)

Hauff, Louis H. *Israel in Bible Prophecy.* Springfield, MO: Gospel Publishing House, 1974. (PRO)

Hay, Malcolm. *Thy Brother's Blood.* New York, NY: Hart Publishing Company, Inc., 1975. (AS)

Heaton, E.W. *Solomon's New Men: The Emergence of Ancient Israel as a National State.* New York, NY: Pica Press, 1974. (GR)

Heiden, Konrad. *Der Fuehrer: Hitler's Rise to Power.* Boston, MA: Houghton Mifflin Company, 1944. (HIT)

Henkin, Louis. ed. *World Politics and the Jewish Condition.* New York, NY: Quadrangle Books, Inc., 1972. (GR)

Herzl, Theodore. *Zionist Writings: Essays and Addresses.* 2 volumes. 1898-1904. New York, NY: Herzl Press, 1973-1975. (HZ)

Herzl, Theodore. *The Jewish State.* Mineola, NY: Dover Publications, Inc., 1988. (HZ)

Herzl, Theodore. *Old-New Land.* New York, NY: Bloch Publishing Company and Herzl Press, 1960. (HZ)

Herzstein, Robert Edwin. *The Nazis.* Chicago, IL: Time Life Books, 1980. (HIT)

Hertzberg, Arthur. *The Jews in America: Four Centuries of an Uneasy Encounter: A History.* New York, NY: Simon and Schuster, 1989. (GR)

Hess, Tom. *Let My People Go.* Washington, D.C.: Progressive Vision, 1987. (PRO)

Higham, Charles. *American Swastika.* Garden City, NY: Doubleday & Co., 1985. (HIT)

Hohne, Heinz. *The Order of the Death Heads: The Story of Hitler's SS.* New York, NY: Random House Inc., 1971. (HIT)

Hugo, Victor. *Les Miserables.* New York, NY: Thomas Y. Crowell Company, 1915. (GR)

Hull, William L. *And It All Began: The Story of Israel's Rebirth 1947.* Ontario, Canada: William L. Hull, 1987. (PRO, CZ)

Hull, William, L. *The Fall and Rise of Israel.* Breezewood, PA: Heralds of Hope, Inc., 1978. (PRO)

Hull, Willliam L. *Israel: Key to Prophecy.* Grand Rapids, MI: Zondervan Publishing House, n.d. (PRO)

Ironside, H. A. Litt. D. *Ezekiel: The Prophet.* Neptune, NJ: Loizeaux Brothers, Inc., Bible Truth Depot, 1974. (PRO)

Isaacson, Dr. Ben. *Dictionary of the Jewish Religion.* Englewood, NJ: Bantam Books, Inc., 1979. (GR)

Jakobovits, Immanuel. *If Only My People: Zionism in my Life.* Washington, D.C., B'nai B'irth Books, 1986. (HZ)

Jolly, Pastor Raymond G. *Anglo-Israelism: A Stong Delusion.* Chester Springs, PA: Laymen's Home Missionary Movement. (10T)

Jones, J. Sydney. *Hitler in Vienna 1907-1913.* New York, NY: Stein and Day Publishers, 1983. (HIT)

Kagan, Benjamin. *The Secret Battle for Israel.* Cleveland, OH: The World Publishing Company, 1966. (GR)

Kantor, Mattis. *The Jewish Time Line Encyclopedia: A Year by Year History from Creation to the Present.* Northvale, NJ: Jason Aronson Inc., 1989. (GR)

Katz, Samuel. *Battle-Ground: Fact and Fantasy in Palestine.* New York, Jerusalem, Tel Aviv: Steimatsky and Shapolsky, 1985. (GR)

Kertzer, Rabbi Morris N. *What a Jew?* New York, NY: MacMillian Publishing Co., Inc., 1973. (GR)

Keter Publishing. *Encyclopaedia Judica.* Jerusalem, Israel: 1972. (GR)

Kimmerling, Baruch and Midgal, Joel S. *Palestinians: The Making of a People.* New York, NY: The Free Press, 1993. (GR)

Kinche, David and Bawly, Dan. *The Sand Storm: The Arab-Israeli war of June 1967: Prelude and Aftermath.* New York, NY: Stein and Day, 1968. (GR)

Kirschen, Ya'Akov. *Trees: The Green Testament.* New York, NY: Vital Media Enterprises, 1993. (PRO)

Klein, Mina C. and H. Arthur Klein. *Israel Land of the Jews: A Survey of Forty-Three Centuries.* Indianapolis, IN. The Bobbs-Merrill Company, Inc., 1972. (GR)

Koestler, Arthur. *The Thirteenth Tribe.* New York, NY: Popular Library, 1978. (10T)

Kolleck, Teddy and Kolleck, Amos. *For Jerusalem: A Life by Teddy Kolleck.* New York, NY: Random House Inc., 1978. (GR)

Lamb, W. *Great Britian in Prophecy and Anglo-Israelism Under the Searchlight.* Sidney, Austraila: The Australian Baptist House, Inc., 1918. (10T)

Lambert, Lance. *The Uniqueness of Israel*. Great Britian: Kingsway Publications, 1980. (PRO)

Langer, Walter C. *The Mind of Adolf Hitler: The Secret Wartime Report*. New York, NY: New American Library, 1973. (HIT)

LaRouche, Helga Zepp. ed. *The Hitler Book*. New York, NY: New Benjamin Franklin House, 1984. (HIT)

Lawrence, Gunther. *Three Million More?* Garden City, NY: Doubleday & Company, Inc., 1970. (GR)

Lee, Albert. *Henry Ford and the Jews*. New York, NY: Stein and Day Publishers, 1980. (AS)

Leese, Arnold S. *My Irrelevant Defence being Meditations Inside Gaol and Out on Jewish Ritual Murder*. London, England: The I. F. L. Printing and Publishing Co., 1938. (AS)

Levin, Nora. *The Holocaust: The Destruction of European Jewry 1933-1945*. New York, NY: Thomas J. Crowell Company, 1968. (HO)

Levy, Henry W. and Postal, Bernard. *And the Hills Shouted for Joy: The Day Israel Was Born*. New York, NY: David Mc Kay Company, Inc., 1973. (GR)

Lewis, David A. *Prophecy 2000*. Green Forest, AR: New Leaf Press, 1990. (PRO)

Lieber, Sherman. *Mystics and Missionaries: The Jews in Palestine 1799-1840*. Salt Lake City, UT: University of Utah Press, 1992. (GR)

Lindsey, Hal. *The Road to Holocaust*. New York, NY: Bantam Book, 1989. (HO)

Lipstadt, Deborah E. *Denying the Holocaust: The Growing Assualt on Truth and Memory*. New York, NY: The Free Press, 1993. (HO)

Lowdermilk, Walter Clay. *Palestine Land of Promise*. New York, NY, and London: Harper and Brothers Publishers, 1944. (GR)

Luther, Dr. Martin. *The Jews and Their Lies*. Erueka Springs, AR: Christian Nationalist Crusade, 1948. (AS)

Maccoby, Hyam. *Judas Iscariot and the Myth of Jewish Evil*. New York, NY: The Free Press, 1992. (AS)

Manvell, Roger and Heinrich Fraenkel. *Adolf Hitler: The Man and The Myth*. New York, NY: Pinnacle Books, 1977. (HIT)

Marsden, Victor E., translator. *Protocols of the Meetings of the Learned Elders of Zion*. Eureka Springs, AR: Christian Nationalists Crusade, n.d. (AS)

Maser, Werner. *Hitler: Legend, Myth and Reality.* New York, NY Harper and Row Publishers, 1971. (HIT)

Maser, Werner. *Hitler's Letters and Notes.* New York, NY: Harper and Row, Publishers, 1973. (HIT)

Mason, David ed. *Hitler.* New York, NY: Balentine Books, Inc. 1970. (HIT)

McKale, Donald M, ed. *Rewriting History: The Original And Revised World War II Diaries of Curt Prufer, Nazi Diplomat.* Kent OH: The Kent State University Press, 1988. (HIT)

McWhirter, James. *A World in a Country.* Jerusalem, Israel: B.S.B. International, 1983. (CZ)

Meyer, F.B. *The Prophect of Hope: Studies in Zechariah.* Chicago, IL: Fleming H. Revell Company, 1900. (PRO)

Miller, Irving. *Israel — The Eternal Ideal.* New York, NY: Farar, Straus and Cudahy, 1955. (GR)

Moszkiewiez, Helene. *Inside the Gestapo: A Jewish Woman's Secret War.* Toronto, Ontario Canada: Macmillan of Canada, 1985. (HIT)

Myers, Philip Van Ness. *Mediaeval and Modern History.* Boston, MA:Ginn & Company, 1905. (GR)

Nelson, Walter Henry and Terence Prittie. *The Economic War Against the Jews.* New York, NY: Random House, 1977. (AS)

Netanyahu, Benjamin. *International Terrorism: Challenge and Response.* Jerusalem, Israel: Transaction Books, 1981. (GR)

Neusner, Jacob. *Israel in America: Too-Comfortable Exile.* Boston, MA: Beacon Press, 1985. (GR)

Nicholls, William. *Christian Antisemitism: A History of Hate.* Northvale, NJ: Jason Aronson, Inc., 1993. (AS)

Oliphant, Mrs. *Jerusalem: The Holy City Its History and Hope.* New York, NY: MacMillan and Co., 1893. (GR)

Olson, Arnold. *Inside Jerusalem.* Glendale, CA: G.L. Publications, 1968. (PRO)

Pache, Rene. *The Return of Jesus Christ.* Chicago, IL: Moody Press, 1955. (PRO)

Parfitt, Tudor. *The Thirteenth Gate: The Travels Among the Lost Tribes of Israel.* Bethesda, MA: Adler and Adler, Publishers, Inc., 1987. (IOT)

Patai, Josef. *Star Over Jordan: The Life of Theodor Herzl.* New York, NY: Philosophical Library, Inc., 1946. (HZ)

Patterson, Charles. *Anti-Semitism: The Road to the Holocaust and Beyond.* New York, NY: Walker and Company, 1982. (AS)

Payne, Robert. *The Life and Death of Adolph Hitler.* New York, NY: Popular Library, 1973. (HIT)

Pennick, Nigel. *Hitler's Secret Sciences: His Quest For the Hidden Knowledge of the Ancients.* Suffolk, England: Neville Spearman Limited, 1981. (HIT)

Peres, Shimon. *The New Middle East.* New York, NY: Henry Holt and Company, 1993. (GR)

Pike, Theodore Winston. *Israel: Our Duty — Our Dilemma.* Oregon, City, OR: Big Sky Press, 1984. (CAS)

Podhoretz, Norman. ed. *The Commentary Reader: Two Decades of Articles and Stories.* New York, NY: McClelland and Stewart Ltd., 1965. (GR)

Posner, Rabbi Dr. Raphael. ed. *My Jewish World: The Encyclopaedia Judaica for Youth.* Jerusalem, Israel: Keter Publishing House Jerusalem Ltd., 1975. (GR)

Prager, Dennis and Telushkin, Joseph. *Why the Jews?* New York, NY: Simon & Schuster, Inc., 1983. (AS)

Price, Charles S. *Palestine: In Picture and Prophecy.* Pasadena, CA: Charles S. Price Publishing Co., 1937. (PRO)

Rausch, David A. *The Middle East Maze: Israel and Her Neighbors.* Chicago, IL: Moody Press, 1991. (CZ)

Rausch, David A. *Building Bridges.* Chicago, IL: Moody Press, 1988. (CJ)

Raush, David A, and Voss, Carl Herman. *Protestantism: Its Modern Meaning.* Philadelphia, PA: Fortress, Press, 1987. (CZ)

Rausch, David A. *A Legacy of Hatred: Why Christians Must Not Forget the Holocaust.* Chicago, IL: Moody Press, 1984. (HO)

Rausch, David A. *Zionism Within Early American Fundamentalism 1878-1918.* New York, NY: The Edwin Mellen Press, 1979. (CZ)

Rawlings, Meridel. *Fishers and Hunters: Exclusive Interviews with PLO Terrorists.* Jerusalem, Israel: World Vistas Inc., 1982. (CZ)

Rawlings, Jay and Meridel. *Gates of Brass.* Chichester, England: New Wine Press, 1985. (CZ)

Read, Anthony, and Fisher, David. *Kristallnacht: The Unleashing of the Holocaust.* New York, NY: Peter Bedrick Books, 1989. (HO)

Reitlinger, Gerald. *The Final Solution: The Attempt to Exterminate the Jews of Europe 1939-1945.* North Vale, NJ: Jason Aronson Inc., 1987. (HO)

Rhodes, Anthony. *Propaganda: The Art of Persuasion: World War II.*

Seacaucus, NJ: The Wellfleet Press, 1987. (HIT)

Rittenhouse, Stan. *"For Fear of the Jews"* Vienna, VA: The Exhorters, Inc., 1982. (CAS)

Roper-Trevor, H. R. *The Last Days of Hitler.* New York, NY: The Berkley Publishing Corporation, 1947. (HIT)

Rose, George L. *Real Israel and Anglo-Israelism.* Glendale, CA: Rose Publishing Company, 1949. (10T)

Rosio, Bob. *Hitler and the New Age: The Coming Holocaust the Extermination of Christendom.* Lafayette, LA: Huntington House Publishers, 1993. (HIT)

Rottenberg, Isaac C. *The Turbulent Triangle: Christians-Jews-Israel.* Hawley, PA: Red Mountain Associates, 1989. (CZ)

Rubin, Alexis P, ed. *Scattered Among the Nations: Documents Affecting Jewish History 1949 to 1975.* Toronto, ONT., & Dayton, OH: Wall & Emerson, Inc., 1993. (GR)

Rushdoony, Rousas John. *Thy Kingdom Come: Studies in Daniel and Revelation.* Fairfax, VA: Thoburn Press, 1978. (CAS)

Russell, Lord, of Liverpool. *The Scourge of the Swastika.* Liverpool, England: Gorgi Books, 1976. (HIT)

Rutherford, Ward. *Hitler's Propaganda Machine.* New York, NY: Grosset and Dunlap, 1978. (HIT)

Samuel, Rinna. *Israel: Promised Land to Modern State.* New York, NY: Golden Press, 1969. (GR)

Schauss, Hayyim, *The Jewish Festivals: History and Observance.* New York, NY: Schocken Books, 1938. (GR)

Schwarzwaller, Wulf. *The Unknown Hitler: His Life & Fortune.* Bethesda, MD: National Press Books, 1989. (HIT)

Shank, Robert. *Until the Coming of Messiah and His Kingdom.* Springfield, MO: Westcott, Publishers, 1982. (PRO)

Sharansky, Natan. *Fear No Evil.* New York, NY: Random House Inc., 1988. (GR)

Shermis, Michael. *Jewish-Christian Relations..* Bloomington, MN. Indianapolis, IN, Indiana University Press, 1988. (CJ)

Shirer, William . *The Rise and Fall of the Third Reich: A History of Nazi Germany.* Greenwich, CT: Fawcett Publications, Inc., 1960. (HIT)

Shorrosh, Anis A. *Jesus Prophecy & Middle East.* Mobile, AL: Anis Shorrosh Evangelistic Assoc., 1979. (PRO)

Sklar, Dusty. *Gods and Beasts: The Nazis and the Occult.* New York, NY: Thomas Y. Crowell Company, 1977. (HIT)

Smith, Gerald L. K. *Satan's New Testament*. Los Angeles, CA: Christian Nationalist Crusade, 1975. (CAS)

Smith, Wilbur M. *Israeli/Arab Conflict*. Glendale, CA: Regal Books Division, 1972. (PRO)

Snyder, Louis L. *Hitler and Nazism*. New York, NY: Bantam Books, 1967. (HIT)

Sollittman. *War Criminal on Trial: The Rauca Case*. Toronto, Ontario Canada: Lester and Orpen Dennys, 1983. (HIT)

Speer, Albert. *Inside the Third Reich: Memoirs*. New York, NY: Macmillan Company, 1970. (HIT)

Speer, Albert. *Spandau: The Secret Diaries*. New York, NY: Pocket Books, 1977. (HIT)

Spiegeman, J. Marvin, Ph.D. and Abraham Jacobson, Ph. *A Modern Jew In Search of a Soul*. Phoenix, AZ: Falcon Press, 1986. (GR)

St. John, Robert. *Tongue of the Prophets*. North Hollywood, CA: Melvin Powers, n.d. (GR)

Steinberg, Milton. *Basic Judaism*. Orlando, FL: Harcourt Brace Jovanovich, Publishers, 1975. (GR)

Steinsaltz, Adin. *The Essential Talmud*. Northvale, NJ: Jason Aronson, Inc., 1992. (GR)

Strom, Yale. *The Expulsion of the Jews: 500 Years of Exodus*. New York, NY: Shapolsky Publishers, Inc., 1992. (GR)

Tal, Eliyahu. ed. *Israel in Medialand*. Tel Aviv, Israel: Tal Communications, n.d. (GR)

Tanenbaum, Marc H., Marvin R.Wilson, and James A. Ruden, ed. *Evangelicals and Jews in an Age of Pluralism*. Grand Rapids, MI: Baker Book House, 1984. (CJ)

Thalmann, Rita and Emmanuel Feinermann. *Crystal Night: 9-10 November 1938*. New York, NY: Coward, McGann and Geoghegan, Inc., 1974. (HO)

Toland, John. *Adolf Hitler*. New York, NY: Doubleday and Company, Inc., 1976. (HIT)

Tsur, Jacob. *Zionism: The Saga of a National Liberation Movement*. New Brunswick, NJ: Transaction Books, 1977. (HZ)

Twain, Mark. *The Innocents Abroad*. New York, NY: Grosset & Dunlap Publishers, 1911. (GR)

Tweedie, Rev. W.K., D.D. *Jerusalem and its Environs: Or the Holy City as it Was and Is*. Boston, MS: The American Tract Society, 1860. (PRO)

Van Der Hoeven, Jan Willem. *Babylon or Jerusalem*. Shippensburg,

PA: Destiny Image, 1993. (PRO)

Varner, William C. *Jacob's Dozen: A Prophetic Look at the Tribes of Israel.* Bellmawr, NJ: The Friends of Israel Gospel Ministry, Inc., 1987. (PRO)

Waite, Robert G.L. *The Psychopathic God.* New York, NY: Basic Books Inc., 1977. (HIT)

Weisel, Elie. *Night.* New York, NY: Bantam Books, 1982. (HO)

Widlanski, Michael. ed. *Can Israel Survive a Palestinian State?* Jerusalem, Israel: Institute for Advanced Strategic and Political Studies, 1980. (GR)

Wilson, Marvin R. *Our Father Abrahram: Jewish Roots of the Christian Faith.* Grand Rapids, MI: William B. Eerdmans Publishing Co., 1989. (CZ)

Wykes, Alan. *Hitler.* New York, NY: Ballantine Books, 1976. (HIT)

Wyman, David S. *The Abandoment of the Jews . . . America and the Holocaust 1941-1945.* New York, NY: Pantheon Books, 1984. (HO)

Yad Vashem, *The Holocaust.* Martyrs' and Heroes' Remembrance Authority. Jerusalem, Israel 1977. (HO)

Zagoren, Ruby. *Chaim Weizmann: First President of Israel.* Champaign, IL: Garrard Publishing Company, 1972. (GR)

Zeligs, Dorothy F. *A History of Jewish Life in Modern Times: For Young People.* New York, NY: Bloch Publishing Company, 1943. (GR)

Zeman, Zbynek. *Heckling Hitler: Caricatures of the Third Reich.* Hanover, England: University Press, 1987. (HIT)

Index

Free Subscription

JERUSALEM COURIER &

Prophecy Digest

Published irregularly 4-6 times per year.

- **Essays of significance**
- **Up-to-date Mideast Reports**
- **Prophecy in the Process**
- **Research & Archaeology**
- **Conference & Seminar News**

•YES! SEND ME THE JERUSALEM COURIER.

Name _____

Address _____

City _____

State/Prov._____ Zip/PC _____

Mail your request to:

David Allen Lewis Ministries, Inc.
P.O.Box 11115 (eleven-eleven-five}
Springfield, Missouri 65808
Phone (417) 882-6470 FAX: (417) 882-1135

SHALOM!

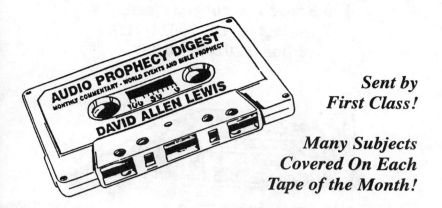

United States
Holocaust Memorial Museum

100 Raoul Wallenberg Place, SW
Washington, DC 20024-2150
Phone: 202-488-0400

Hours: 10 a.m. to 5:30 p.m. daily
Admission: Free

Visitor Services: Visitor Services staff (in maroon
jackets) are available to answer questions and provide
special assistance.

David A. Lewis is a member of the
Church Relations Committee of the
United States Holocaust Memorial Council